Approaches to Teaching the Works of Assia Djebar

Approaches to Teaching the Works of Assia Djebar

Edited by

Anne Donadey

The Modern Language Association of America
New York 2017

Library of Congress Cataloging-in-Publication Data

Names: Donadey, Anne, editor.
Title: Approaches to teaching the works of Assia Djebar / edited by Anne Donadey.
Description: New York : The Modern Language Association of America, 2017. | Series: Approaches to teaching world literature ; 144 | Includes bibliographical references and index.
Identifiers: LCCN 2016050770 (print) | LCCN 2017010389 (ebook) | ISBN 9781603292955 (cloth : alk. paper) | ISBN 9781603292962 (pbk. : alk. paper) | ISBN 9781603292979 (EPUB) | ISBN 9781603292986 (Kindle)
Subjects: LCSH: Djebar, Assia, 1936-2015—Study and teaching.
Classification: LCC PQ3989.2.D57 Z528 2017 (print) | LCC PQ3989.2.D57 (ebook) | DDC 843/.914—dc23
LC record available at https://lccn.loc.gov/2016050770

Approaches to Teaching World Literature 144
ISSN 1059–1133

Cover illustration of the paperback and electronic editions: photograph of Assia Djebar © Ulla Montan, Stockholm, Sweden, 2002.

Published by The Modern Language Association of America
85 Broad Street, suite 500, New York, New York 10004–2434
www.mla.org

In memory of Assia Djebar,
Clarisse Zimra, Farida Abu-Haidar, and Robert Markin

CONTENTS

PREFACE

Assia Djebar is the foremost francophone Arab woman writer and filmmaker. Her first, notorious novel, *La soif* (*The Mischief*), was published in 1957, and her last book, the autobiographical *Nulle part dans la maison de mon père* ("No Place in My Father's House"), appeared in 2007. In the span of her fifty-year literary career, she published over fifteen critically acclaimed fictional and autobiographical books, which were translated in many languages. What is arguably her most elaborate masterpiece, *L'amour, la fantasia* (1985; *Fantasia: An Algerian Cavalcade*), stands as one of the great novels of the twentieth century; it is of the same caliber as Gabriel García Márquez's *Cien años de soledad* (1967; *One Hundred Years of Solitude*) and Toni Morrison's *Beloved* (1987). Djebar received many international literary prizes, and she was elected to the elite French Académie Française in June 2005, the first Algerian and second African person to achieve this honor. She was considered for the Nobel Prize for Literature several times.

In North America, Djebar is one of the most commonly taught women writers from Arab or Muslim backgrounds. Her works are included in French, comparative literature, English, and women's studies courses. There are three major reasons for the interest in adding her works to the curriculum. The first is the intrinsic literary quality of her writing. The second is the move to internationalize the United States higher education curriculum, a move whose origins can be traced to the rising influence of feminist, multicultural, and postcolonial paradigms in the humanities in the 1980s and 1990s. Finally, in the post-9/11 world, representations of Muslim women have acquired a new political centrality. In this ideologically saturated context, voices of writers such as Djebar are particularly important because they make it difficult for Western readers to fall back on stereotypical images of veiled women oppressed by the twin forces of Islam and Muslim men while still mounting feminist criticisms of patriarchy.

Part 1 of this volume, "Materials," contains a biobibliographic section and a section on editions and translations of Djebar's works as well as secondary sources. Part 2, "Approaches," opens with an introduction that presents critical and theoretical debates regarding interpretations of Djebar's works and discusses the challenges and rewards in teaching her texts. Sixteen essays are structured around four major pedagogical constellations of issues that arise when Djebar's works are taught: historiographical contexts, interdisciplinary contexts, comparative contexts, and cultural and linguistic contexts.

Djebar was trained as a historian, and most of her fiction entails a creative rewriting of colonial, decolonial, and postcolonial Algerian history. The politics of history writing looms large in her works, and her fragmented fictional revision of a history that is very foreign to North American students is a major challenge in teaching her works. The essays in this volume by Martine Guyot-Bender, Najat Rahman, Mildred Mortimer, and Hanan Elsayed exemplify various complementary approaches to this aspect of Djebar.

Part of what makes Djebar's works both rewarding and difficult to teach is the wide range of literary, visual, and musical references to things that are mostly unknown to North American students. Her method is interdisciplinary, drawing on historical texts and archives, painting, music, architecture, and religious texts, as well as Middle Eastern, European, and Mediterranean literary traditions. She incorporates a wealth of intertexts, some rather obscure, that are evoked but not didactically presented. The essays in this volume by Diya Abdo and Maria Bobroff, Thérèse De Raedt, Christa Jones, Dominique D. Fisher, and Annica Schjött Vonèche deal with this aspect of her work.

Various contexts are important to help students understand Djebar. The third section of this volume, the essays by Kathryn Lachman, Dana Strand, and Vlatka Velčić, focuses on teaching her work in dialogue with that of other writers for purposes of comparison. The fourth section, the essays by Carine Bourget, Valérie J. Budig-Markin, Maya Boutaghou, and Alison Rice, presents her work in the light of Islamic feminism as well as the politics and pedagogy of language use and translation.

A concluding overview on teaching Djebar is given by the postcolonial feminist theorist Gayatri Chakravorty Spivak.

For help in the assembling and editing of this volume, I am grateful to David G. Nicholls, Margit Longbrake, Katherine Kim, Michael Kandel, Hanan Elsayed, and Peter C. Herman.

Part One

MATERIALS

Her Life

Clarisse Zimra has provided much information on Djebar's personal and literary trajectory (Afterword [to Djebar, *Women*]). Assia Djebar was born Fatima Zohra Imalhayene on 30 June 1936 and grew up in Cherchell, a coastal city west of Algiers—she often refers to Cherchell as Césarée, the French version of Caesarea, its name during the Roman occupation in antiquity. Her family is of Arab and Berber (indigenous North African) descent. Djebar's father, an elementary school teacher for Algerian boys (French schooling did not become coed until much later), took his precocious daughter to school with him and taught her to read and write in French. (In the 1996 special issue of the journal *World Literature Today* devoted to her works, Djebar shared a school picture from that time [*Assia Djebar: 1996 Neustadt International Prize* 786].) Like many other Arab feminist writers, she presents her father as a vector of female emancipation, though she also criticizes the limits of his progressiveness. This kind of tribute rarely occurs in Western European and North American women's writing (Djebar, "Territoire" 26–27). A brilliant student, she entered the prestigious École Normale Supérieure in Sèvres, France, in 1955, at a time when only a handful of Algerian women achieved a college education.

At age twenty, at the height of the Algerian war of decolonization from the French, Djebar shocked North African male critics by publishing a novel in French about a young, elite Algerian woman's search for personal liberation, *La soif* (1957; *The Mischief* [1958]). That French critics compared her work with Françoise Sagan's similarly disillusioned 1954 *Bonjour tristresse* did not help her with critics on the home front, who found the novel's topic inappropriate in the midst of the country's search for national liberation. Djebar's second novel, *Les impatients* (1958; "The Impatient Ones"), was written along the same lines and included autobiographical material that she would mine again in later texts. Perhaps as a response to her critics, her next two novels, *Les enfants du Nouveau Monde* (1962; *Children of the New World: A Novel of the Algerian War* [2005]) and *Les alouettes naïves* (1967; "The Naive Larks") both dealt with the war of national liberation from the French, which by then was over, and its effects on male-female relationships in Algeria (Zimra, Afterword [to Djebar, *Women*] 168–69). In 1969, she published a collection of poetry, *Poèmes pour l'Algérie heureuse* ("Poems for a Happy Algeria"), and a play coauthored with Walid Garn, her husband at the time, *Rouge l'aube* ("Red Dawn"), neither of which has received much critical attention. She claimed that she wrote in order to hide herself ("Assia Djebar" 236; Zimra, "Writing Woman" 70, 76). Critics interpreted this statement, which may have been made because early reviews simplistically assumed an equation between author and protagonist (Lançon 125), to mean that her writing was entirely fictional, but later works revealed that autobiographical traces were present even in the earliest texts. She taught history at the University of Algiers in the 1960s and 1970s but left that position after the Algerian government decided to enforce the use of Standard Arabic rather than French in instruction. She lived between Paris and Algiers for the following decade, writing and working for the Centre Culturel Algérien in Paris.

Desiring to reach more Algerian women than writing novels in French would allow, Djebar turned to film. She directed one feature-length film, *La nouba des femmes du Mont Chenoua* (1978; "The Nouba of Women from Mount Chenoua"), and a documentary, *La zerda et les chants de l'oubli* (1982; "Zerda and the Songs of Forgetting").[1] In *La nouba*, an experimental film that straddles the line between documentary and fiction, a female narrator interviews her female relatives about their memories of their experiences during the war of national liberation from the French (the relatives being interviewed were actually Djebar's). The film highlights themes that she had addressed earlier, such as the difficulty of male-female relationships in Algeria, and themes that would come to dominate her later fiction, such as the need for women to come together in solidarity and speak to one another about the traumas of the past and the present. The film's avant-garde aesthetics, which include slow duration, lack of plot-driven action, complex structure, complex use of sound, overlapping past and present scenes, and mixing of languages, marked her collection of short stories *Femmes d'Alger dans leur appartement* in 1980 (*Women of Algiers in Their Apartment* [1992]), which is taught frequently and has received much critical attention. *La zerda* takes colonial French newsreel footage of North Africa, reorganizes it, and adds a musical and narrative track that destabilizes orientalist tropes. She cowrote the screenplay with Malek Alloula, who was her husband then and an Algerian writer best known in the United States for *Le harem colonial* (*The Colonial Harem*). The costs and technical difficulties of filmmaking, coupled with the rigidity of state expectations about Algerian cinema, led her back to writing when future film projects never materialized.

In 1985, Djebar published *L'amour, la fantasia*. A "historiographic metafiction" (Hutcheon 105), the novel weaves the narrator's story of her relation to the French and Arabic languages and how she came to write with episodes from the colonial and decolonial history of Algeria and France, which focus on the presence of women in various wars. The personal-historical binary structure is subverted in the third part, which incorporates some of the testimonies from the film *La nouba*. The book is the first volume of a projected quartet, the fourth of which was never published. The second volume, *Ombre sultane* (1987; *A Sister to Scheherazade*), explores the intersecting trajectories of two women who, married at different times to the same man, are dissimilar in many ways but end up coming together in solidarity. Djebar's quartet was interrupted in 1988 by the Algerian people's demonstrations and their bloody repression by the state. As the country sank further into violence as a result of fundamentalist Islamist groups' bid for power and the Algerian military's brutal use of repressive measures, and as this violence began to target French-writing intellectuals and women, Djebar felt compelled to address the issue in her writing. The result was *Loin de Médine: Filles d'Ismaël* (1991; *Far from Madina: Daughters of Ishmael* [1994]), which with her collaboration was made into an opera, *Filles d'Ismaël dans le vent et la tempête / Figlie di Ismaele, nel vento e nella tempesta* ("Daughters of Ishmael in Wind and Storm") in Italy in 2000. In *Loin de Médine*, she goes back to another troubled time, right after the death of the Prophet, when the community of believers had to decide which road to take among bids for power by various groups. Interpretations of women's role in Islam became more conservative then. Perspectives are given of several historical and fictional women on the changes taking place around them.

The 1990s and early 2000s were a prolific time for Djebar. In 1995, she published *Vaste est la prison* and *Le blanc de l'Algérie*. The third installment of her quartet, *Vaste est la prison*, was translated as *So Vast the Prison* in 1999. It continued the tripartite structure of *L'amour, la fantasia* and its intersection of autobiography and history. The most directly autobiographical of all of Djebar's works up to that point, the novel also dealt with the situation of the Berber ethnic minority in Algeria and included reflections on the making of the film *La nouba*, an experience that still inspired Djebar almost twenty years later. *Le blanc de l'Algérie*, translated as *Algerian White: A Narrative* in 2000, is Djebar's elegy for the fallen intellectuals of Algeria. She was moved to write it after three male Algerian intellectuals who were very close to her were assassinated by fundamentalist Islamists during the civil unrest that began in the early 1990s. She organized her chapters around the deaths of Algerian intellectuals over a period of four decades, making subversive parallels between deaths caused by fundamentalist Islamists and those caused by the Algerian state. She added the French-Algerian intellectual Albert Camus and Josie, the white wife of the theorist of decolonization Frantz Fanon, into her pantheon of fallen Algerian intellectuals (her book was one of the first to reassess Camus's Algerian legacy in a positive light). Beginning with *Le blanc de l'Algérie*, her works were increasingly marked by despair over the level of violence and the status of women in postcolonial Algeria. She also lost her beloved father in 1995. Jane Hiddleston and other critics have argued that from *Le blanc de l'Algérie* on, her works were all poised between mourning and melancholia and that the psychoanalytic framework of trauma and haunting is appropriate to their study (*Out of Algeria* 120–80).

In 1997, Djebar published *Les nuits de Strasbourg* ("Strasbourg Nights") and *Oran, langue morte* (*The Tongue's Blood Does Not Run Dry: Algerian Stories* [2006]), which is Djebar's last book to be translated into English. (A more literal translation of the title is "Oran, Dead Language.") *Les nuits de Strasbourg* returns to her early focus on couples, this time in the French border city of Strasbourg, including a Frenchman and an Algerian woman. It is the most erotic of her novels. In contrast, the collection of short stories *Oran, langue morte* deals with the trauma of postcolonial and gendered violence in Algeria at the time. In 1999, she published her only book of essays, a compilation of lectures given and short pieces written over the years, *Ces voix qui m'assiègent: En marge de ma francophonie* ("The Voices That Besiege Me: From the Margins of My *Francophonie*"). It is a revision of her PhD dissertation, undertaken after she moved to the United States as a university professor in the mid-1990s because she felt targeted by the Algerian violence. She exiled herself to a land whose language she never mastered. She directed the Center for French and Francophone Studies at Louisiana State University between 1996 and 2001, then was a professor at New York University. She arrived in New York City shortly before September 11, 2001, and was a faculty member at the university until she retired in 2011. Her essays discuss the literary aspects of her work and her relation to language.

At the turn of the century, Djebar was still publishing. *La femme sans sépulture* (2002; "Woman without a Grave") is a historiographic metafiction of the life and death of Zoulikha Oudai, a real-life female freedom fighter during the war of national liberation from the French. The novel follows a fragmented structure in which various female characters remember Zoulikha and piece her story together. As in the film *La nouba*, a female narrator and filmmaker gathers the women's testimonies (note that *La nouba* was dedicated in part to Zoulikha Oudai and included a short section on her). The novel also highlights the difficulty of talking about the trauma of violence and torture, even decades after the fact. Djebar's *La disparition de la langue française* (2003; "The Disappearance of the French Language") mines similar terrain but with a major difference: for the first time since the 1967 *Les alouettes naïves*, the novel's narrator is a man. In 2005, Djebar was inducted into the Académie Française, a body composed only of forty members, most of them white men from France. Djebar's last work is the lengthy autobiographical *Nulle part dans la maison de mon père*, in which many of the fictional scenes of her earlier work, including a suicide attempt at age seventeen, are revealed to have been based on her life. The title has multiple valences, as explained by Maya Boutaghou (229) and Mary Jean Green (52). *Nulle part* continues to highlight Djebar's difficult relation to trauma, memory, and language. Her health started to deteriorate around that time. She passed away in Paris at age seventy-eight on 6 February 2015 and was buried in her hometown of Cherchell a week later.

Editions, Translations, and Secondary Sources

Most of Djebar's works from 1980 to 2007 and some of the earlier ones are available in French paperback. The contributors to this volume used the most available editions (e.g., from the cheap Livre de Poche paperback series) for the great majority of the texts discussed. Readers should keep in mind that these editions are frequently updated and that a newer edition may have slightly different pagination. Books also tend to go out of print, and some may have been reedited. We used the original editions of *Vaste est la prison*,

Nulle part dans la maison de mon père, *Oran, langue morte*, and *Ces voix qui m'assiègent*.

Many of Djebar's works were translated into English by a number of different translators. The admirably gifted and culturally knowledgeable Marjolijn de Jager translated *Women of Algiers in Their Apartment*, *Children of the New World*, and, in collaboration with David Kelley, *Algerian White*. The first two volumes of the quartet, *Fantasia: An Algerian Cavalcade* and *Sister to Scheherazade* (the translation of *Ombre sultane*), as well as *Far from Madina* appeared in British English translations by Dorothy S. Blair. The third volume of the quartet was translated as *So Vast the Prison*, by Betsy Wing, who, like De Jager, is a reputable and talented translator of francophone postcolonial literature. Djebar's first novel, *La soif*, was translated as *The Mischief* by Frances Frenaye, and her collection of short stories *Oran, langue morte* was translated by Tegan Raleigh as *The Tongue's Blood Does Not Run Dry*. A couple of pieces from other books have also been translated. With the help of Christi Merrill, I translated an earlier version of Djebar's chapter "Anamnèse" (in *Ces voix*) in 1999 ("Anamnesis"), and Farida Abu-Haidar translated Djebar's afterword to *Nulle part* into English in 2008 ("'Silence'"). While most translations appeared within five years of the original, some (e.g., *Women of Algiers in Their Apartment* and *The Tongue's Blood Does Not Run Dry*) were published about ten years later, at a time when Djebar had become more famous in the anglophone world. The translation *Children of the New World* was more than forty years overdue. The translations generally provide additional materials, such as glossaries, that can help an instructor contextualize Djebar's works for an audience unfamiliar with North Africa and Arabic. Blair adds a historical time line, a map, and a useful introduction to *Fantasia*. Both of De Jager's published translations contain invaluable afterwords by Zimra. Zimra's afterword to *Women of Algiers* contains a lengthy and revealing interview with Djebar. Because no book has been translated into English more than once, there is currently no choice between translations.

Many scholarly books and hundreds of articles and book chapters on Djebar have been published throughout the world. Despite her popularity, only a few scholars have written about the pedagogical joys and challenges of teaching her complex prose, whether in the original French or in translation. Dana Strand discusses how the novel *La femme sans sépulture* can be effectively used as a point of entry into teaching undergraduate students central issues in postcolonial theory that is gentler than the more abstract, sometimes opaque theoretical works of Homi Bhabha, Gayatri Spivak, or Édouard Glissant. She covers the ambivalences of rewriting history through memory and fiction, the role of women in the anticolonial struggle and their place in the postcolonial nation, the use of fragmented narratives that incorporate many voices, and questions of identity and hybridity as postcolonial mainstays that are articulated in an engaging manner in Djebar's "historiographic metafiction." Mary Vogl shows how to teach Djebar's multimedia prose, which often reflects on the tradition of orientalist painting. Vogl's pedagogy includes painting, photography, art criticism, and North African music and film, turning the literature class into a truly interdisciplinary cultural experience. Because Djebar's use of a multitude of intermedial intertexts from various cultural traditions magnifies the complexity of her writing, this volume fully explores this dimension.

There have now been three generations of Djebar scholars. In the 1980s, a handful of critics such as Jean Déjeux in France and Mildred Mortimer and Zimra in the United States contributed to making Djebar noticed in academic circles. In the 1990s and early 2000s, a larger group of scholars established itself as Djebar's works became more widely recognized. It includes Beïda Chikhi (Algeria and France), Mireille Calle-Gruber (France), Ernstpeter Ruhe (Germany), and, in the United States, Reda Bensmaia, Anne Donadey, John Erickson, and Hafid Gafaiti. Since 2005, there has been an explosion of scholarship on Djebar. Among the major scholars in this group are Hiddleston in the United Kingdom and Boutaghou, Dominique Fisher, Ranjana Khanna, Michael O'Riley, and Alison Rice in the United States.

Secondary sources on Djebar that the MLA survey respondents recommended most frequently as useful to instructors are the works of Mireille Calle-Gruber, Anne Donadey, Lise Gauvin, and Mildred Mortimer. Hiddleston, H. Adlai Murdoch, Jenny Murray, and Zimra were also mentioned by more than one respondent. Most respondents placed the study of Djebar in a postcolonial and feminist framework (with reference to Alloula, Bhabha, Cixous, Fanon, Khatibi, Lionnet, Memmi, Mohanty, Said, Spivak, and Young), in a Muslim feminist framework (with reference to Badran and Mernissi), in a poststructuralist framework (with reference to Derrida and Lacan), or in a historical framework (with reference to Horne and Stora).

According to the MLA survey, Djebar's works are most often taught in conjunction with texts by other Maghrebian writers, such as Tahar Ben Jelloun; by twentieth-century French and francophone writers, such as Leïla Sebbar; by writers who are women of color; by Arab women writers; and by English-language postcolonial women writers. The film that is most often screened together with Djebar's works is Gillo Pontecorvo's classic 1966 *Battle of Algiers*. The Tunisian filmmaker Moufida Tlatli's beautiful *Silences of the Palace* (1994) as well as Djebar's own *Nouba des femmes du Mont Chenoua* (1978) are also frequently screened in classes that include her writings. Feature films and documentaries are often used in the classroom, but few online resources are mentioned.

NOTE

[1] A *zerda* is a North African feast, a celebration with an abundance of food. A *nouba* is both intertwined songs or tales by women about their lives and an ancient Andalusian musical form.

Part Two

APPROACHES

Introduction

Anne Donadey

In the opening pages of her highly regarded and often-taught volume of short stories *Femmes d'Alger dans leur appartement* (*Women of Algiers in Their Apartment*), Djebar makes the following statement regarding her project of writing about Algerian women as a French-educated, Algerian woman: "Ne pas prétendre 'parler pour,' ou pire 'parler sur,' à peine parler *près de*, et si possible *tout contre*" (9; "Don't claim to 'speak for' or, worse, to 'speak on,' barely speaking next to, and if possible *very close to*" [*Women* 2]). The ethical, dialogical injunction she sets for herself is one that the postcolonial feminist theorist Gayatri Chakravorty Spivak has also called for in landmark essays such as "Can the Subaltern Speak?" This injunction, coupled with Djebar's exquisitely complex literary style, explains Spivak's interest in her works (Spivak, "Acting Bits," "Echo," "Examples," and "Ghostwriting"). Djebar and Spivak both refuse to be complicit with the illusion of narrative transparency, choosing to highlight the presence of the intermediary voice that conveys the message and to remain as aware as possible of the constant danger of appropriation involved in carrying a message across. Indeed, as Mireille Rosello astutely notes, Djebar's suggestion that the writer place herself "tout contre" carries with it both an antagonistic potentiality (in the sense of being "up against") and a loving one ("very close to") (7). Diya Abdo and Maria Bobroff suggest in this volume that Djebar's ethical stance is one that all her Western readers, and all Western readers of Arab-Muslim literature by women, would do well to make their own.

Conceptual Framing

Scholars do not all agree about how to interpret the works of Djebar. Their disagreements fall into two categories: one concerns the assessment of the evolution of her writing over its fifty-year span; the other has to do with the choice of theoretical approach to her writing.

Assessment of Her Evolution

Most critics divide Djebar's written works into two periods, those published before and those published after her foray into film in the late 1970s, a division marked by a ten-year hiatus. Although at the level of theme there is arguably much difference between her first pair of novels and her second, the works from 1957 to 1969 are stylistically close to one another: in style and structure they can be characterized as classical. In 1980, *Femmes d'Alger dans leur appartement* marked a turning point in her career, both in terms of her new focus on women's solidarity rather than on the male-female couple as the hope for the future and in terms of the work's avant-garde aesthetics and kinetic style (Gafaiti, *Femmes* 163; Donadey, *Recasting* 43–44). Clarisse Zimra, however, has insisted that Djebar's works should not be divided in such a way and that there is a continuity of preoccupations throughout her oeuvre ("In Her Own Write" and "Writing Woman").

In interviews, Djebar explained why she stopped publishing (if not writing) between 1969 and 1980, providing two main reasons. One was that she wished to write in Arabic but was unable to master literary Arabic in the way she had mastered French, so she switched to film as a way to reach Algerian women who could not read, let alone read her complex French (Zimra, "In Her Own Write" 208; "Entretien" [by Mortimer] 199). She also explained her self-silencing as related to the difficulty of writing—especially about sexual pleasure—in the autobiographical mode: because a section of *Les alouettes naïves* ("The Naive Larks") dealing with a couple's sexual pleasure was autobiographical, she feared this kind of self-revelation in a context in which modesty is key to an individual's, particularly a woman's, sense of self ("Assia Djebar" 238; Zimra, Afterword [*Women*] 168–73; Redouane and Bénayoun-Szmidt 28–30). Filmmaking, then, allowed her to go back to writing in French ("Assia Djebar" 242–43) and to continue exploring her complex relations to autobiography.

Theoretical Approaches

Scholarship on Djebar falls into two main theoretical groups: postcolonial feminist and poststructuralist, and there is both overlap and controversy within and between them. Postcolonial feminist approaches to Djebar are the most common, especially outside France. Some scholars feel that Djebar is too accommodating to colonialist, orientalist, patriarchal, or poststructuralist frameworks (Page; Altes; Woodhull 116); others argue that her ambivalent responses to orientalist and patriarchal structures in themselves constitute a postcolonial feminist approach (Donadey, *Recasting*). Writing from a postcolonial feminist standpoint, I have criticized poststructuralist approaches for equalizing varying groups' differential access to power that Djebar highlights in her works (*Recasting* 50–51). In turn, Zimra has taken exception to my use of the term *postcolonial* to refer to Djebar's works, which she sees as transcending all categories and needing to be assessed primarily for their aesthetic value ("Hearing" 159). In "Hearing Voices; or, Who You Calling Postcolonial? The Evolution of Djebar's Poetics," Zimra relates Djebar's writing to an Algerian and French poststructuralist tradition.

Other debates extend beyond the academic realm. Whenever postcolonial writers publish in what Djebar has called "la langue adverse" ("Assia Djebar" 232; "the inimical language"), the language of the former colonizer, they are often accused of betrayal. This accusation was made particularly in postindependence Algeria, where Arabic was soon selected as the only national language (see Berger for a careful delineation of these language politics). In

France, moreover, the term *francophone literature* is often used in a dismissive manner. Djebar is taught mainly in French and francophone literature and culture classes, but like other writers from formerly colonized countries, she had a vexed relation to being classified as a francophone writer (to being classified at all, for that matter). In *Ces voix qui m'assiègent: En marge de ma francophonie* ("The Voices That Besiege Me: From the Margins of My *Francophonie*"), she insists that she is "en marge" (7; "on the margins") and "sur les frontières" (27; "on the borders") of *francophonie* (the French-speaking world) yet chooses the possessive "ma" ("my") to refer to *francophonie*, claiming and disowning ownership at the same time. She ends up applying to herself the coined term "*francographie*" (29; "writing in French"). To an extent, this term allows her to escape the overdetermined space of *francophonie*, which connotes the continued imperial hegemony of the French language, as Spivak indicates in her afterword to this volume. Like Maya Boutaghou and Spivak, Djebar makes it clear in *Ces voix* that her work cannot be reduced to the francophone sphere by claiming "l'entre-deux langues" (32; "an in-between language").

Another controversy is that Djebar's version of feminism has not always been welcomed by critics. Although her *La nouba des femmes du Mont Chenoua* ("The Nouba of Women from Mount Chenoua") was recognized at the Venice film festival, it was criticized by Algerian male critics, who objected to the power reversal in the representation of the main male character. Hafid Gafaiti has expressed uneasiness at some of the feminist aspects of her works. In particular, he found *Ombre sultane* (*A Sister to Scheherazade*) to be too didactically and simplistically focused on woman-to-woman feminist sisterhood in opposition to men. He also took issue with Djebar's staging of women's subjectivity and speech and with the corollary objectification of male characters. He favored Djebar's complex historical rewriting of French colonization and Algerian resistance in *L'amour, la fantasia* (*Femmes*). Also, that Djebar dared to voice Algerian women's desire, beginning as early as 1957, has constantly disturbed critics. Her expression of the possibility of Algerian women's sexual desire, especially for European men in *L'amour, la fantasia* and later texts, in a context of colonial violence raised questions not just for Algerian male critics but also for some feminist scholars, who felt that the author was being irresponsible. There is a fine line between voicing the complexities of female desire in Arab-Muslim women and erasing the difference between consensual sex and rape, for example (Page; Altes). Djebar never gives her readers comfortable resolutions, whether the issue be female desire, colonialism, or nationalism. She raises difficult questions about women's agency—including sexual agency—in colonial and postcolonial contexts. For instance, in *La femme sans sépulture* ("Woman without a Grave"), she has the freedom fighter Zoulikha Oudai describe how a French police officer questions her in terms reminiscent of the dance of sexual attraction (Donadey, "African American and Francophone Postcolonial Memory"). Djebar always seeks to position her texts at the border between the oppositional and the complicit, in matters of sexuality as in matters of colonization.

Theoretical approaches that are not discussed at length in this volume but raise important issues are the psychoanalytic, autobiographical, and queer. Psychoanalytic approaches in general and trauma studies in particular have become an important prism through which to teach Djebar's later works, as Jane Hiddleston convincingly demonstrates in *Out of Algeria*. Kathryn Lachman briefly mentions trauma in her essay in this volume, which places *Oran, langue morte* (*The Tongue's Blood Does Not Run Dry*) and Djebar's essays on Albert Camus in *Ces voix qui m'assiègent* in the context of Algerian literature and the rise of religious fundamentalism since the 1990s. Ranjana Khanna reassessed the relevance of psychoanalytic and trauma frameworks for postcolonial contexts in general and for Djebar studies in particular, as have Rita Faulkner, Jenny Murray (*Remembering*), and I ("Introjection" and "Expression").

Even though Zimra, in good poststructuralist fashion, has continually cautioned us not to read Djebar too autobiographically ("Hearing" 157–58, "Still Besieged"), it is clear that Djebar's writing has become more and more autobiographical as time passes, culminating in her last book, *Nulle part dans la maison de mon père* ("No Place in My Father's House"). Djebar began with an understanding of writing as a way to hide the self (Djebar, "Assia Djebar" 236; Zimra, "Writing Woman" 70, 76). In 1991, Gafaiti clearly articulated the ways in which her autobiographical forays told of her relation to the French language instead of revealing events in her life ("Écriture"). By 1995, perhaps radicalized by the violence taking place in Algeria at the time or freer to write in the first person after her father's passing, she no longer felt the need to hide behind a narrator in *Vaste est la prison* (*So Vast the Prison*) and *Le blanc de l'Algérie* (*Algerian White: A Narrative*). Many scholars have addressed the complexities of her signature mix of autobiography and history and her shuttling back and forth between individual and collective autobiography (Geesey; Hornung and Ruhe; Asholt, Calle-Gruber, and Combe). The essays mentioned above, and others, provide excellent springboards to help instructors teach about this aspect of her work. The deft analysis by Mildred Mortimer of what she calls the evolution of Djebar's autobiographical project is particularly recommended ("Writing"). The connections Mortimer establishes between trauma and Djebar's difficult relation to autobiography are insightful, as are Lachman's view of Djebar's "[a]utobiography as an intertextual project" (88) and Murray's assessment of *Nulle part* as "a self-penned epitaph" ("'Mort'" 80).

There have also been a few queer approaches to Djebar. Zimra discussed potentially queer aspects of Djebar's novels before the term was coined. About Djebar's early fiction, she said, "Her heroines yearn for a prelapsarian universe of 'homoerotic' (rather than homosexual) love" ("In Her Own Write" 208). Zimra traces the homoerotic in Djebar's fiction between 1957 and 1980 in her important essay "Writing Woman" (see also Abdo and Bobroff in this volume). Although Djebar did not write explicitly about same-sex love, Jarrod Hayes has demonstrated that there is enough in her texts to warrant a queer approach to them. Like Zimra, he mentions that Djebar's descriptions of women in the hammam are often "homoerotic" (198). He relates them to Adrienne Rich's concept of the lesbian continuum (208–11) and to the work of queer scholars. He also notes that Djebar occasionally refers to the homosexuality of male writers or filmmakers, such as Jean Sénac and Pier Paolo Pasolini (212–13). Similarly, in her 2002 "historiographic metafiction" *La femme sans sépulture* (Hutcheon 105), there is one mention of a gay relationship between two young men, one Algerian and one French, which was apparently a fictional addition to a text based on historical realities (Mortimer, "Tortured Bodies" 116n9). Djebar evidently felt the need to add the story of a cross-cultural gay male relationship to her retelling of Zoulikha's engagement and death. She makes this story circulate by having it told by one Algerian woman to another within the space of her French-language novel. As always, she is making borders between sexualities and nationalities porous through telling and writing.

Challenges and Rewards of Teaching Djebar's Works

The formal experimentation in Djebar's style, especially evident in *L'amour, la fantasia* (*Fantasia: An Algerian Cavalcade*), makes her works challenging to teach. In Roland Barthes's characterization, we are dealing with "writerly" rather than "readerly" texts, texts that demand active participation and research on the part of the reader to elucidate them (*S/Z* 4). The difficulties occur on several levels.

Djebar's postmodern and avant-garde stylistics provide us with fragmented texts and exploded narratives. This is particularly true of *L'amour, la fantasia*, which includes some highly poetic passages relying on esoteric French vocabulary to refer to language and sexual pleasure: "Mots coulis, tisons délités, diorites expulsés des lèvres béantes, brandons de caresses quand s'éboule le plomb d'une mutité brutale, et le corps recherche sa voix, comme une plie remontant l'estuaire" (156; "Molten words, splintered firestones, diorites expelled from gaping lips, fire-brand caresses when the harsh leaden silence crumbles, and the body seeks for its voice, like a fish swimming upstream" [*Fantasia* 109]). The translator selected less arcane vocabulary in English ("molten" for "coulis," "splintered" for "délités," and "fish" for "plie"), which facilitates the reader's understanding. In an interview with Lise Gauvin, Djebar explained her selection of obscure vocabulary in that chapter as relating to her desire to recall the alliterative qualities of Arabic poetry ("Territoire" 24–25). In the above example, the repetition of *s* sounds is particularly well rendered by Dorothy Blair. Essays in this volume by Martine Guyot-Bender, Abdo and Bobroff, and Alison Rice will help instructors lead students through close readings of original and translated Djebar excerpts.

Djebar's works are multilingual: her idiosyncratic French language is inflected with Arabic as well as with touches of Berber and Turkish. In a stylistically beautiful passage, Djebar explicitly describes these languages as vying for dominance in her body, a struggle that is part and parcel of the process of colonization in *L'amour, la fantasia*:

> [L]a langue française, corps et voix, s'installe en moi comme un orgueilleux préside, tandis que la langue maternelle, toute en oralité, en hardes dépenaillées, résiste et attaque, entre deux essoufflements. Le rythme du "rebato" en moi s'éperonnant, je suis à la fois l'assiégé étranger et l'autochtone partant à la mort par bravade, illusoire effervescence du dire et de l'écrit. (299–300)

> [T]he French tongue, with its body and voice, has established a proud *presidio* within me, while the mother-tongue, all oral tradition, all rags and tatters, resists and attacks between two breathing spaces. With the rhythm of the *rebato* spurring me on, I am both the besieged foreigner and the native swaggering off to die, in the illusory effervescence of the spoken and written word. (*Fantasia* 215; trans. modified)

I have termed this multilingual style Djebar's Algerian palimpsest (Donadey, "Multilingual Strategies"). In this volume, Najat Rahman discusses her writing as translation, and Boutaghou provides guidance on further unraveling her multilingual arabesques, especially at the syntactic level. Boutaghou's essay, the first to elaborate in detail how Djebar's French often follows Arabic syntax, will be an invaluable resource to instructors, most of whom are not fluent in Modern Standard Arabic let alone Algerian dialectal Arabic. Instructors may also be interested in reading Boutaghou's "Le style en arabesque d'Assia Djebar."

Reading Djebar in French is thus already reading a translated-transmitted-transcripted text, in the sense that she brings to her French prose the oral inflections of her female relatives speaking in dialectal Algerian Arabic and Berber as well as the ornate nineteenth-century French of her archival sources and ekphrastic painterly descriptions (Al-Nakib; Donadey, *Recasting*; see Rahman, Boutaghou, and Rice in this volume). Her style is not only multilingual but also highly idiosyncratic and intricate. The sentences are long and winding, interrupted by the ample use of ellipses and dashes. To translate her into English is to make constant creative compromises between the rhythmic, breathy flow of her lengthy, juxtaposed sentence fragments and American English's tendency to favor efficient expression and avoid run-on sentences. Djebar often uses the metaphor of the *fantasia*, the ritualistic exhibition of horsemanship, to qualify her writing. In a chapter in her book of essays *Ces voix qui m'assiègent* titled "Anamnèse" ("Anamnesis"), she writes:

> Ce serait donc une écriture de fuite, disons une écriture de coursière (quelle monture pour ma fièvre inlassable et mon doute? . . .): écrire d'un souffle scandé par poussées, par brassées, par apnées. . . . Peu à peu, le rythme lent s'emporte, je ne sais plus si ce sont les autres en moi

> (les mères, les soeurs, les aïeules) qui nous emportent—la langue et moi sa cavalière—ou si c'est la langue d'écriture, ni dominée ni ensauvagée, simplement habitée, donc transformée, qui nous emmène, nous entraîne. (138–39, 150)

With the help of Christi Merrill, I rendered the passage as follows:

> This would be writing in flight, let us say, writing as riding (but what mount could carry my tireless fever, and my doubt?): to write to the beat of my breath, exhaling, inhaling, pausing. . . . Step by step, the slow rhythm gains momentum, and I no longer know if it is the others that I carry (the mothers, sisters, foremothers) who pull the language and I, its rider, along, or if it is the language of writing, neither dominated nor driven wild, simply inhabited and thus transformed, that sweeps us along and carries us away. ("Anamnesis" 179, 188)

The text includes alliterations such as "souffle scandé" ("the beat of my breath"). The rhythm of the sentences embodies their meaning: "par poussées, par brassées, par apnées" ("exhaling, inhaling, pausing") follows the scansion of one's breath. In the last sentence, the flow becomes more and more ample and the sentence appears to go from trot to gallop as "le rythme lent s'emporte" ("the slow rhythm gains momentum").

The challenges are compounded when Djebar is taught in the original French to students who are learning French or when her works in translation are taught in a context in which students know little about colonization in general and about Algeria and France in particular. The essays in this volume by Valérie Budig-Markin and by Rice address these pedagogical challenges.

Finally, teaching Djebar's nuanced feminist critiques of Algerian patriarchy can be especially thorny when students come to her texts with entrenched stereotypes of the Muslim woman seen in simplistic terms as always already oppressed by her male compatriots, religion, and culture. Feminist texts from Muslim cultures inscribe themselves in an overdetermined context because the so-called plight of the Muslim woman has been a mainstay of colonialist ideology in the West at least since the nineteenth century and continues to be used to justify Western economic and military intervention today (for an outstanding articulation of this issue in the French context, see Kemp). How to teach Djebar (or any feminist writer from a Muslim or Arab background) in North America or Europe, especially post-9/11, in ways that resist this dominant, imperialist, pseudo-feminist paradigm effectively is a difficult task indeed. Several essays in this volume propose a range of useful strategies to counter Islamophobia, help students acquire intercultural competency, and promote ethical listening to the multiple perspectives of Muslim or Arab women through teaching various works by Djebar (Rahman, Abdo and Bobroff, Jones, Elsayed, Bourget). This volume contributes both intellectually and pedagogically to the countering of such stereotypes in teaching not just Djebar but also, and more generally, texts by Arab or Muslim writers who deal with gender issues.

Sequence of Reading

The organization of this volume—historiography, interdisciplinary approaches, comparative approaches, and cultural and linguistic contexts—provides different lenses through which to view Djebar. Teachers interested in learning more about postcolonial, transnational, or postcolonial feminist approaches to her oeuvre would do well to focus on the essays by Rahman, Mortimer, Abdo and Bobroff, Dominique Fisher, and Annica Schjött Vonèche. Those looking to uncover poststructuralist approaches to Djebar may be most interested in Rice's essay. Both Boutaghou and Rahman put their studies of Djebar's works in the context of Abdelkebir Khatibi's theory of *bi-langue* (bilingualism and multilingualism), and Abdo and Bobroff, Schjött Vonèche, and Carine Bourget consider Djebar in reference to Said's concept of orientalism. Rahman reads her alongside Spivak, Abdo and Bobroff and Bourget through Islamic feminism, and Schjött Vonèche through Roland Barthes's *Mythologies*. Djebar's essays and speeches have also been used productively as a theoretical lens into her fiction (see the essays in this volume by Guyot-Bender, De Raedt, Lachman, Boutaghou).

Thérèse De Raedt, Fisher, and Guyot-Bender place Djebar in the context of French literature and painting; Christa Jones, Fisher, and Schjött Vonèche in reference to cinema; Lachman and Mortimer in the context of North African literature, film, theory and history; and Elsayed and Bourget in reference to Islamic and Middle Eastern sources. Interesting interpretive intersections arise among various essays in the volume. For instance, Fisher, Elsayed, and Bourget all raise the question of how to teach Djebar's signature mix of fiction and history and the ethical issues that arise from it. Jones and Fisher discuss how teaching Djebar in an interdisciplinary manner can help students seeking corporate global competencies learn to value the complex world perspectives that the humanities have to offer. Jones places Djebar's works in the context of journalistic as well as literary materials, including interviews, letters to the editor, and journal and newswire articles. Instructors of world literature will be particularly interested in the essay by Vlatka Velčić. Instructors of women's literature will profitably read essays by Abdo and Bobroff; Bourget; Jones; Dana Strand, who teaches Djebar alongside works by Hélène Cixous and Charlotte Delbo; and Velčić, who offers thoughts on teaching Djebar in the wider context of works by writers such as Toni Morrison and Gloria Anzaldúa. Those focusing on film will be interested by pairings of Djebar's works with Gillo Pontecorvo's classic docufiction *The Battle of Algiers* (Fisher's essay), Julien Duvivier's colonial classic *Pépé le Moko* (Schjött Vonèche's essay), and by a variety of documentary films on Algeria (Jones's essay) or on Muslim women (Bourget's essay).

Finally, instructors who teach Djebar exclusively in English will be well served by the essays by Abdo and Bobroff, Rice, Rahman, and Boutaghou.

While there are many secondary sources that illuminate the complexities of Djebar's texts, the purpose of this book is to provide pedagogical resources that will assist in instructor preparation and enhance the student learning experience. Many contributors offer original, classroom-tested ways to teach Djebar. Abdo and Bobroff describe hands-on exercises to illustrate for students Djebar's foundational use of the figure of the palimpsest. De Raedt shares a grid she created to show students how to perform a close analysis of a painting so they can explore the painterly quality of Djebar's prose. Bourget describes prereading activities she designed to raise students' awareness about stereotypes of Muslim women. Budig-Markin discusses a variety of scaffolded activities to teach Djebar's short story "Il n'y a pas d'exil" ("There Is No Exile") (*Femmes d'Alger*) to less-experienced readers of French and shows how to assess student learning effectively. Rahman's contextualization of *L'amour, la fantasia* should be of help to instructors new to teaching Djebar.

Many contributors use prereading activities, which they describe in this volume, and tend to teach Djebar toward the end of the semester in order to contextualize her works and make them more accessible for non-native speakers of French and students in the lower-division language classroom (Budig-Markin). Contributors to the volume and to the MLA survey on teaching Djebar consider that short texts (short stories or excerpts) work well with students at the lower level (see Guyot-Bender, Elsayed, Lachman, Abdo and Bobroff, and Bourget).

The responses to the survey indicate that Djebar's pre-1980 works are rarely taught (only one survey respondent has taught *Les enfants du nouveau monde* [*Children of the New World: A Novel of the Algerian War*]), whereas *Les nuits de Strasbourg* ("Strasbourg Nights") was her only post-1980 novel not mentioned by any respondent (an excellent study of this text by Ottmar Ette is recommended to interested readers). Djebar's *Femmes d'Alger dans leur appartement* and *L'amour, la fantasia*, often taught in tandem, appear with by far the most frequency in the survey, followed by *Ombre sultane*; *Oran, langue morte*; *Ces voix qui m'assiègent*; *La femme sans sépulture*; and *Loin de Médine* (*Far from Madina: Daughters of Ishmael*).

L'amour, la fantasia, Djebar's most acclaimed novel and a central text in her corpus, is an extremely complex book, even for a French-speaking audience; it therefore demands significant pedagogical effort to illuminate it. When I was preparing a special issue of the journal *L'Esprit Créateur* dedicated to her, Djebar suggested that the focus be placed on that novel's pivotal role in her works. The issue was accordingly titled "*L'amour, la fantasia*—avant et après" ("Before and after *Fantasia: An Algerian Cavalcade*"). Instructors preparing to teach *L'amour* should consult the essays in this volume by Abdo and Bobroff, De Raedt, Guyot-Bender, Rahman, and Rice (see also Thiel, "Querelle"; Fernandes; Murdoch; and Tageldin). Those preparing to teach *Femmes d'Alger* will be most interested in the essays by Abdo and Bobroff, Bourget, Boutaghou,

Budig-Markin, De Raedt, and Rice. Bourget's excellent comparative analysis of the two editions of the book is also recommended ("Réédition"). In this volume, Bourget and Boutaghou both discuss *Ombre sultane* (see also Prabhu); Boutaghou, Jones, Lachman, and Rice discuss *Oran, langue morte*; Lachman discusses *Ces voix qui m'assiègent* (see also Lionnet, "Ces voix"); Fisher and Strand discuss *La femme sans sépulture* (see also Mortimer, "Tortured Bodies"; Martin; and Milkovitch-Rioux); and Elsayed and Bourget discuss *Loin de Médine*. For less frequently taught works, Velčić focuses on *Vaste est la prison*, Fisher and Schjött Vonèche on *La disparition de la langue française* ("The Disappearance of the French Language"), Bourget on *La beauté de Joseph* ("Joseph's Beauty") and "Nuits de Ramadan" ("Ramadan Nights"), Mortimer on *Les enfants du nouveau monde*, and Strand on *La nouba des femmes du Mont Chenoua* (see also Bensmaia; Weber-Fève) and *Nulle part dans la maison de mon père* (see also Asholt, Calle-Gruber, and Combe; Hiddleston, "Mother"). Budig-Markin briefly discusses *La zerda et les chants de l'oubli* ("Zerda and the Songs of Forgetting"; see also Calle-Gruber, *Assia Djebar ou la résistance*, esp. ch. 10).

All but one of the twenty-two respondents to the MLA survey were located in United States institutions. About half taught in research universities, about forty percent at private liberal arts colleges and universities, and the rest at other types of institutions (one was an AP high school teacher). Contributors to this volume similarly include faculty members teaching in a variety of institutions (research universities, liberal arts colleges, and comprehensive-regional schools). Some are esteemed Djebar scholars (Mortimer, Fisher, Bourget) and well-known critics of French and francophone literature (Rice, Strand, Guyot-Bender) or of Arab literature and film (Rahman); others are emerging teacher-scholars who bring new insights to the field. All present a range of creative ideas for teaching various aspects of Djebar's complex works.

NOTE

Translations are mine, unless otherwise indicated.

HISTORIOGRAPHICAL APPROACHES

Finding One's History: Beyond Chronology in *L'amour, la fantasia*

Martine Guyot-Bender

This essay proposes concrete strategies to discuss the intertwining historical layers in *L'amour, la fantasia* (1985; *Fantasia: An Algerian Cavalcade* [1989]), a complex rendering of the colonization and decolonization of Algeria from an autobiographical narrative perspective. Many readers, including French natives, find reading *L'amour* somewhat difficult. However, and despite my own moments of self-doubt, I have found teaching it in its original French to non-native undergraduate students quite rewarding. I use *L'amour* as the concluding text in a multidisciplinary senior seminar in French titled Picturing War: Representations of France's Twentieth-Century Wars, a course that examines tools of representation of wars in a variety of media. By the time we get to *L'amour*, students have acquired fluency in various representations of World War II and of the Nazi occupation of France through films, novels, and other media, such as soldiers' letters, postcards, songs, Web sites, and maps. I have also provided them with enough background about the Algerian war of liberation from the French (1954–62) to tackle *L'amour*'s convoluted style of addressing historical questions and paradoxes. In earlier attempts, when I offered little or no prereading activities, students' first response was often rejection. Consequently, and although I usually rely on open discussion as the basic pedagogy for my literature classes, for this particular text I now include specific exercises in the early stages of our study. After identifying the multiplicity of influences on Djebar's vision through her own testimony, I have adopted a cumulative approach to the novel's contextual framework, one that could, I believe, be applied to a variety of pedagogical environments, including teaching the novel in its English translation to students with less knowledge of French or of the historical period.

Frameworks

Almost all we need to know about Assia Djebar to read *L'amour, la fantasia* can be gleaned from the inaugural speech she gave at the Académie Française, to which she was elected in 2005—the first member of Arab descent and only one of seven women chosen since the creation of the elite institution in 1635. The speech, ostensibly written in honor of her predecessor, the lawmaker Georges Vedel, provides a valuable backdrop to understanding better her position as a historian-novelist. In addition, it provides guidelines into the motifs behind *L'amour*'s complex, nonlinear narrative voice. Giving students excerpts of this testimony-speech (readily available on the Internet, but in French only so far [*Discours de réception*]), makes the issues of *L'amour* more comprehensible and more stimulating.

Citing Denis Diderot, Djebar identifies herself as being "à la fois en-dehors et au-dedans" 'both an outsider and an insider.' This reference to France and Algeria is doubled by crucial questions around language—Berber is her ancestors' language, Arabic her family's language, and French her adopted language—as well as of the conflict between traditional and modern ways of life in Algeria. The solemn assertion she makes to her audience of fellow *académiciens* that she is inhabited by a "désir ardent de langue" 'burning desire for language' brings us back to her ceaseless interrogations about language in *L'amour*. Her words are even more critical when put in the context of the Arabization process, the deliberate weaning of Algerian educational and administrative discourse from the French language. This policy was first announced in the initial 1963 Algerian Constitution and has been reaffirmed since then in each of its versions (1976, 1989, 1996 with its revision in 2008):

> L'Islam et la langue arabe ont été des forces de résistance efficaces contre la tentative de dépersonnalisation des Algériens menée par le régime colonial.
>
> L'Algérie se doit d'affirmer que la langue arabe est la langue nationale et officielle et qu'elle tient sa force spirituelle essentielle de l'Islam.
>
> (Preamble)

> Islam and the Arabic language were effective forces of resistance against the attempt to depersonalize Algerians led by the colonial regime.
>
> Algeria must reaffirm that the Arabic language is the official national language and that it draws its basic spiritual strength from Islam.

For Djebar, the universal human search for one's origins was clearly obstructed by the colonial imposition of French monolingualism onto local populations; this obstruction seems to have led to her interest in the history of her homeland (*L'amour* 14).

Immediately after evoking Vedel's imprisonment during the Nazi occupation, Djebar declares point-blank that for over a century France was also an occupier, "une immense plaie" 'a deep wound' in her country (*Discours de réception*). With an uncharacteristic burst of anger, she reminds her audience of the dismembering of Africa by European powers—except, she notes with a touch of irony, for Germany—and of the unnecessary violence of decolonization, which caused a "lourd passif de vies humaines écrasées" 'a heavy toll of crushed human lives.' The speech, with its explicit references to *L'amour* and *La nouba des femmes du Mont Chenoua* ("The Nouba of Women from Mount Chenoua"), her 1978 film documentary on women's testimonies of the Algerian war of decolonization, calls for the recognition of the origin and form of sources that historians have at their disposal when constructing historical accounts. The narrative voice in any historical account is unquestionably of crucial importance to her.

Indeed, embedded in this speech is a cue that, when *L'amour, la fantasia* was published in the mid-1980s, little had been written in French on the independence war from an Algerian perspective, and even less through intersecting historical and autobiographical discourses. This is not to say that Djebar wrote her novel in a total vacuum but that it tackled "le passé qui ne passe pas" (5; "the past that is not passing"), a past still on hold because no one has yet found a way to represent it definitively.

A *Progressive Approach*

Considering the convoluted form of *L'amour*, a cold reading of the book is risky for undergraduates who are not native speakers of French. Accessing a range of source materials, including the Académie speech; examining visual representations of the colonial experience, such as Eugène Delacroix's paintings (a clear influence on Djebar; see De Raedt's essay in this volume); and developing a variety of prereading activities make its examination more effective.

Unfolding the Multilayered Narrative

Readers generally agree that the organization and the mix of first- and third-person narrators in *L'amour* do not invite a smooth reading. Djebar's point is to engage readers, including educated French readers, in an epistemological questioning of how information about any past reaches future generations, through a style Maya Boutaghou calls "en arabesque" (216; "arabesque-like"). In an attempt to alleviate some of that confusion and infuse an inspiring way of considering *L'amour*, I ask students to predict the perspective and context of each subdivision of the book. They look through the entire text and take note, in each chapter, of the narrative voice, the presence or absence of dates, proper names, geographic locations, and so on. In the first part, titled "La prise de la ville ou l'amour s'écrit" (9; "The Capture of the City or Love-letters" [*Fantasia* 1]), chapters alternate autobiographical story lines, which are titled, with untitled but numbered historical accounts of episodes of the French invasion, internal conflicts among Algerian factions, and episodes of the war of independence. Sections of the second part, which is titled "Les cris de la fantasia" (71; "The Cries of the *Fantasia*" [47]), are inverted: autobiographical chapters are now numbered while historical ones are titled. This reversal of format keeps readers on their toes and suggests that any structure is a construction. The third part, "Les voix ensevelies" (159; "Voices from the Past" [111]), is made up of short parts, numbered as "Mouvements" 'Movements,' that include sections called "Voix" 'Voices.' The "Voix" sections may be described as a string of testimonies from previously ignored women survivors and invisible activists of the independence war, people Djebar searched for and then listened to before transcribing their stories, using a double translation from oral to written mode and from Arabic or Berber to French. Unearthing and dispersing those testimonies turn out to be the ultimate purpose of *L'amour*.

When actively involved in a close examination of the structure of a fragmented text, students assume the role of historians sifting through archives. It is up to them to find a rhyme and reason to nonlinearly organized documents.

Reading Closely

The first part of the novel provides an illuminating context to understanding the autobiographical and historical double take of *L'amour* and is worth reading slowly, almost one line at a time.

The first section, titled "Fillette arabe allant pour la première fois à l'école" (11; "A Little Arab Girl's First Day at School" [3]), raises the question of cultural and linguistic *métissage*, which permeates the narrator's position as she unveils both recent-personal and distant-national pasts. Students usually respond well to questions around the mise-en-scène of contrasts such as *fillette arabe / école*, *fez/cartable / costume européen*, *fillette/père*, *école française / village du Sahel algérien* (11; Arab girl /school, fez/ bag of schoolbooks / European suit, daughter/father, French primary school / village in the Algerian Sahel [3]). The absence of verbs and minimalist descriptions create vivid visual snapshots. Elsewhere in the novel, future, imperative, and interrogative verb forms reproduce the voices of inescapable tradition still echoing in the adult narrator's mind.

Going to school in the middle of the Sahel region frees her from the older generations of Arab women who deplored girls' education. The fez marks her father as Algerian, while his European suit and book bag situate him in the French context and provide a visual contrast with a traditional culture that hides and veils "la fille nubile" 'the nubile girl.' He too is both inside and outside his society. Embracing the French colonial education, "le père audacieux, . . . le frère inconséquent" (11; "the foolhardy father, the irresponsible brother" [3]) challenge and endanger tradition. Together, father and daughter lead the intradiegetic historian's quest for a multilayered past: her personal past, the past of her cultures, of her nation, of languages that make her who she is. The sentence that closes this first part, "Ma fillette me tenant la main, je suis partie à l'aube" (13; "I set off at dawn, with my little girl's hand in mine" [5]), says that we are all our past. Students tend to remember this sentence.

The first historical episode comes immediately after. It is the French armada's attack on Algiers on 13 June 1830, the abrupt start of the colonial period. Narratively speaking, it is marked by a clear rupture with the introductory autobiographical part. The date stands out, suggesting that factual information will follow. However, what comes next is not a series of dates and battles but an embedded vision of orientalist painting—which students love discovering, especially if they have some familiarity with Delacroix. In the first hour of the day, from the deck of their schooners, French soldiers observe—and artists sketch—Algiers, the object of European fantasy (thus the interest of using Delacroix's paintings liberally); on land, the unrecorded gaze and questions of an imagined community under attack are highlighted by Djebar. We find the same contrast that was in the first paragraph of "Fillette arabe," a gaze of traditional Algeria doubled by the impact of European presence. While the French officer Amable Matterer explains in his journal, "J'ai été le premier à voir la ville d'Alger comme un petit triangle blanc couché sur le penchant d'une montagne" (15; "I was the first one to catch sight of the city of Algiers, a tiny triangle on a mountain slope" [6]), the vision of Hussein, the district governor, can only be the subject of questioning: "Contemple-t-il en personne l'armada étrangère? Juge-t-il cette menace dérisoire? . . . Le dey se sent-il l'âme perplexe?" (16; "Is he personally watching the foreign armada approach? Does he consider this threat beneath contempt? . . . Is the Dey at a loss?" [7]). Adding another layer to this construction, Djebar imagines some of the women audaciously fantasizing about French soldiers through "rêves d'amour [qui] s'allument en elles" (17; "dreams of romance [that] are lit in their hearts" [8]). The arrival of the French armada, with observers on all sides, lays the basis for Djebar's insistence on ambiguity as an inherent component of any account of the past.

Students, at first baffled, will become familiar with how Djebar presents moments in history: they will ask themselves who writes, in what form is the writing, and which parts can only be imagined.

Drawing a Matrix

Note-taking in the form of a visual matrix helps students recognize the constellation of clues brought out by the book and how they intersect: episodes of personal reminiscences, episodes of the war of independence, reflections on the narrator's linguistic and cultural affiliations, transitions or absence of transition, blatant contrasts or mere nuances. Students enjoy creating their matrix, which can take various forms, such as arborescence, columns, or bubbles, as they attempt to uncover the text's underlying architecture. They quickly abandon this drawing as they gain independence in their reading. The point is not to complete a matrix (although completing it would be an interesting exercise) but for them to use it to ease into the first stage of reading. Sifting through the various levels with the aid of student-created visual structures focuses the readers' attention on the juggling of various times, spaces, and perspectives: this exercise helps students identify significant details on colonization that emerge through the tortured levels of the narrative voices.

Embracing Incomplete Understanding

We, instructors of literature, know the benefits of retroactive reading. Don't we all wish our students would do this spontaneously or at least willingly? The preparation I propose—making a preliminary inspection, doing a close reading, and drawing a matrix in a notebook—is not equivalent to a complete first reading but lays the groundwork for students to understand the reasons for the complexity of the text. This is not to say that their understanding will ever be full. The form of *L'amour* is, after all, a mirror image of anyone's relation to the past and of anyone's multicultural background. When we consider our own past (and students love to do that), questions arise, such as where one draws a line between periods, where and how one accesses information about this past, which filters enhance one's understanding and which block it, and how a personal perspective can alter the way one considers larger issues. These are all questions Djebar asks herself, readers, and implicitly historians in Algeria and elsewhere. *L'amour* thus emerges as postmodern history, in which pure facts are unattainable; This unattainability leaves some readers unsatisfied and some, hopefully, intrigued. *L'amour* does provide some answers, even if they are not, as usually expected from historical accounts, chronological or summarizing clear relations of cause and effect.

The narrative does not rely on outrage. Rather, both first- and third-person narrators adopt a clinical tone, one that could almost be confused with indifference—but we know it is not—about the documents she finds, the descriptions she reads, and the pictorial representations she comes across. In one of the most heart-wrenching passages, when families of shepherds, refusing to negotiate with French soldiers, are trapped in a mountain cave and killed by smoke, she borrows the words of a Spanish soldier who has difficulty representing the event he witnessed: "Quelle plume saurait rendre ce tableau? Voir, au milieu de la nuit, . . . un corps de troupes françaises occupé à entretenir un feu infernal ! Entendre les sourds gémissements des hommes, des femmes, des enfants et des animaux" (103; "Whose pen could do justice to this scene? To see, in the middle of the night, . . . a body of French soldiers, busy keeping that hellfire alive! To hear the muffled groans of men, women, children, beasts" [71]). That Djebar reproduces the witness's words and fatalistic tone carries more power than would any comment or analysis of the tragedy.

Djebar implicitly criticizes the omniscient, self-assured voice that was still typical of historical accounts in the 1980s, when she was researching and assembling *L'amour*. Instead, she chose, as a legitimate path to talk about Algeria, the entanglement of her personal multicultural background and the political past of her native land. Her Algerian father's determination to send her to school in the Sahel at a very young age led her ultimately to Strasbourg, to the École Normale Supérieure in Paris, to elite institutions of higher education in the United States, and then to the Académie Française, one of the most highly regarded institutions in the country that colonized her own. Paradoxically, her father's decision allowed her to recover lost parts of the story of her country and to transcribe testimonies of illiterate women in the Sahel. The irony is that only French, the colonizer's language, makes it possible for her to share with a French audience these women's testimonies on the war and for an Algerian audience to understand the role of women, even when they were at home, in the resistance to the French during the war and before that, in cultural resistance to the colonial order.

No linear story of the colonial period in Algeria emerges from *L'amour*, yet readers gather meaningful fragments that can fit on a time line (another possible exercise for students). As late as the 1980s, oral testimonies of aging illiterate women whose traditional way of life restricted them to their homes were rarely heard or recognized as legitimate historiographical sources. These witnesses were disappearing fast. Included in texts such as *L'amour*, their testimonies now constitute an invaluable body of knowledge. Students are quick to notice that Djebar's status of being both an outsider and an insider was essential to this process. Had she been entirely an outsider, she could not have accessed the testimonies. Had she been entirely an insider, they would have been lost forever.

Concluding More Broadly

In *L'amour* more than in any of her other texts, Djebar leads readers through concrete historical events by means of poetic, fluctuating, meandering ways that carry more than a hint of fantasy, seduction, and nostalgia. Subtle expressions of bewilderment and disbelief draw readers, regardless of their grasp of the historical context, to participate actively in the construction of knowledge. As we read *L'amour*, we find ourselves, like historians, using mismatched fragments from different sources to understand the past.

Djebar's goal in *L'amour* is less to provide a clear-cut history of Algeria than to invite readers to a dynamic journey. As Djebar clearly states it in her acceptance speech, her only power as a writer is to get closer to the past, not to create the illusion that she can make it emerge intact and univocal (*Discours de réception* 4). This is one lesson that students can take away from *L'amour*: because personal bias is inevitable, no writer can completely represent real life events, especially tragic ones. Conversation about that impossibility will likely lead to a discussion of the media representation of events more recent and more familiar to students than Algerian colonization and decolonization, such as the war in Vietnam, Iraq, or Syria. *L'amour* will also lead to a discussion of colonial legacies. Students often dwell on the paradox that the narrator of *L'amour* on the one hand recognizes her indebtedness to the French educational system and on the other hand appears both nostalgic for and distant from the traditions that still restrict many Algerian women to domestic life. The paradox is a hard realization for those students who are familiar with postcolonial theories, which are less ambiguous and rarely acknowledge the benefits derived from colonization.

Often, at the end of the semester, it is my turn to be surprised at how some students manage to unravel multiple layers of *L'amour* and use the issues it presents to discuss questions that pertain to their own lives; at how they, initially skeptical of the meaningfulness of *L'amour* or doubting their ability to grasp the novel, become impassioned advocates of it; and, most important, at how they gain a greater understanding of the many ramifications of historiography.

NOTE

All translations are mine, unless otherwise indicated.

"Attending to the Past, the Future Is Always around the Corner": Narrative Intervention in Assia Djebar's *L'amour, la fantasia*

Najat Rahman

Assia Djebar's literary works, it can be argued, coalesce in *L'amour, la fantasia* (1985; *Fantasia: An Algerian Cavalcade*). For Djebar writes in this novel of her enduring literary preoccupations, her longing to redress Algeria's historical past and the impossible limits of writing the self: "Je ne m'avance ni en diseuse, ni en scripteuse. Sur l'aire de la dépossession, je voudrais pouvoir chanter" (202; "I do not claim here to be either a story-teller or a scribe. On the territory of dispossession, I wish that I could sing" [*Fantasia* 142]). She wonders how one confronts the past, both the personal past of her childhood and of the collective memory, that of the 1830 invasion of Algeria and of the 1954 war of liberation, all marked by dispossession (*L'amour* 69). She is most forceful when she observes the span of history or of culture. It is from this unstated starting point that I teach her novel.

I begin by outlining this theme: the fracturing of heritage and of identity and the suturing of them through solidarity, mourning, and writing. The fracturing is the burial of the past, violence, absence, exile, the rift of the self from the collective, and the challenges to sustaining women's quest for selfhood—all manifested in the problem of language that she foregrounds. The suturing is the task of recovering a voice as a writer, as a woman, as an Algerian; the task of becoming free while remaining connected. Her literary intervention points to a future despite the past, where love rather than violence takes precedence, where liberation is more than independence, where struggle is continuous, and where imagination plays a vital role in pushing beyond the historical impasses.

At the University of Montreal, a francophone institution, I teach *L'amour* in the seminar Comparative Arabic Literature, at the graduate level.[1] At the undergraduate level, I teach it in courses such as Comparative Postcolonialisms, Introduction to Comparative Literature, and World Literature. In the seminar, I teach Arabic literature as multilingual and transnational. Placing Djebar's novel in this context shows the plurality of Arabic literature and of the world from which it ensues. It also highlights how history affects literature and vice versa: in this case, French colonialism in Algeria has left its marks on language, and the language has been reclaimed against itself. The approach also notes the damage of an imposed "Arabness" on an identity clearly more complex than it presents itself. Already in the first words of the novel, we are introduced to a "[f]illette arabe" (11; "[a] little Arab girl" [3]).

Focusing on multilingualism, we address translation as an intervention in history. Abdelkebir Khatibi writes that "toute cette littérature maghrébine dite d'expression française est un récit de traduction. Je ne dis pas qu'elle n'est que traduction, je précise qu'il s'agit d'un récit qui parle en langues" (*Maghreb* 186; "All this literature from the Maghreb, said to be of French expression, is a narrative of translation. I do not mean that it is only a translation, but it is a narrative that speaks in tongues"). For Khatibi, the Arab writer of French does not write his own language: "[I]l transcrit son nom propre transformé, il ne peut rien posséder . . . ni son parler maternel qui ne s'écrit pas, ni la langue arabe écrite qui est aliénée et donnée à une substitution, ni cette autre langue apprise et qui lui fait signe de se désapproprier en elle et de s'y effacer" (201; "He transcribes his transformed proper name, he can possess nothing . . . neither his maternal speech, which is not written, nor the written Arabic language, which is alienated and given as substitution, nor his other learned language, which signals to him to disown and efface himself within it").

One cannot do justice to such texts if one treats them only in one linguistic tradition or disciplinary approach. Works like *L'amour* demand new readings and new theories of translation. Djebar's text translates the fragments of the past into the present, the historical into the personal and the literary, and the oral into the written. In crossing borders of language, time, national cultures, genres, and strict gender demarcations, it crosses forbidden limits. But the limits themselves become the writing of imbricated borders. Djebar interlocks fragment and narrative, history and translation, testimony and fiction. A historian herself, she sees the translator as the one who reads the past with the present in order to probe its discontinuities (*L'amour* 63).

Emily Apter considers Djebar's writing as a translation of "the traumatic proximity of love and violence . . . manifest as exploded holes in language or translation gaps . . . aporias [that] disrupt predication" (*Translation Zone* 247). Apter draws out the significant political implications of such disruptive acts of literary translation, which reform the subject and reposition her "in the world and in history" and which create political change (6). Gayatri Spivak compellingly argues that translation, "an incessant shuttle that is a 'life,'" does even more, translating violence into conscience (*Aesthetic Education* 241). Moreover, she conceives of translation in Djebar's work as a possibility for healing and reparation:

> When a translator translates from a constituted language, whose system of inscription and permissible narratives are "her own," this secondary act, translation in the narrow sense, as it were, is also a peculiar act of reparation—toward the language of the inside, a language in which we are "responsible," the guilt of seeing it as one language among many.
> (243)

In my undergraduate courses, we address translation only after ample discussion of the novel. The number of students as well as the pedagogical culture sometimes dictate more of a lecturing format, though I tend to involve students in collaborative efforts of reading and discussion. They are drawn to questions of how one tells a story about oneself, how one approaches one's past, and how one's individual story intersects with that of the collective one.

Introducing Djebar and *L'amour*, I outline how during the war in Algeria and shortly thereafter she published her early novels *La soif* (1957; *The Mischief* [1958]), *Les impatients* (1958; "The Impatient Ones"), *Les enfants du Nouveau Monde* (1962; *Children of the New World: A Novel of the Algerian War* [2005]), and *Les alouettes naïves* (1967; "The Naive Larks"). After many years of silence, in which she experimented with films, she published *Femmes d'Alger dans leur appartement* (1980; *Women of Algiers in Their Apartment* [1992]) and autobiographical novels also centered on women and the history of Algeria: *L'amour, Ombre sultane* (1987; *A Sister to Scheherazade* [1987]), and *Vaste est la prison* (1995; *So Vast the Prison* [1999]).

As a writer, filmmaker, and scholar who gained international recognition and was admitted to the Académie Française in 2005, Djebar inscribed women's voices into the history of Algeria in her quest for freedom.[2] *L'amour* addresses Algeria's history from the war of conquest in 1830 to the war of liberation, 1954–62. She relies on her archival research and eyewitness accounts written at the time by participants in the war of conquest. The oral testimonies of the women who participated in the struggle form the basis of covering the war of independence and are at the center of her narrative.

The first volume of a projected quartet, *L'amour* is simultaneously an autobiography, a historical narrative of the effacement of Algerian history under French colonization, a rewriting of French archives, and a transcription of oral testimonies by Algerian women. My students are mostly Quebecois, French, or from former French colonies. The French students often point out the near absence in France today of public debate on the subject. For the students who may be uncritical of the preponderant narratives of settler colonialism, including its purported civilizing mission, I emphasize colonialism as a political structure and an economic system of power. I give examples of other colonialisms—in *L'amour*, the Arab expansion in Algeria. Colonialism is a subject that draws students and that also can make them uncomfortable if they are unprepared.

Students can simplify Djebar's gender narrative of seclusion and silencing, because it reinforces the kind of gender narratives that have been proliferating. The most effective way to resist this simplification is to begin with a discussion of Djebar's literary style and strategies. I introduce the term *aporia* and give ample gender examples. This approach interests students and becomes a way of complicating their understanding of the novel, going beyond the lulling polarity of oppressed Algerian women and their purported liberated French counterparts.

I define *aporia* as a conflict in meaning that cannot be altogether resolved, where one meaning cannot be privileged over another. For instance, the French invasion is evoked both as a "viol" ("the ghosts of the raped") and "amour non avoué" (28; "unacknowledged love" [16]). In evocative language, such as "j'ai coupé les amarres" (13; "I cut myself adrift" [5]), the image liberates but also separates, sends one into exile and recalls the ships of conquest.

Although I do develop student interest in stories such as those of the bride of Mazuna or of the grandmother and Djebar's critical vision as presented through them, I focus on the opening representation of the war of conquest, the Pélissier segment in part 2, the Abraham rendition, the story of Chérifa, and the closing sections, especially the evocations of Pauline Rolland. All this allows me to show the virtuosity and imagination of the writer, the profound historical vision that is inextricable from them, and her intellectual intervention into the present.

I link particular cultural customs to philosophical problems—for instance, the prohibition on writing (love letters)—so that such practices are not seen simply as ethnographic. Rather, the self-critique of traditional practices becomes an invitation to assume that same distance from one's own cultural practices. I do not linger on the sections that may introduce cultural benevolence but maintain power structures intact, such as the French and Algerian neighbors' exchanging recipes. This is a touching and timeless story of connection in times of conflict, but it does not have the same force as that of Rolland on the power of political and social solidarity through imagining difference otherwise. Also I avoid exotic elements, which might unwittingly reinforce orientalist preconceptions. Careful students quickly grasp these critical strategies.

I begin with structure, noting the alternation between the historic and personal parts in the novel and eliciting the significance of such a choice from students—for example, the impossibility of relating a story of self without a story of the collective, the realization of how the past still acts on the present. Djebar writes, "Avant d'entendre ma propre voix, je perçois les râles, les gémissements des emmurés . . . ils m'interpellent . . . pour qu'au signal donné, mon chant solitaire démarre" (302; "Before I catch the sound of my own voice I can hear the death-rattles, the moans of those immured. . . . They summon me . . . so that at the given signal my solitary song takes off" [217]). I then focus on the multiple and hybrid genres that complicate the propensity to tell the story of Algerians as unified. The style of narration, such as that of a palimpsest or fragment, highlights the complex nature of the history of Algeria and of the difficulty of access to the past.

Questions of representation and language ensue—notably, the violence of language and the violence of representation. In this novel, language is that through which violence speaks, and it is language that ultimately testifies to this violence. For there is no language of interiority for the narrator. In transforming language, she points to its duplicity: "La langue encore coagulée des Autres m'a enveloppée, dès l'enfance, en tunique de Nessus, don d'amour de mon père qui, chaque matin, me tenait par la main sur le chemin de l'école. Fillette arabe, dans un village du Sahel algérien" (302; "The language of the Others, in which I was enveloped from childhood, the gift my father lovingly bestowed on me, that language has adhered to me ever since like the tunic of Nessus: that gift from my father who, every morning, took me by the hand to accompany me to school. A little Arab girl, in a village of the Algerian Sahel" [217]). It is a gift of love that unknowingly inflicts violence. And yet she transforms language again so that it speaks creatively.

Djebar is fully aware of the paradoxes of her autobiographical novel, of revealing the self in the language of the other, "l'ennemi d'hier" (302; "the former enemy" [216]); thus, her autobiographical work announces itself, in an exemplary gesture of testimonial, as a fiction: "Ma fiction est cette autobiographie qui s'esquisse, alourdie par l'héritage qui m'encombre. Vais-je succomber? . . . c'est dans le silence des mots d'amour, jamais proférés, de la langue maternelle non écrite . . . que l'imagination . . . s'accroupit" (304; "My fiction is this attempt at autobiography, weighed down under the oppressive burden of my heritage. Shall I sink beneath the weight? . . . the imagination crouches in the silence when loving words of the unwritten mother-tongue remain unspoken" [218]). Implied in this narrative is the impossibility to speak from the inside. What is being testified to is absence, absence as the burden of heritage. Djebar nonetheless attempts to translate this silence in her venture of reconstruction. Testimony is unveiled as a duplicitous intervention. It is a language that, in attempting to witness, cannot escape the repetitive act of violence, revealing a central aporia: if one represents, one risks reproducing, however slightly, the act. But if one does not speak, one risks erasing the traces of the act.

And yet Djebar points to the many limitations of her role as witness: How does one testify over a distance of time and place? How does one testify to other testimonies? She writes, "Vingt ans après, puis-je prétendre habiter ces voix d'asphyxie?" (283; "Can I, twenty years later, claim to revive these stifled voices? And speak for them?" [202]).

After a discussion of narrative and examples of how Djebar foregrounds the construction of her novel, so students are now attentive to how a story does not just give itself, I turn to representation. Djebar stages romantic representations of Algeria that elide its terribly violent reality (17). She denaturalizes that staging and shows ideology at work, precisely in such violent representations that dominate (66, 67). Students can become uncomfortable, especially when she describes how the French doctor, delivering Western medicine, fails to persuade the father to treat his son, who was injured in the first place by colonial violence: students recognize that such narratives endure today precisely in contexts of war and occupation.

It is Matterer, an archival writer, who sees the city of Algiers as an odalisque (14–15), establishing the analogy between sexual and military conquest. Problematically, violence is rendered romantically like mutual seduction.[3] This idea is developed through close reading and attention to the novel as a literary text.

I then focus on how Djebar attempts to revisit her heritage before it solidifies again into tradition. The paternal heritage she highlights includes the father as a figure of transmission, mediation, and hybridity—he wears a Turkish fez and a European suit and separates her from her own language but reveals another world to her through a French education (11); Pélissier as the "bourreau-greffier" (114; "butcher-and-recorder" [78]) who inscribes the violent erasure he perpetuates into memory; Abraham as the aporetic figure whom tradition has recuperated too quickly and too often as a figure of patriarchal submission over love and that she reclaims for his love for his son. Ibn Khaldun is a forerunner of the writing of self in the language of the other. Saint Augustine is an Algerian whose confessional writing in Latin is emblematic. In the third part, Djebar looks to women who participated in the war of liberation as voices of revolt and of survival, of struggle and of solidarity, who may open the way out of past and present impasses. Rolland becomes a figure of solidarity who sets a different path for freedom.

Djebar's disappointment with the postindependence responses to the struggle of women like Chérifa is evident: "la paix soudain comme un plomb" (201; "peace suddenly descending like a lead weight" [141]). Djebar ends her novel with an anticipation of deadly violence. The narrator's internal exile echoes that of women like Chérifa. Djebar's emphasis on women is a necessary and constitutive part of a historical struggle for freedom. As Spivak points out, colonizing powers perpetuated rigid precolonial laws to reinforce patriarchy and gender oppression (*Aesthetic Education* 109).

Djebar encounters her past as fractured, divided between a paternal heritage where love recedes and a maternal heritage always in effacement. Another juxtaposition is made between the testimonies of Algerian women and that of Abraham, whose ballad is at the center of these testimonies. Djebar reads the story of Abraham to valorize love over submission and to point to the threatening possibility of foreclosing one's future for one's past. It is this inherited cultural moment that will lead her to point to the rupture in her inheritance and to attempt a new reading of its story.

Djebar recognizes that the fracturing of her paternal heritage has created a divided self and that language, a marker of absence and of historical violence, reflects this division: ". . . je suis à la fois l'assiégé étranger et l'autochtone partant à la mort" (299; ". . . I am alternately the besieged foreigner and the native swaggering off to die" [215]). She intervenes through autobiography "as a recovery of women's voices," where identity is revealed through language as a "wound" (Spivak, *Aesthetic Education* 181). For if writing gives voice, it remains "hiéroglyphes de la voix collective et sauvage" (*L'amour* 83; "hieroglyphs of a wild, collective voice" [56]). Spivak insists that the "recovery of a woman's voice" has to take into account how woman "may be the site of internalized phallocracy": " . . . Djebar gives to the supercolonized woman the task of a-phonie: not a writing, not a graph, but not the phonocentric . . . unmediated woman's voice either" (*Aesthetic Education* 231). She also intervenes through solidarity. Rolland, an 1848 French revolutionary imprisoned and then deported to Algeria as a dangerous rebel, is claimed as one of her ancestors, because Rolland's struggle and writing speak of sisterhood with Algerian women (*L'amour* 308–09; *Fantasia* 223). For Djebar, the words of Rolland, so promising of a future, "libèrent" (309; "finally set . . . free" [223]), allowing for a quest for identity tied to a greater quest for solidarity.

Opposite to Rolland is the nineteenth-century painter Eugène Fromentin, "seconde silhouette paternelle" (313; "like a second father figure" [226]), whose journal Djebar evokes for her narrative. Fromentin gathers from the dust a severed hand of an Algerian woman, a hand of memory, and Djebar reclaims this mutilated fragment from the past that he throws away. Writing, for her, is that hand extended by the father, a borrowed thing that can neither be completely possessed nor appropriated to the present: ". . . je me saisis de cette main vivante, main de la mutilation et du souvenir et je tente de lui faire porter le 'qalam'" (313; ". . . I seize on this living hand, hand of mutilation and of memory, and I attempt to bring [to] it the *qalam* ['reed pen']" [226]). Yet the severed hand is also testimony to the inability to narrate what resists narration.

Djebar's intervention into history implies not only solidarity in collective struggles but also mourning, which requires "exhumer des cris" (93; "exhuming buried cries" [63]) of the dead through a writing of love. Following Edward Said and Giambattista Vico, if we consider that the term *human* derives from "the root to bury," then our humanity also finds its fulfillment in proper mourning (Said, *Beginnings* 373). Djebar redeems writing, which allows her to hear and "ressuscite" (273; "resurrect" [204]) the buried cries of protest and to awaken the voice.

For a new future to become possible, it is imperative to recapture a cultural past in order first to mourn, but this is exactly the figure of the impossible according to Spivak: "an experience of the impossibility of recapturing a cultural past in order to mourn it so that new life can begin. Yet . . . the figure of the experience of the impossible *is* the condition of possibility of deciding. In the aporia or double bind, to decide is the burden of responsibility" (*Aesthetic Education* 109). Beyond aporia is responsibility predicated on consciousness, for consciousness is also liberation. The need to struggle for liberation persists; liberation cannot be limited to national independence, as the emblematic case of Algerian independence has shown. Said writes, "Liberation is consciousness of self, a never-ending process of 'discovery and encouragement' leading to true national self-liberation" (*Culture* 274). A new beginning lies in language, as creative possibility, beyond violent history, "to transform (language) from a force for identity statement into a transgressive, disruptive . . . mode" (*On Late Style* 84).

Djebar's writing imagines beyond the buried violence, reminding us, in the words of Spivak, that the "the future is always around the corner, (and that) there [are] only victories that are also warnings" (*Aesthetic Education* 16). The quest for freedom needs to remain in tandem with a vision of attending to the past (and to the present) to open onto a future. Djebar's work invites us to rethink history, and the self imbricated within it, poetically.

NOTES

All translations are mine, unless otherwise indicated.

[1]I also taught *L'amour* and other works of Djebar in such seminars as Problems of Representation and Introduction to Advanced Literary Studies. Before that, I taught her novel at James Madison University in the course Major Authors.

[2]The unfinished quartet also includes *Ombre sultane* and *Vaste est la prison*.

[3]In a detailed criticism, Page accuses Djebar of unwittingly reproducing Western perspectives. Gabara responds to Page's argument (198n70).

Seeds of Change: Assia Djebar's *Les enfants du nouveau monde / Children of the New World: A Novel of the Algerian War*

Mildred Mortimer

Assia Djebar published four novels, a play, and a collection of poetry before achieving international recognition in the 1980s with her book of short stories *Femmes d'Alger dans leur appartement* (1980; *Women of Algiers in Their Apartment*) and her novel *L'amour, la fantasia* (1985; *Fantasia: An Algerian Cavalcade*).[1] Yet numerous critics make no mention of her earlier writings in their study of her work.[2] As Clarisse Zimra notes in her afterword to *Children of the New World* (the English translation of *Les enfants du nouveau monde*), the lack of critical recognition accorded Djebar's pre-1980 texts has given readers an incomplete picture of her oeuvre (203).[3] It is fitting to return to Djebar's early texts, examining them for thematic and stylistic elements that will add to, if not complete, the picture.

Djebar's third novel, *Les enfants du nouveau monde*, is her first to treat events of the Algerian Revolution. A fresco of Algeria in the throes of war, it is overtly anticolonial and feminist, supportive of Algeria's struggle for independence from France, and critical of the oppressive nature of indigenous patriarchy. Exploring the process of decolonization in her country, the writer discerns a significant gender gap between Algerian men and women: men struggle to throw off the yoke of French colonialism; women, the captives of both a colonial structure and a native patriarchy, seek agency in their family and society as well as political independence from the colonial power. The narrative is fragmented and multiply voiced, a mode for which the novelist came to be known.

In this essay, I argue that *Enfants* not only provides scholars with germinating seeds—political, feminist, and aesthetic elements that will define her later work—but also merits greater attention in the classroom as a well-crafted, thoughtful text that is politically correct in its anticolonial stance yet subversive in its feminist objectives, expressing the writer's belief that Algerian independence alone will not liberate women.

Written in 1960 as the Algerian war raged and published in 1962, the year the war for independence came to an end, the novel is constructed as a *témoignage* ("testimony"), a realistic chronicle of one day's events in Blida, a small city southwest of Algiers. The date is 24 May 1956, two years into the struggle for independence. As the story unfolds, twenty characters appear, men and women connected to one another by family ties. Charting the intricate meshing of their lives, the novel offers readers a panoramic view of a community awakening to the psychological demands of revolution yet unable to predict its outcome.

My pedagogical approach is to situate the text historically, bringing anticolonial and feminist theory into the discussion. I introduce the novel by focusing on the opening chapter, which gives readers a panoramic view of the war often experienced indirectly by women cloistered in their homes:

> Il arrive aux femmes qui, dans la fraîcheur de leur chambre, ne bougent pas, de se tendre un instant, les yeux grands ouverts, le regard fixe, avec une palpitation enfantine, et d'imaginer leur mari debout contre un mur, au soleil de midi, secoué sans doute d'une peur qu'il doit s'efforcer de ne point révéler, mais que l'épouse retrouve en lui, le soir lorsque tout est fini, que la montagne reprend sa nudité orgueilleuse. (16)

> In the coolness of their room, the women sometimes don't move; they grow tense momentarily, eyes wide, staring into space, hearts pounding like those of the children as each imagines her husband up against a wall in the sun at high noon, no doubt shaking with a fear that he must make every effort to conceal. But the wife recognizes it at night, when everything is over, when the mountain once again assumes its arrogant nakedness. (*Children* 3)

Significantly, Djebar illustrates the gap between male and female experiences in spatial terms: women witness the devastation in the shelter of their homes as men face danger directly in streets patrolled by the French army. She reinforces the sense of the immobility of women by depicting them huddled in their rooms as they watch "la montagne dans les feux de la lutte" (13; "the mountain under fire" [3]). As descriptive passages transmit the immediate effect of the war on the population, they reveal the reasons for women's inability to act. A rigid patriarchal society that cloisters women, requiring their submission and promoting passivity in their formative years, prevents them from maturing emotionally and politically. The war, however, is a catalyst for change.

Instead of situating all her female characters in confined space, Djebar broadens the social spectrum as the text progresses to include "modern" as well as "traditional" women, all of whom are forced to meet new challenges. Although the latter remain in closed interiors, the former have access to the city. Yet the boundary between closed and open is often porous: women who become militants, in cities or the countryside, may later find themselves confined to another form of enclosure—for example, to life behind prison walls when they are captured by the French military.

Readers find that as the war gains intensity, when there are arrests and torture, when some individuals and families flee the war zone and others join the resistance, women are forced to adopt new strategies for survival. After men leave home to join the resistance and are imprisoned or killed, women assume greater authority in their families: "il se trouve toujours une femme, jeune, vieille, peu importe, qui prend la direction du chœur" (14; "there is always one woman—young, old, it makes no difference—, who conducts the choir" [2]).

To present a cross section of Algerian women, Djebar introduces Salima, an imprisoned militant; Hassiba, a militant about to join the revolutionaries in the countryside; Suzanne, a French intellectual who espouses the anticolonial cause; Touma, a prostitute; Amna, an Algerian police officer's wife; Cherifa, a militant's wife; and Lila, a university student whose husband has joined the underground. Some choose to participate in the revolution (Salima, Hassiba); others are thrust into new, often dangerous situations (Amna, Cherifa, Lila). Whether by choice or circumstance, all are swept up by the winds of political change and must respond to them. Amna, when her husband tells her to denounce her neighbor, lies to him (never having deceived him before), then warns the militant's wife of his imminent arrest. Cherifa immediately sets out across town to warn her husband and urge him to flee:

> Elle a oublié le danger lui-même; peut-être n'est-ce pas lui, en vérité qui l'a poussée, mais un désir sournois de savoir soudain si elle ne peut être vouée qu'à l'attente dans sa chambre, à la patience et à l'amour. Ainsi, elle a traversé la ville entière, cette présence pour elle aux yeux multiples, hostiles et au terme de cette marche, elle a découvert qu'elle n'est pas seulement une proie pour la curiosité des mâles—une forme qui passe, mystère du voile que le premier regard sollicite, faiblesse fascinante qu'on finit par haïr et sur laquelle on crache—non, elle a existé. (201–02)

> She'd forgotten the danger itself. In truth, it's perhaps not that which drove her, but rather a gnawing desire to suddenly know whether she could really spend her life waiting in her room, in patience and love. That's why she crossed the entire town, bared her presence to so many hostile eyes, and at the end of her trek discovered that she was not only a prey for the curiosity of men—a passing shape, the mystery of the veil accosted by the first glance, a fascinating weakness that ends up being hated and spat upon—no, she now knows that she has existed. (143)

Class discussion of this passage focuses on Cherifa's growing sense of self. Students find that Cherifa not only meets the challenge of venturing into public space alone but also understands how participating in the political struggle has transformed her: "toutes ces sensations violentes qui ont alimenté sa volonté de plus en plus tendue et qui, de plus en plus, la découvraient à elle-même, l'ont introduite dans un état second" (201; "All the violent emotions that had fed her increasingly strained willpower and that had revealed her temperament, pushed her beyond herself" [143]).

Examining the interplay between a veiled woman in the streets of Blida and the "hostile eyes" of her countrymen, students become aware that Djebar alerts her readers to traditional male resistance to women's freedom of movement in public space. The city street becomes a metaphor for women's possibilities and limitations. Cherifa gains a new sense of self-worth by venturing into public space, but Touma dies in the street, murdered by a brother committed to cleansing the shame that her loose behavior has cast on her family. Since FLN revolutionaries (FLN stands for Front de Libération Nationale ["National Liberation Front"]) have made this honor killing a requirement for the young man to join their cell, the implementation of an archaic code, as Evelyne Accad aptly notes, represents a disquieting omen for women's rights in postcolonial Algeria (807). Algerian women, Djebar warns, face an indigenous patriarchal structure so deeply rooted that it may not change with independence; they must be prepared to continue the struggle.

Broadening the social spectrum of Algerian women by introducing Lila, a young woman whose education and worldliness contrast vividly with Cherifa's life experiences, Djebar exposes the similarities as well as the differences between the two characters. Lila, like Cherifa, confronts a dangerous political situation not of her making. Once her husband joins the underground, she chooses to live alone. When she provides refuge for her young cousin, a rebel on the run, she is arrested for harboring a fugitive. She resists her interrogators in prison, showing the same courage that Cherifa has shown. Each woman faces a different test, but both mature politically. Djebar describes this maturation realistically: Lila and Cherifa awaken to political action in moderate steps. Lila chooses not to follow her husband into the maquis. Cherifa, on learning from her husband that women are actively engaged in the rebellion, does not ask to join him; she will wait patiently for his return but with a greater sense of self.

The parallel journeys of Cherifa and Lila toward self-knowledge and political engagement foreshadow the eventual bonding between Hajila, the traditional woman, and Isma, the "modern" woman, in Djebar's *Ombre sultane* (*A Sister to Scheherazade*). In that novel, Isma, a well-educated professional Algerian who married and then left the man of her choice, helps Hajila, trapped by poverty and illiteracy, break free from an unsatisfactory arranged marriage to the same man, a marriage that Isma herself helped broker earlier. Watching Hajila defy overt oppression, Isma recalls her own struggle against patriarchal domination, though it was more subtle and indirect. The memory of her father's anger at her inadvertent display of bare legs on a fairground swing when she was a child makes her realize that she and Hajila share common ground. Hajila's revolt therefore supports Isma's quest for self-understanding.

Djebar reminds her readers that Scheherazade, storyteller of the *Arabian Nights*, needs the help of her sister, Dinarzade, to succeed in telling tales so inventive that the sultan spares her life. Djebar reconfigures this legendary complicity between sisters in the relationship between Isma, the largely autobiographical self, and Hajila, the primarily fictional self. If Lila prefigures Isma, the relationship between Isma and her father depicted in *L'amour, la fantasia* begins in *Enfants* as the narrator describes an Algerian father proudly walking his daughter to school: "Lila se souvient de son père qui lui portait son cartable et la conduisait, main dans la main, à l'école primaire" (182; "Lila remembers that her father used to carry her book bag and, her hand in his, take her to elementary school" [129]).[4]

Although some characters, relationships, and events depicted in *Enfants* recur in later texts, others do not. For example, the friendship between Lila and her cousin Bachir remains unique. Lila, having experienced love for her husband, Ali, as a stifling emotion—"le faisceau de liens que l'emprisonnait à Ali" (251; "the cluster of links that enslaved her to Ali" [183])—comes to value her friendship with her cousin as a sentiment as profound as romantic love. After his death, she recalls their last night in her apartment, when they talked until dawn: 'Parler avec transparence, avec palpitation, au cœur de la nuit, quelles belles heures cela faisait! elle y pensa ensuite, bien plus tard" (251; "Speaking honestly, with passion, in the deep of the night—those were beautiful hours she realized, later on, much later" [182]). Their relationship, however, is destroyed by war: Bachir is assassinated, Lila imprisoned. We debate the following question in class: Is Djebar telling readers that true friendship between a man and a woman can rarely, if ever, endure?

Djebar's readers find in *Enfants* a structure far more complex than the linear first-person narrative of the first two novels, *La soif* (*The Mischief*) and *Les impatients* ("The Impatient Ones"), and narrative strategies that Djebar never used in her previous works. The author has explained that the multiplicity of characters, use of flashback, and *chassé-croisé* or reshuffling in time were new to her ("Entretien" [Mortimer] 198). By depicting many female characters with different viewpoints, she introduces a gendered perspective that offers a nuanced interpretation of Algerian women's capabilities and limitations and, most important, that eschews any reductive analysis. Gordon Bigelow suggests that the analysis of gender systems that emerges in the novel leads to an analysis of colonial Algeria's cultural practices and historical transformation that is more complex than those provided by Frantz Fanon and Pierre Bourdieu in their theoretical writings (14). Although Fanon and Bourdieu (*Algerians* and *Sociologie*), like Djebar, represent the anticolonial struggle as a process that destabilizes the foundations of identity and community, the novelist, Bigelow argues, understands most fully the strong claim of embedded cultural norms on Algerian society, particularly those related to gender. Thus, if the tone of the novel is optimistic, conveying the belief that the colonized will win the war, this optimism remains qualified in the realm of women's rights.

Djebar's most important stylistic innovation in *Enfants* is the use of fragmentation in narrative: as we move quickly between chapters titled with different characters' names, the inner thoughts of the characters form a succession of fragments. Jane Hiddleston notes that the novel offers a collective vision of modern Algerian women whose voices are neither definitive nor fully evolved (*Assia Djebar* 40). I suggest to my students that Djebar chooses a narrative strategy that conveys the sense of a revolution in the making. In 1956 in Algeria, men and women caught up in the conflict have not yet assimilated their experiences, have not yet reached political and emotional maturity. Hence Djebar's narrative captures the drama of a moment in history, one day's events reflecting a volatile, rapidly changing political struggle.

As we probe the effect of the novelist's choice of the fresco, I ask the class to consider whether the text that resists the obvious stereotype of courageous male combatant versus timid female observer nevertheless creates stereotypes by sketching each character too briefly. This question leads some students to voice the opinion that Djebar avoids stereotypes by portraying her characters in varying stages of psychological awakening. They note, for example, that the personal transformation of Cherifa begins when she leaves her first husband, an act of rebellion and self-affirmation that predates by several years her decision to cross town to warn her second husband of his imminent arrest.

To ground Djebar's fictional world in the reality that subtends it, I reference Danièle Djamila Amrane-Minne's work on Algerian women's active participation in the liberation struggle. The Algerian historian's study combines personal testimony with archival research: documentation from the Algerian ministry's files on the combatants, the Algerian press of the period, and her collection of eighty-eight interviews with Algerian women combatants (*Femmes*).[5] In the theoretical realm, Fanon's "L'Algérie se dévoile" ("Algeria Unveiled") provides a provocative introduction to a discussion of women's empowerment. In his analysis of the changing significance of Algerian women's veiling practices during this period, Fanon asserts that the revolutionary experience will radically transform the people engaged in it. Although Djebar depicts Cherifa's journey as such a transformational experience, she cautions against the optimism that he expresses. In this regard, Fatima Mernissi's analysis of the division between the public universe—the *umma* (the community of Muslim believers), which, she notes, is composed principally of men (*Sexe* 156 and *Beyond the Veil* 138)—and the domestic universe of women helps students grasp the complexity of the struggle for women's rights in a society divided by gender. The Moroccan sociologist explains that spatial rules for that division are so fundamental to the Muslim social order that they cannot be easily dismantled.

To bring the immediacy of the Algerian war into the classroom and further illustrate the emergence of women in public space, I often show *The Battle of Algiers* in conjunction with this text. As students compare the representation of Algerian men and women in Djebar's novel with that in Gillo Pontecorvo's film, they recognize women's important contribution to the war effort. Text and film combine to destroy the stereotype of war as an exclusively masculine activity and of Algerian women as bystanders to their nation's history.

Before we conclude our analysis of the work, I pose a question that may serve as an essay topic. Does this anticolonial novel speak to today's readers, and if so, why? The answer, students find, lies in its focus on emerging female empowerment as women move into new situations and enter new spaces. Having followed Djebar's characters through difficult emotional transitions in trying times, they now view Algerian women's struggle against patriarchal domination with greater clarity and compassion, thereby rejecting the stereotype of the forever subjugated and submissive Muslim woman. Djebar's novel is clearly relevant to students, particularly young women students, who are seeking their way in today's world. I therefore urge my colleagues to teach this text, which, by skillfully articulating women's varied perspectives on a crucial anticolonial war of our time, confirms Assia Djebar as a leading Algerian writer.

NOTES

[1]The preceding works were *La soif* (1957), *Les impatients* (1958), *Les enfants du nouveau monde* (1962), *Les alouettes naïves* (1967), *Rouge l'aube* (1969), and *Poèmes pour l'Algérie heureuse* (1969).

[2]Among these critics are Anna Rocca, Soheila Kian, and Nicholas Harrison.

[3]On *Enfants*, see Accad; Mohammedi-Tabti; and Bigelow.

[4]Djebar stated in an interview, "La position de Lila, à côté et en même temps dedans et témoin, c'est un peu moi" ("Entretien" [Bouzar] 160; "Lila's position, on the periphery and at the same time within and a witness, that's somewhat me" [my trans.]).

[5]Amrane-Minne's historical studies have not been translated into English. For classes in English, I suggest her "Women and Politics in Algeria."

Early Islamic Historiography: The Background and Sources of *Loin de Médine*

Hanan Elsayed

Set in the seventh century in the Arabian Peninsula, *Loin de Médine* (1991; *Far from Madina*) stands out from Assia Djebar's other works. The historical setting, early Islam with its sacred sites (Mecca and Medina), and the presence, albeit briefly, of the Prophet Muhammad (570–632) represent an entirely new direction for Djebar. More than any of her novels, the context of *Loin de Médine* presents particular challenges to readers unfamiliar with early Islamic history. In fact, the very richness of the narrative, with its seventy-seven characters, risks alienating readers. To avoid such a response from my students, I paid attention to the activity of prereading in the classroom when I taught *Loin de Médine* in an upper-division French undergraduate course on Arab francophone works. However formidable its difficulties, an examination of its literary precedents and an illumination of its background and sources will help students access the novel productively. It will also help them understand Djebar's creative use of historical materials.

Precedents and Challenges

Loin de Médine has no precedents in francophone literature; they can be found in Arabic literature. The novel also offers an opportunity to break with the monolinguistic approach adopted in francophone studies, which Madeleine Dobie justifiably describes as "Eurocentric if in the process these works' affinities with other regions, cultural traditions, and, perhaps most fundamentally, other languages, are obscured" (33). Djebar's novel appears in line with previous works published in Arabic and that dealt with early Islam. These works were all based on early Arabic historiography. Thus *Loin de Médine* differs from works on early Islam produced in the West, for they generally rely on Western sources, which are antagonistic to Islam. An example is Salman Rushdie's *Satanic Verses* (1989), which reproduced the epithet "Mahound," which means "monster" or "demon" and was used by medieval European clerks to designate Muhammad, the Prophet.

How authors before Djebar used the early Arabic sources varies immensely. If we consider the example of the إسلاميات (Islamiyyat), the twentieth-century corpus of prose texts in Arabic that is probably best known and that presents accounts of early Islam, the treatment of the history and life of Muhammad differs from one work to another. The Islamiyyat were written in the 1930s by prominent Egyptian writers such as Taha Hussayn and Tawfiq al-Hakim, whose interest in early Islam stemmed from a desire to assert a collective cultural identity at a time of foreign occupation. As M. M. Badawi points out, these various works are of uneven quality: some authors engaged in creative work while others did not. Badawi is rightly critical of writers interested in rebutting the attacks of orientalists and Christian missionaries and who, as a result, opt for polemic and defensive tones (164, 166).

Another literary precedent that deserves to be mentioned is the work of a woman, the Egyptian Islamic scholar and author ʿA'isha ʿAbd al-Rahman (1913–98), who wrote under the pseudonym Bint al-Shati'. In her multivolume تراجم سيدات بيت النبوة (1956–84; Tarajim sayyidat bayt al-nubuwwa; "Biographies of the Women of the Prophet's Household"), Bint al-Shati' draws attention to the roles of women and presents their portrayal of the Prophet. Unlike her male predecessors, she gives voice to women's perspectives. Moreover, she shows no interest in addressing the accusations leveled in the West against the Prophet. Her work seems to be the closest to Djebar's *Loin de Médine*, which also foregrounds women's voices. Yet there are major differences between the two works both in the language of the writing and in the targeted audience. Bint al-Shati''s work was published in Egypt primarily for an Arab and Muslim readership with at least some familiarity with the subject, whereas *Loin de Médine* was published in France for francophone readers, at least initially.[1]

The early period of Islam is considered sacred because it is the time of the Qur'anic Revelation. In 610, at around the age of forty, Muhammad received the first Revelation in a cave in the Mountain of Hira' on the outskirts of Mecca. The Revelation continued until 632. For believers, both the form and content of the Qur'an are sacred because both were revealed; therefore, the Qur'an exists only in Arabic. In addition, the time and sites of the Revelation (Mecca, Medina, and the road from Mecca to Medina) are sacred. The sacredness of the Revelation, of its time period, and of its sites demand faithful transmission. But creative writing implies freedom of invention. How can a novelist harmoniously marry the demands of orthodoxy and freedom of invention? Proximity to sacred history allows for more maneuver and creativity on the writer's side. Djebar's *Loin de Médine* is marked by its proximity to Islamic sacred history, more specifically the two years following the Prophet's death, 632 to 634.

Early Islamic Historiography

A successful introduction to *Loin de Médine* requires a brief discussion of the historical sources and of their particularities. Historical writing, like the Islamic religious sciences, developed under the general rubric of حديث (hadith).[2] Hadith is a vast collection of sayings and deeds attributed to the Prophet; its purpose is to demonstrate how to apply Qur'anic teachings and to clarify some Qur'anic verses. Women in the life of the Prophet, especially his wife ʿA'isha, played an important role in the transmission and dissemination of hadith. A single hadith is composed of the إسناد (isnad; "chain of transmitters") and the متن (matn; "substance"). The *isnad* can look like the following: "Ibn Humayd—Salamah—

Ibn Ishaq—ʿAbd al-Rahman b. Qasim—his father—ʿA'isha the Prophet's wife." From an early time, hadith criticism emerged as a science whose aim was to ensure the accuracy of hadith by classifying each as either sound, weak, or fraudulent, in accordance with a set of principles. This criticism was important, given that sectarian rivalry and regional interests, among other motives, led to the fabrication of thousands of hadith. Of critical importance to the assessment of hadith is the soundness of the *isnad*. Distortion of the *isnad*, however, was not uncommon.

Early historical writing (roughly from the eighth to the tenth century) adopted the same form as hadith. As a result, the خبر (khabar; the plural is أخبار [akhbar]), which is an individual report of a single event, includes the *isnad*. The *isnad* can be complete or partial, even giving the name of only one of the transmitters. Authoritative sources on early Islam belong to the first phase of Islamic historiography; therefore the *isnad* is common in them.

In the foreword to *Loin de Médine*, Djebar names her sources: Ibn Hicham (or Ibn Hisham, d. 833), Ibn Saad (or Ibn Saʿd, d. 845), and Tabari (d. 923). What is commonly referred to as Ibn Hisham's السيرة النبوية (al-Sira al-nabawiyya; "The Biography of the Prophet") is in fact an abbreviated, annotated edition of the work of Ibn Ishaq (d. 761). The original version of this major biography of the Prophet is lost, although some portions of it were uncovered in the last decades. Ibn Saʿd's كتاب الطبقات (Kitab al-Tabaqat; "The Book of Generations") on the other hand, is a compilation of biographical material. It provides entries on 4,250 important persons, including women. Finally, Tabari's ambitious تأريخ الرسل و الملوك (Ta'rikh al-rusùl wal-muluk; "The History of Prophets and Kings") is a multivolume narrative of universal history that begins with creation and ends in 915. Tabari applied the annalistic form to Muslim history. His annals are by far the most important source; they reproduce versions of the works of several of his predecessors, including Ibn Ishaq and Ibn Saʿd. Tabari is also the most frequently named historian in Djebar's narrative. The collaborative annotated English translation of his *Taʿrikh* contains thirty-nine volumes and is available in the libraries of most research institutions.

Historical Background

The early Arabic sources provide detailed information about the life of Muhammad, his family and friends, as well as his lineage, which they trace back to Ishmael. He was born in Mecca around the year 570 and grew up an orphan under the care of his uncle. His family (Banu Hashim) belonged to Quraysh, the ruling tribe of Mecca but not its powerful branch. Muhammad was a trader and was also known as الأمين (al-ameen; "the trustworthy"). He married a well-to-do widow engaged in trade, Khadija. After her death, he remarried, and only one daughter, Fatima, survived him. The sources narrate the formation of a community around Muhammad following the Revelation, their trials at the hands of

Meccans who did not tolerate Muhammad's call for an end to paganism, for the worship of God, and for the acceptance of God's moral demands. The sources provide ample information about the last years of the Prophet and subsequent caliphates.

Many episodes in *Loin de Médine* are set in the period surrounding or after the death of the Prophet, but some, such as "La fugueuse d'hier" ("The Erstwhile Runaway") and "La laveuse des morts" ("She Who Lays Out the Dead"), go further back in time and refer to important events then—for example, the emigration of many of Muhammad's followers to Abyssinia around 615 because of persecution by Meccans. The Prophet had urged his followers to seek refuge in Abyssinia, as the Christian king there was known for his mercy. Another major event was الهجرة , the Hijra or emigration of the Prophet and his followers from Mecca to Medina in 622. The Hijra took place in secrecy after the Prophet received a warning about the Meccans' plan to assassinate him in the middle of the night. That year marks the first year of the Islamic (Hijri) calendar and thus constitutes a new beginning for the nascent Muslim community.

Of importance, also, are the wars of الردة (al-riddah; "apostasy") that took place mostly after the death of the Prophet. Four chapters in *Loin de Médine* deal directly with the *riddah* wars, which were to a large extent a test for the emergent Islamic state. Fred Donner, a historian, explains:

> Some tribes claimed that they wished to remain Muslims in the religious sense—by performing prayer, for example—but would not send to Abū Bakr [the first caliph] the tax payments that Muḥammad had requested of them in his last years. Others repudiated both the political and the religious leadership of Medina; they wished simply to go their own way, now that the Prophet was dead, in some cases choosing to follow other figures who claimed, like Muhammad, to be prophets (and whom the Muslim tradition, naturally, condemns as "false prophets"). Still others, it seems, hoped simply to take advantage of the turmoil in Medina to raid the town, enriching themselves with plunder and ending what they perhaps felt to be vexatious demands for tribute. (xii–xiii)

This is a portion of an excerpt on the *riddah* wars that my students found useful before reading the first part of *Loin de Médine*, "La liberté et le défi" ("Liberty and Defiance"), which includes four episodes on the topic. In these chapters, Djebar draws attention to the different roles played by women, Muslim and non-Muslim, during times of military conflict. In "La reine yéménite" ("The Yemenite Queen"), the protagonist plays a significant role in putting an end to the life of an apostate named Aswad. In "Celle qui attend Gabriel" ("The Woman Who Waits for Gabriel"), however, Nawar, the wife of a rebel, assumes the role of a mere spectator. "Selma, la rebelle" ("Selma the Rebel") highlights the leading military role of the female protagonist when she learns of the death of her brother. Finally, "La prophétesse" ("The Prophetess") focuses on Sadjah from Mesopotamia, who claims to receive divine inspiration and who is known for her poetic talent.

These fictional reconstructions, like the rest of the narrative, present Djebar's rendition and vision of events as different from the historical accounts in the sources. Djebar argues in the foreword that early male historians silenced women's voices, but this contention should not be accepted uncritically. Her claim is in fact historically invalid (see Elsayed). She also states in the foreword that she used fiction to recreate those stories. For my students, I define the contours of fiction and of early historiography by contrasting two opposing writing styles, the historical and the literary, and narration. My goal is to make my students more attentive to the particularities of the literary text.

Comparison and Contrast

Another reference to the *riddah* wars appears later in the narrative, in "Celle qui préserve parole vive" ("She Who Preserves the Living Word"). ʿA'isha laments the loss of her husband, the Prophet, who died in her arms; she also contemplates the precarious situation that her father, as first caliph, has to face. I ask my students to read this passage closely:

> Son père combat la *ridda*, c'est-à-dire le retour des tribus au paganisme. Il n'arrête pas. Conseillé par Omar à la rigueur tranchante à sa droite, par Obeidallah ibn el Jerrah et Abderahmane ibn Auf à sa gauche, il ne cesse pas : il décide, il agit, il sévit, il se veut irréductible. (*Loin* 295)

> Her father is fighting the *ridda*, the return of the tribes to paganism. He does not give up. Advised by Umar, harsh, tyrannical, on his right, by Obaidallah ibn al-Jarrah and Abderahman ibn Auf on his left, he presses on unceasingly: he makes decisions, he acts ruthlessly, his aim is to be invincible. (*Far* 265)

The aesthetic quality of the last sentence especially is remarkable: the parallel structure ("à droite," "à gauche") and the rhythmic repetition of the pronoun "il" (the last "il" is lost in translation), coupled with the frequency of the sound /i/ in the verbs, produce an undeniable musical quality. Djebar's style contrasts with the plain style of the early sources, which used hadith as a model. Furthermore, the spontaneity of the present tense contrasts with the ubiquitous past tense in those sources. Her narrative connects and reshapes several *akhbar* in the source. Modern historians have examined the fragmented quality of the *akhbar*: because each *khabar* stands as an independent unit, a series of *akhbar* is not a connected narrative of events. Franz Rosenthal links the absence of "causal nexus" between events to the nature of the *khabar* form (66). By contrast, the chapters in *Loin de Médine* develop and elaborate on the events discussed.

Another stylistic feature in the novel, which my students quickly notice, is the generous use of interrogation. The function and formulation of interrogation vary, as illustrated in the following passage, which gives us insight into ʿA'isha's thoughts on the new role of her father, Abu Bakr:

> Comment ce père qu'elle a connu surtout dans sa douceur, son indulgence, se mue-t-il en homme d'État à l'esprit rapide, à la parole sévère, à la ténacité infatigable ? Ne va-t-il pas s'user à la tâche? (295)

> How has her father, whom she has known especially in his gentle moods, his indulgence, been transformed into a statesman, quick-thinking, harsh-speaking, of indefatigable persistence? Will he not wear himself out in this task? (266)

The first question serves an informative purpose: readers learn more about the first caliph and his sensitive side, which he suppressed as he assumed the role of statesman. The shift from the past tense to the present highlights this transformation. The elegant symmetry and repetition of the three prepositional phrases remind us of its literariness. The next short rhetorical question, expressed in the near future (*le futur proche*), is speculative. Yet its negative form affirms the speculation, while its brevity seems to parallel Abu Bakr's short caliphate (little more than two years). Overall the passage reveals the narrator's strong presence in the reconstruction of events.

The prevalent speculative tone of the third-person narrator contrasts sharply with the neutral tone adopted by the early historians. The *akhbar* consist of assertions about the past by those who, removed, perceive their role as that of a transmitter. One of the advantages of the verbatim method used extensively in early Islamic historiography is that it "allows a writer to avoid committing himself too publicly on any given issue." The verbatim quotations also give the historical report an immediate quality: "Tabarî's story does not become boring, for almost every report is humanly vivid" (Hodgson 353). We see this immediacy in the following passage:

> ʿAbdallāh b. Masʿūd states: Our beloved Prophet announced his [approaching] death a month before he died. When the separation drew near, he gathered us in the house of our mother ʿĀ'ishah, looked at us intensely while his eyes were shedding tears, and said, "Welcome to you. May God treat you with compassion, shelter you, protect you. . . .
>
> We asked, "When is your appointed time (*ajal*)?" "The separation [from you] and return to God and the Lote Tree have drawn closer," he replied. (Tabari 9: 173; the bracketed text is in the translation)

The vividness of dialogues and detailed descriptions stand out in Tabari's work. Yet the original Arabic language of the *akhbar* remains simple and accessible. It shows no effort of embellishment, in contrast with later historical writings influenced by أدب (adab; "belles lettres"). More important, the early historian neither comments on nor interprets what he reports.

In *Loin de Médine*, one notes the penchant for interior monologue, which is an index of fictionality (see Genette, *Fiction* 67). Interior monologue gives access to the subjectivity of the female character, as we see in the following quote attributed to the newly widowed ʿA'isha: "Ne suis-je pas toute amour envers l'Aimé, envers l'Absent ? Lui dont la séparation me tient, au cœur de chaque nuit, éveillée. Lui pour qui ne me calme aucune prière surérogatoire" (295; "Am I not all love for the Beloved, towards the Departed? From whom my separation keeps me awake in the heart of every night. For whom no supererogatory prayer can bring me peace" [265]). The intimate thoughts of ʿA'isha do not figure in the historical sources, but biographical details about her do. Djebar uses the biography as background to imagine the inner feelings that the new widow likely had after the death of her husband.

The presence of the narrator is equally strong in "Celle qui dit non à Médine" ("The Woman Who Said No in Madina"), one of two chapters devoted to Fatima, the Prophet's daughter. Before we consider this particular episode, I ask my students to read the following *khabar* from the source:

> Abū Ṣāliḥ al-Dirārī—ʿAbd al-Razzāq b. Hammām—Maʿmar—al-Zuhrī—ʿUrwah—ʿÃ'ishah: Fāṭimah and al-ʿAbbās came to Abū Bakr demanding their [share of] inheritance of the Messenger of God. They were demanding the Messenger of God's land in Fadak and his share of Khaybar['s tribute]. Abū Bakr replied, "I have heard the Messenger of God say: 'Our [i.e., the prophets' property] cannot be inherited and whatever we leave behind is alms [i.e., to be given in charity]. The family of Muḥammad will eat from it.' By God, I will not abandon a course which I saw the Messenger of God practicing, but will continue doing it accordingly." Fāṭimah shunned him and did not speak to him about it until she died. ʿAlī buried her at night and did not permit Abū Bakr to attend [her burial].
>
> (Tabari 9: 196; the bracketed text is in the translation)

Djebar extensively develops and interprets this account according to her own vision. Her fictional reconstruction opts for a dramatic tone: ". . . Fatima va vivre la déshérence qui lui est, d'une façon bien spécieuse, imposée, comme une dépossession tout à fait illégitime" (78; ". . . Fatima is, in fact, to be deprived of her inheritance completely illegally, through specious argument" [67]). The subjective language of the interpretation reveals once again a strong presence of the narrator, who assumes a gendered perspective. But rereading of canonical texts in that way seems not to pertain here: the *khabar* makes no reference to gender; moreover, Abu Bakr's decree applies to both Fatima and al-ʿAbbas, her male relative, who is conveniently omitted in the novel. Djebar is no transmitter; she uses fiction to recreate, mold, and shape historical events according to her vision.

Attention to prereading as a teaching strategy prepares students for this rich and complex text. *Loin de Médine* can be and has been read in many ways. My interest in the interplay of the historical sources and traditions with the fictional narrative is only one approach. Given the tendency to read historical fiction from other parts of the world as historical documents, I have found this particular strategy to be useful in the classroom. It encourages my students to be more sensitive to the text's literariness and more aware of its fictionality.

NOTES

[1] *Loin de Médine* has been translated into the following languages: Turkish (1992), Spanish and Italian (1993), English and German (1994), and Bosnian (2003). There is no Arabic translation. In 2000 *Loin de Médine* was staged in the *Teatro di Roma* under the title *Figlie di Ismaele nel vento e nella tempesta* ("Daughters of Ishmael in Wind and Storm").

[2] According to Tarif Khalidi, a contemporary historian, there are three other dominant epistemic modes: أدب (adab; "belles lettres"), from the ninth to the eleventh century; حكمة (hikma; "philosophy"), during the tenth and eleventh centuries; and سياسة (siyasa; "politics"), from the twelfth to the fifteenth century. Khalidi, however, highlights the variation in methods and historical styles in addition to the overlap of different epistemic modes.

Don't Claim to "Speak for" Algerian Women: Reading Djebar across Disciplinary Borders

Diya Abdo and Maria Bobroff

Teaching and studying Arab women writers in a Western context is a fraught endeavor, if not downright problematic. Often, students come to such courses with preconceived and stereotypical notions about the Arabo-Islamic world, especially its women. An approach that helps mitigate these difficulties is teaching across disciplinary borders. As faculty members in French and English (and both in women's, gender, and sexuality studies) at a small liberal arts college, we bring together English and French majors in advanced courses that include Maghrebi women writers. While there will always be administrative roadblocks, the pedagogical advantages of coteaching make worthwhile the trouble of overcoming them. Since there is no distinct disciplinary home that Djebar's work inhabits (French, English, postcolonial studies, women's studies, Arab and Maghrebi women writers, etc.), interdisciplinarity is essential. Our collaborative efforts enrich not only the students' experience and learning but also our knowledge as instructors. For most of our class sessions, we meet together, though we also schedule separate sessions to give the French students an opportunity to discuss the material in French. In a small French department, students typically take classes only with one another at the upper level, but in our course they can interact with a new group of voices at that level (as opposed to an introductory general education course). Reducing their interaction in French is a compromise worth making to expose them to an additional way of exploring the text. We have found that a combination of interdisciplinary theoretical groundwork and hands-on activities is essential for guiding students to approach a text with an awareness of their politics of location.

We teach Djebar's *Femmes d'Alger dans leur appartement* (*Women of Algiers in Their Apartment*) and *L'amour, la fantasia* (*Fantasia: An Algerian Cavalcade*). We read *Femmes d'Alger* first, both because it is more accessible than *Fantasia* and because of what Djebar outlines in the "Ouverture" ("Overture"). Before we begin reading and discussing either of the texts, we spend some time studying orientalism. Students read the introduction to Edward Said's *Orientalism* and watch *On Orientalism*, an interview with him (Said, Jhally, and Talreja), and then through guided questions they are asked to define orientalism and identify its features and characteristics, its functions and purposes, and its modern-day manifestations. To emphasize how orientalism intersects with issues of gender, we watch Tania Kamal-Eldin's *Hollywood Harems* and read articles on the representations of Arab and Muslim women,[1] especially the narratives constructed around them locally, even by other Arab and Muslim women, and in the West. To complicate the students' view of Arab women, we read various secondary sources on Arab and Islamic feminisms as well as primary texts by Arab and Muslim/Islamic feminists.[2] We read about Algeria's history and the role of Algeria's women and watch Parminder Vir's *Algeria: Women at War* or Faouzia Fekiri's *Algiers 1957: The Lady Carriers of Fire*. These documentaries offer testimonials by women from different social classes who participated in Algeria's struggle for independence; moreover, they bring to life the women we read about in Djebar's *Femmes d'Alger* and embody her objective of recording and reconstituting the voices and histories of these "porteuses de feu" (*Femmes* 118; "fire carriers" [*Women* 44]). Our pedagogical aims are to understand the historical roots of current and popular narratives about Arab women, to engender greater self-awareness of prejudice and expose the damaging narratives that students might have internalized and that might affect their reading of the literary texts, to understand the climate in which and against which Arab women must write, and to paint a complex picture of the Arab and Muslim world and its women as active agents of change rather than passive victims. While enlightening, this extensive groundwork often results in student anxiety: they become afraid of taking a wrong step, of saying something that sounds imperialist, racist, sexist, or orientalist.

We never wish to silence students, but an active listening silence can be productive, and it is essential when dealing with Djebar's *Femmes d'Alger*. To emphasize this "trajet d'écoute" (7; "journey of listening" [1]), we spend some time digesting the overture and discussing Djebar's goal as an Algerian woman writing about women in Algeria: "Ne pas prétendre 'parler pour,' ou pis 'parler sur,' à peine parler près de, et si possible tout contre" ("Don't claim to 'speak for' or, worse, to 'speak on,' barely speaking next to, and if possible *very close to*"). Surely, if an Algerian woman who has gained "la liberté de mouvement, du corps et de l'esprit" ("freedom of movement, of body and of mind") finds it problematic to speak, indeed must actively resist speaking, for and about other Algerian women "qu'on incarcère" ("who are incarcerated") but who have "des âmes plus que jamais mouvantes" (9; "souls that move more freely than ever before" [2]), then the American student must initially cease speaking altogether about these seemingly benighted women and instead listen to them and to Djebar's words. To facilitate that listening, we ask students to simply read aloud, without any analysis or explanation, lines or excerpts that strike or move them. We do not ask them why they selected those particular lines; we simply listen to the words. This attention to the text also makes us more aware of the formal and aesthetic qualities of Djebar's intricate and complex prose.

The next exercise brings us to a place of analyzing the text, of speaking about it, yet still in the framework of active listening: we consider how Djebar's text acts as counternarrative, as countervoice to Eugène Delacroix's painting *Femmes d'Alger dans leur appartement* (1834), which is reproduced on the novel's cover. We begin, aided by our previous groundwork discussion of imperialism, orientalism, patriarchy, and colonialism, to explore the painting: What is its history? How was it produced? What historical moment does it represent? What does it suggest about the women who are its subject? We use the section entitled "Regard interdit, son coupé" ("Forbidden Gaze, Severed Sound") to help us with these questions, but we also allow the students to engage with the painting directly. Often they will discuss the way the women appear, using adjectives like *idle*, *lazy*, *distracted*, *unfocused*, *inside*, *silent*, *vacant*, and *motionless*. Our next step is to explore the text as counternarrative to the painting. How does Djebar respond to the painting? Where and how does she subvert its orientalist representation? Where does the text speak against the painting's silence and stillness? How does it reclaim the forbidden gaze and attempt to re-member the severed sound of Algerian women? Where in the text do we see how the women "ne cessent de nous dire, depuis, quelque chose d'insoutenable et d'actuellement présent" (242; "have not stopped telling us something that is unbearably painful and still very much with us today" [136])? But also, how might the text show us the ways in which such silencing and segregation still continue in postindependence Algeria and how these women "demeurent absentes à elles-mêmes, à leur corps, à leur sensualité, à leur bonheur" (244; "remain absent to themselves, to their body, to their sensuality, to their happiness" [137])? Perhaps the most challenging question we ask is how the text itself engages in this very silencing and hiding, to reinforce or perpetuate them instead of subverting them. An interesting text to discuss here alongside Djebar's is *The Colonial Harem*, a book by Malek Alloula, her ex-husband, in which he responds to French colonial postcards of Algeria and the damaging narratives they embodied and attempts to exorcise the colonial ghost, to "return this immense postcard to its sender" (5). Does Djebar attempt to send the painting back to its sender? Although both Alloula's and Djebar's texts engage with Algeria's colonial legacy, Djebar's text engages with Algeria's Islamic and patriarchal realities as well.

The above analysis is valuable, but unfortunately it can gloss over the literary and creative merits of the works of Arab women writers. Students sometimes read with an eye only for what a literary text has to teach them about Arab and

Muslim women. It should always be emphasized that a work of art, a piece of literature, is not simply a window into the real world, a way for us to gain knowledge about, for example, the veiled and exotic Other. A close reading assignment—a deep focus on the literary, formalistic, and aesthetic qualities of a text, in both the original French and translated English—is therefore essential.

We ask the English students to pick an excerpt, one no longer than a paragraph, from "For a Diwan of the Water Carrier" (*Women* 37–43) and to perform a close reading of its formal elements. This exercise, focusing as it does on language, acknowledges the legitimacy of the translation as a new text. Students write on figures of speech, images, word choices, punctuation, and syntax. We then ask the French students to give oral presentations on their close reading of Djebar's story "Femmes d'Alger dans leur appartement." Then we assign pairs of students approximately ten pages each; they must analyze the sensory images and rhythms of Djebar's French, then compare the original text with the English translation. We encourage them to consider two questions: What might a reader of the English version miss if unable to access the French? What might a reader of the French version gain with the addition of the English? The French students are surprised that we expect them not only to study a text in English translation but also to present their findings in English. Our guidance keeps them from dwelling on the supposed errors in the translation before them; we instruct them instead to consider the English translation as one interpretation of Djebar's writing, neither flawed nor definitive in its perspective. In their study, they will essentially work with three texts: Djebar's original French, the English translation provided to them, and their interpretation of the two together.

We are convinced that this assignment leads the French students to a better appreciation of Djebar's French. Two students who focused on the sensuality of the bathhouse in "III" (*Femmes* 95–108; *Women* 29–37) chose the following passage:

> Baya sourit avec *coquetterie*. Sarah s'absenta de la conversation, *désira* entrer à son tour dans *la chambre chaude*. . . .
>
> Anne, quand Sarah la rejoignit et que, assise sur les genoux, elle *fit glisser* son pagne, aperçut la cicatrice large et bleuâtre de son amie.
>
> —Une brûlure ? demanda-t-elle en la touchant *lentement*, tout le long de l'abdomen. (104; emphasis added)

> Baya smiled *flirtatiously*. Sarah moved away from the conversation, also *wanting* to enter *the steam room* at last. . . .
>
> Sarah joined Anne, who, when Sarah kneeled and *let* her pagne *slide off*, noticed her friend's wide, blueish scar. "A burn?" she asked, touching it *lightly* all along her abdomen. (34; emphasis added)

They were initially drawn to this passage because the word *coquetterie* was translated with "flirtatiously." At their first reading of the French they had overlooked the sensuality of *coquetterie*, understanding it as "prettily" or "vainly." The translation therefore surprised them, and they reconsidered the passage. Putting the two versions side by side, they noticed other evocative elements of the French, which have been italicized above. They had expected to dismiss the translation as overly sexualized but instead discovered the eroticism of the original French. There was discussion of how their discomfort with the intimacy of the bathhouse led them to deny at first the passage's sensuality. In their wish to avoid a Western gaze, they had overcompensated and forgotten to listen to Djebar's words.

We then ask the English students to write a short paper, this time contrasting their results in close reading the English version with those of the students working with the French text. Many note the different readings produced by the additions and deletions, by changes in sentence structure and punctuation, and by the translator's decision to opt for a particular English word over another. One student found a decidedly homoerotic undertone in the English version that was not as obvious in the French. We discuss not only the reasons for Djebar's language choices and their larger implications but also the ways in which translation in general produces refracted texts that can afford readers a new perspective on the original.

As we conclude our study of *Femmes d'Alger*, we revisit its final section, "Regard interdit, son coupé" ("Forbidden Gaze, Severed Sound"), which provides a good bridge to our study of *Fantasia*. It is one of many prereading activities that serve to set the tone and prepare students for what lies ahead. We project Delacroix's *Femmes d'Alger dans leur appartement* alongside Pablo Picasso's *Les femmes d'Alger, Version O* (1955) and invite students to compare, not analyze, the two paintings, then compare both with Djebar's description of them. From there we lead students through an activity that is meant to elucidate the palimpsest embedded in *Fantasia*. We provide each student with a sheet of unlined white paper and a pencil with a substantial eraser. For a full minute we project Delacroix's *Femmes d'Alger dans leur appartement*, then remove the image and ask students to draw it from memory. At the end of the allotted time, students pass their drawings to a neighbor who must erase it. We then project Picasso's *Les femmes d'Alger, Version O*. After a full minute of study, students recreate Picasso's image on top of the erased depiction of Delacroix. At the end of the allotted time, students pass their drawing to a new neighbor, who erases it. We repeat this process twice more, using lesser-known artworks that mimic Delacroix's style.[3]

At the end of the fourth drawing we ask students not to erase but instead to look carefully at their piece of paper and describe what they see. Some will note that they can still make out parts of the drawings underneath the last or that they cannot distinguish between the final drawing and its predecessors. We use these observations as a segue into a discussion of appropriation and interpretation. Students debate how a perspective becomes definitive and what problems arise when successive interpretations are based on a first that is incomplete or incorrect. With guidance, they will eventually realize that our metaphor of the palimpsest has placed the entire class in the position of colonizers claiming authority over a story about which they have limited knowledge. With this exercise, students become more open to the layered narration of *Fantasia*.

As a second prereading activity, we focus on the title of the work, *L'amour, la fantasia*, and on its translation, *Fantasia: An Algerian Cavalcade*. Students of both languages immediately question the absence of *love* and the presence of a subtitle in the English. We ask them to suspend judgment of the altered title until after they have read the work. We then have them consider the common element of the two titles, "fantasia," and to brainstorm on their associations with the term. Some will link it to classical Western music. Even if students zero in on the Disney animated film, they can recall that it consists of separate segments of music that ebb and flow together. We then play for them a Western fantasia and ask them to describe what they hear.[4] Because some students will not be comfortable talking about music, we remind them that we are not looking for informed critiques but rather their impressions. As they share their comments with the class, we hope to arrive at a collective understanding of the fantasia as a free-form piece with repeating motifs that are unpredictable in their tempo and duration.

We turn to video clips from *YouTube* to show examples of the equestrian *fantasia* as practiced in the Maghreb. It is useful to first show a clip without the sound so that students can focus on the visual aspects of the performance: the formal costumes, the speed of the horses, the synchronized blasts of gunpowder. A second viewing, this time with sound, brings the energy of the spectacle into the classroom as students listen to the horses galloping, the crowd ululating, and the rifles firing. We briefly explain that the *fantasia* was once executed by Berber warriors and is now staged in cultural celebrations. Once the students have heard both a fantasia and a *fantasia*, they are better equipped to tease out the significance of the title of Djebar's work: the interplay of Western and Arab cultures, the conflicting forces of beauty and destruction.

A final preparation is to have students work with the table of contents of part 3, "Les voix ensevelies" ("Voices from the Past"). We provide them with a worksheet on which we have outlined a chart with six columns and seven rows. At the top of each column, we print the main subdivisions: first movement, second movement, and so on. Under each movement we list its constituent parts. Down the first column, we would have "First Movement," "The Two Strangers," "Voice," "Clamor," "Aphasia of Love," "Voice," and "Embraces." We push this visual aid further by changing fonts or styles in each row so that the similarities from movement to movement are easier to see. This simple charting serves as a powerful visual testimony to the rhythms of Djebar's work. As students work through part 3 on their own, they must put a descriptive phrase in each square of the chart, thereby marking the relation of each subsection to those above, below, and beside it. We have found that this reading guide helps students see where the text has been and where it is headed.

In bringing our two groups of students together, we hope to enrich, but not ease, their experience engaging with Arab women writers. We see our cross-disciplinary teaching as mirroring the *métissage* ("hybridity") of meaning in Djebar's works. It highlights the texts' problems of accessibility and denies students the false sense of security of a totalizing comprehension that can easily become the surveying gaze of the orientalist painter or the pitying stare of the sympathetic Self. In constantly unsettling them in their role as voyeurs or readers, we remind them to resist the desire to speak about and for these Other women, and to listen to them instead.

NOTES

In this essay, *Other* and *Self*, when capitalized, refer to specific identities constituted by the discourses of (neo)colonialism, (neo)imperialism, and (neo)orientalism.

[1]See Ahmed, "Western Ethnocentrism" and *Women and Gender*; Amireh; Lazreg; Nader.

[2]See Ahmed, "Feminism"; Badran, "Feminisms," *Islamic Feminism*, and "Islamic Feminism"; Badran and Cooke; Cooke; Darraj; El Saadawi; Sabbagh; Saliba.

[3]The specific images are not important, so long as they interpret Delacroix. Any number can be found through an online search of "Femmes + Alger + D'après + Delacroix."

[4]Any fantasia will suffice, though we typically use one by Chopin.

Visual and Textual Interplay: Delacroix, Picasso, Djebar, Balzac, and Fromentin

Thérèse De Raedt

In my upper-level French course titled Visual and Textual Interplay, my students and I examine the mutual influence between image and word. By focusing on selected case studies, I show them how paintings inspire writers and how texts inspire visual artists. My approach is semiotic: I consider both art forms to be equal, consisting of signs in their respective languages. I rely on the concepts of ekphrasis and its modern form, *transposition d'art* ("art transposition"), which relate literature to the visual arts (Pappas 171). Throughout the course I stress the fact that works of art are received and perceived differently depending on specific sociopolitical, historical, ideological, and cultural contexts. In our analyses, I combine close reading with thematic discussions. I also focus on the importance of what Gérard Genette has defined as paratext: "what enables a text to become a book and to be offered as such to its readers and, more generally, to the public" (*Paratexts* 1).

My primary objective for the course is to make students aware of the interrelatedness between image and text and of the changing nature of this interaction. I provide them with critical tools for analyzing various types of visual and literary documents, and I help them develop their visual perception skills. The course engages them in interdisciplinary thinking and broadens their way of envisioning literature.

In this essay, I concentrate on the section of the course where we examine the influence of orientalist paintings on French-language writers, in particular on Assia Djebar.

Introduction: Covers and Orientalism

We begin with the illustrated covers of Djebar's books, discussing their function as advertisements, as esthetic envelopes that announce the content of the texts. I point out that Djebar chose both the titles and covers for her novels (Zimra, "Disorienting" 162). Students notice that the covers from *Femmes d'Alger dans leur appartement*; *Oran, langue morte*; *L'amour, la fantasia*; *Ombre sultane*; *Vaste est la prison*; and *La femme sans sépulture* reproduce paintings.[1] I explain how Djebar, who was also a historian and film director, used nineteenth-century art to express the underlying ethos we find throughout her oeuvre about women's place in Algerian society. Then I introduce the term *orientalism*.

Students, liking categories, usually ask if orientalism is an artistic movement. I answer that it is a nineteenth-century term that refers to the source of an artist's inspiration, the Orient, regardless of the movement that the artist is connected with (realism, Romanticism, neoclassicism, etc.). After the students read the introduction of Edward Said's *Orientalism* (2003), we conclude that *orientalism* can be roughly defined as the Western perception of the East. I focus on the years 1798 and 1830, which are vital for understanding French orientalism. I stress the importance of Napoleon's Egyptian military expedition for the rediscovery of the Orient in France, and I explain that this expedition was also ideologically driven, since historians, botanists, biologists, et cetera were involved in order to record Egypt. Next we discuss France's incursions into North Africa, starting in January 1830, during the reign of Charles X, and continued by Louis Philippe after the July Revolution of 1830.[2] The students learn key facts about France's invasion of Algeria, which lasted until 23 December 1847, when Emir Abd-el-Kader surrendered. I show them paintings that relate to this invasion. Most paintings from that time period depict France's military victories as epic accomplishments. We analyze, for example, Horace Vernet's immense painting in Versailles, *Capture of the Smalah of Abd-el-Kader by the Duc d'Aumale May 16, 1843*, an event that marked a turning point in the Algerian conquest. This official propagandist painting conveys the confusion that was created by the surprise attack of Louis Philippe's son, Duc d'Aumale (Henri d'Orléans). It shows France's victory and emphasizes the power, organization, and prestige of France. In contrast to this painting, I introduce Eugène Delacroix's orientalist paintings.

Femmes d'Alger dans leur appartement: *Images*

We consider Delacroix's 1834 *Women of Algiers in Their Apartment*, which is in the Louvre, and compare it with his 1849 version, which is in the Musée Fabre in Montpellier. We then analyze one of Pablo Picasso's fifteen reinterpretations (executed between 13 Dec. 1954 and 14 Feb. 1955) of the painting. By doing so, we follow the same order as Djebar's interpretations of these paintings in the essay "Regard interdit, son coupé" ("Forbidden Gaze, Severed Sound"), which belongs to the short story collection *Femmes d'Alger dans leur appartement*.

I teach my students how to analyze visual documents. Many have learned how to read literary texts closely but have not been trained to look at paintings carefully, critically, and rigorously. I therefore ask them to follow a formal grid that reflects the mental process involved in the act of reading a painting (see app.). When students compare their analyses of the paintings with Djebar's, they can better appreciate how Djebar uses Delacroix's paintings and Picasso's reinterpretations of them to convey her ideas about the role of women in Algeria's colonial past and postcolonial present.

Our analysis of the painting in the Louvre begins with an objective description. The work shows four exotic women, dressed in luxurious attire, in an opulent interior setting. It is a large oil painting, measuring 180 cm x 229 cm. The depicted scene seems near, though no link is created with us. We continue with the technical question of how the artist represents his ideas visually. The painting's composition is stable; its several triangles create a sense of unity, solidity, and balance. In the middle ground, two women sit on carpets around the hookah; in the foreground on the left, a woman rests on cushions; on the right, also in the foreground, a black servant, who is seen from the back, is about to leave. The light source is not defined but appears to come from the left, slightly highlighting the white blouse of the woman holding the hookah. The perspective is linear; the vanishing point is located in the middle of the background. Vertical lines (the red doors, the upright position of the seated woman in the middle) as well as diagonals (the curtain, the resting women in the front) structure the painting. A sense of quietness and secrecy emanates from this closed composition. All the colors are dimmed, but white, red, yellow, and blue dominate. These warm but subdued colors indicate the luxury of the fabrics and add to the exoticism of the scene. The scene seems accurate (the proportions are correct) and realistic. We, the spectators, seem to watch it from an open door.

Then we move to the interpretation of the painting and discuss the cultural and historical contexts. I tell students that the depicted scene is in fact a constructed rendition of reality based on sketches made two years earlier when Delacroix was in Morocco and Algeria.[3] It is commonly accepted that Delacroix, by then thirty-four and well-established, was allowed to enter a harem when he was visiting the newly conquered city of Algiers in June 1832.[4] We discuss what it would mean for a French painter to visit a harem, how its women might respond to being seen by a male foreigner, what they might think and feel. Some students say that they cannot read the women in the painting; others comment that the women do not appear real. We speculate on why Delacroix depicted them with a veil of mystery. To conclude with an aesthetic reflection, Delacroix was able to transcend an anecdotal scene, giving a feminine closed interior a universal meaning by rendering its enigmatic nature, by keeping its secrets. The scene is close to its viewers and at the same time hermetic. The students clearly see the differences between this painting and Vernet's commissioned celebration of France's military success.

Delacroix's *Women of Algiers in their Apartment* in Montpellier shows the same four women in nearly the same pose and wearing almost exactly the same clothes, but they are depicted in a less precise and detailed way, with blurred outlines (sfumato). The students work in groups to analyze this painting, using the grid I have given them. Together we focus on the differences between this painting and the one in the Louvre. Being smaller (84.5 cm x 112 cm, less than half the size of the Louvre painting), this painting creates a more intimate link with the viewer. The black servant, whose headdress here is differently knotted, holds the curtain as if to unveil the scene. She seems to be an intermediary between the painter and the women who are painted. The absence of tiles and of the wall cabinet with the red doors gives this interior space a more somber aspect. The bare wall reflects light that gives the entire scene a gold-orange glow. This bronze color palette, obtained by painting on the varnish, makes the enclosed space more nocturnal (as in some of Rembrandt's paintings), which enhances the idea of mystery and emphasizes that the artist is intruding into the women's solitary lives.

Next we look at Picasso's variations (titled *Les femmes d'Alger* [*Women of Algiers*]) on Delacroix's *Women of Algiers in Their Apartment* and focus on version O, the last and arguably most accomplished painting, done 14 February 1955. Students do group work and use the grid to analyze it. This oil on canvas, 114 cm x 146.4 cm, is bigger than the Montpellier painting but smaller than the Louvre one. The general impression is profusion and fragmentation. Students notice that the four women are positioned differently than in Delacroix's versions, that the woman in the center of the Delacroix painting is moved to the foreground and holds the hookah, and that the resting woman on the left is now represented with her legs up in the air on the right. The servant, who carries a tray with a pot of coffee or tea, is in the middle ground. The fourth woman is relegated to the background, in an opening where she merges with the alcove. The decoration of tiles or mosaics on the right, which appear among the figures as well, opens up the space like a kaleidoscope. The color palette consists of shimmering harmonies of bright red, blue, and yellow.

I give a brief talk about cubism, the avant-garde movement that was created by Picasso. With the exception of the woman on the left, the three other women are depicted as if they were viewed simultaneously from numerous angles. That their breasts and buttocks are accentuated marks a confrontational but also free and open eroticism. The woman seated on the left appears hieratic and sexually powerful. Her face is more detailed in version O than in the other versions. She has a demeanor that demands from the spectator awe and deference. We conclude that Picasso, in his own pictorial language, has made the scene more dynamic and the women more assertive.

Femmes d'Alger dans leur appartement: *Djebar's Short Stories*

These analyses of paintings lead the students to discuss Djebar's second edition of the collection of short stories written over forty-three years but assembled in one book entitled *Femmes d'Alger dans leur appartement*. Students immediately notice that the cover reproduces a detail of Delacroix's *Women of Algiers in Their Apartment* kept in the Louvre.[5] The book is divided into five parts, but Djebar relies throughout on the three paintings we discussed above to develop and elaborate her thoughts on women's imprisonment and liberation in Algeria. We start with the essay "Regard interdit, son coupé" ("Forbidden Gaze, Severed Sound"), written in February 1979, "a kind of textual meditation that would serve as a reflective background to the stories [she] had just put together" (Zimra, Afterword [*Women*] 175). Though the essay appears at the end of the book, I decided for pedagogical reasons that the students should study it first.[6]

We discuss how a "révolution visuelle" (*Femmes* 237; "visual revolution" [*Women* 133]) took place in Morocco for Delacroix.[7] We look at his paintings from that time and briefly analyze his earlier exotic paintings that Djebar mentions: *Death of Sardanapalus* (1827), inspired by Byron's tragedy, and *The Massacre at Chios* (1824), which was based on contemporary events. We ask what "Regard interdit, son coupé" means in relation to the paintings titled *Women of Algiers in Their Apartment*. Students usually say first that a painting is by definition silent and that in Delacroix's paintings they do not see the women talking to one another or interacting with the spectator. The "forbidden gaze" may allude to the fact that these women are not allowed to be seen, that they remain hidden in a confined room, which is unlike Picasso's version. I ask the students to keep this question in mind as they read the entire short story and consider its overall structure, progression, and patterns, such as repetitions, contradictions, and similarities.

We analyze the text closely, in particular the encapsulating sentence in which Djebar states that the essence of Delacroix's painting "se joue dans le rapport qu'entretiennent celles-ci [les trois femmes] avec leur corps, ainsi qu'avec le lieu de leur enfermement" (241; "is played out in the relationship these three [women] have with their bodies, as well as with the place of their enclosure" [135]). Most students notice the relation between body and environment, but few have reflected on the constraints to body that women experience. Our discussion of this sentence helps them better grasp Djebar's later references to repressed female sexuality and forbidden enjoyment and her way of interpreting Delacroix, who captured in his masterpiece "quelque chose d'insoutenable et d'actuellement présent" (242; "something that is unbearably painful and still very much with us today" [136]). It is not clear if the servant, whom Djebar describes as "personnage presque accessoire" (241; "an almost minor character" [135]), is "espionne ou si elle est complice" (254;"is spying on them or is an accomplice to them" [145]).

We compare our interpretation of Picasso's painting with Djebar's. For Djebar, Picasso "renverse la malédiction, fait éclater le malheur, inscrit en lignes hardies un bonheur totalement nouveau. Prescience qui devrait dans notre quotidien, nous guider" ("reverses the malediction, causes misfortune to burst loose, inscribes in audacious lines a totally new happiness. A foreknowledge that should guide us in our everyday life"). Even the spying servant has been replaced by "simplement une autre femme, espiègle et dansante" (260; "simply another woman, mischievous and dancing" [149]). She curiously does not mind that Picasso's servant is carrying a tray with a pot of coffee or tea, a clear sign of subjugation (Bourget, "Réédition" 97). Djebar may be imposing—perhaps intentionally—her interpretation of the painting as a celebration of the anticipated freedom of all women. She sees in his disrobing the women not only "le signe d'une 'émancipation,' mais plutôt celui d'une renaissance de ces femmes à leur corps" (260; "a sign of an 'emancipation,' but[, more,] of these women's rebirth to their own bodies" [149–50]). She then moves her discussion to the role that women played in the war of independence by carrying bombs (she observes that Picasso exaggerates their breasts to the extent that they look like bombs). We discuss that she extrapolates from Picasso's painting another theme that is common throughout her oeuvre: a hymn to the heroism of women.

We turn to the short story "Femmes d'Alger dans leur appartement," which was written in July–August 1978 and appears in the section "Aujourd'hui" ("Today"). Students, as they read, consider the Delacroix and Picasso paintings as well as Djebar's interpretation of them. We discuss how the Algerian women who fought and suffered during the war of independence still cannot be free in their daily lives but remain trapped in silence, mirroring the women in the Delacroix paintings. I point to the scene that takes place in the public baths, the only place where women are free to speak their minds, and suggest that there is a connection between the way that Djebar develops the women's stories and the way that Picasso rearranges and redesigns the women of Delacroix's paintings. He moves the woman in the middle of Delacroix's painting to the left and represents her, in Djebar's words, as "olympienne" ("Olympian"). We wonder if the "Olympian" is an allusion to Sarah in the story. Sarah, married to a surgeon and now working as a musicologist recording traditional songs, was a fire carrier during the war of independence. At the baths she reveals herself, literally (by showing her scar) and figuratively (by disclosing her painful secrets), and appears as "un roc de puissance intérieure" ("a rock of inner power"). Fatma, the water carrier at the public baths, could embody Picasso's servant, whom Djebar depicts as "dansante" (260; "dancing" [149]). Fatma, though "l'exclue" (117; "the excluded one" [43]), is Sarah's ally. Djebar tells her story in a "divan" (108; "diwan" [37]) of several pages, thus granting her an important role, as did Picasso by making a separate portrait of the servant in his *Women of Algiers*, version G.[8] That he represents the women simultaneously from many viewpoints may also parallel the story, because the women Djebar describes led different lives during the war and now. We speculate that Sarah's husband's friend, the painter who frees Leila from a mental institution, may refer to Picasso.

We discuss that Picasso's formal aesthetic of fragmentation can be found in both the content and the form of Djebar's short story. His painting resembles the physical aspect of this short story, which is fractured: certain passages seem intended, others accidental; there are intermezzos in italics and other interruptions.

The four short stories grouped in the section "Hier" ("Yesterday") describe the life of silence and confinement of oppressed women, as in Delacroix's painting, who are often doomed to mourn and lament. In her "Ouverture" ("Overture"), Djebar calls on contemporary Algerian women to free themselves: "Et ne pas oublier que celles qu'on incarcère de tous âges, de toutes conditions, ont des corps prisonniers, mais des âmes plus que jamais mouvantes" (9; "And don't forget that those who are incarcerated, no matter what their age or class, may have imprisoned bodies, but have souls that move more freely than ever before" [2]). She hopes that readers will consider her "La nuit du récit de Fatima" ("The Night of Fatima's Story"), which appears first in the collection but was written last, a light "pour éclairer la solidarité de toute parole feminine, notre survie" (11; "to illuminate the solidarity of each feminine speech, our survival" [my trans.]). In the penultimate paragraph of "Ouverture" she asks us, when we read the short story, to open the door wide "si possible au rythme de la danse de la servante nue des *Femmes d'Alger* de Picasso" (10; "if possible, according to the rhythm of the dance of the naked servant of Picasso's *Women of Algiers*" [my trans.]).[9] Students observe that Djebar now refers to Picasso's "servant." The servant is physically imprisoned but has an unrestrained soul. I use this paragraph to lead into our class discussion of "The Night of Fatima's Story."

Femmes d'Alger dans leur appartement: *Nineteenth-Century Texts*

For the next class session, I assign Honoré de Balzac's *La fille aux yeux d'or* (1835; "The Girl with the Golden Eyes"), which is dedicated to Delacroix. I remind students that a dedication is also a paratext and explain that the two artists knew each other, although "the exact nature of their friendship remains elusive" (Linton 46). Students recognize the two women seated around the hookah of Delacroix's *Women of Algiers in Their Apartment* on the cover of the Fleuron Collection edition (published by Slatkine).[10] By now they know the painting well and are eager to learn why it was used to illustrate Balzac's novel.

I ask them to read the novel through a visual lens, noting the word choices, the use of colors, and especially how enclosed spaces are described. We focus on the four encounters between Henri de Marsay and Paquita: the first encounter, which takes place in an old apartment in the presence of Paquita's mother and Christemio; the second, third, and fourth encounters, in Paquita's oriental boudoir. We discuss the fact that Paquita, like the Delacroix women, fits in the boudoir and that, like them, she remains enigmatic. We establish a link between this story and Djebar's references to the silence and confinement depicted by Delacroix.[11]

We finish the class session with an excerpt from Eugène Fromentin's fictionalized diary *Une année dans le Sahel* (1858; "One Year in the Sahel"), in which there is an explicit reference to Delacroix's *Women of Algiers in Their Apartment*. Fromentin, who was also a painter, went to Algeria three times (in 1846, 1847–48, and 1852–53), and, like Delacroix, his North African journeys profoundly influenced him. During one of his stays in Algeria, Fromentin befriended Haoûa, "*une Mauresque*" (227; "a Moorish woman" [my trans.]), whom he met by accident at a shop and whose voice seduced him. He describes his first encounter at her place—he wonders in advance if it will look like Delacroix's depicted space in *Women of Algiers in Their Apartment*—as follows: "Arrivée devant la chambre de sa maîtresse [Haoûa], la noire servante [Assra] tourna la tête à demi de mon côté, et fit exactement le geste que tu peux voir dans le tableau de Delacroix, pour écarter le rideau de mousseline à fleurs" (290; "Arriving in front of her mistress's room, the black servant [Assra] turned her head halfway toward me, and made the same exact gesture to open the flowery muslin curtain that you can see in Delacroix's painting" [my trans.]). This reference allows me to conclude by summarizing Djebar's statements about women's silenced voices, subordination, possible emancipation, and kept secrets. Fromentin thought he knew Haoûa, but when her husband, of whose existence he was unaware, kills her intentionally during a *fantasia*, he realizes how little he knew her. The way he describes her being killed, "Il y eut un cri déchirant—je l'entends encore" (381; "There was a piercing cry—I can still hear it" [my trans.]), serves as the epigraph to Djebar's *L'amour, la fantasia* (*Fantasia: An Algerian Cavalcade*), the novel we study next, along with other excerpts from Fromentin's two Algerian novels and paintings.

NOTES

[1]With the exception of *Vaste est la prison* and *La femme sans sépulture*, all covers reproduce paintings (or details of paintings) by Delacroix. The cover of the 2006 Albin Michel edition of *Ombre sultane* represents a detail of Delacroix's *Women of Algiers in Their Apartment*. The cover of its 2006 Livre de Poche edition reproduces a drawing in lead pencil from Delacroix's Moroccan album, *Portrait de femme juive de face (Jamila Bouzaglo)*.

[2]Most students know Delacroix's painting *Liberty Leading the People*, and I explain that it was painted to celebrate the July Revolution, after which Louis Philippe took over.

[3]In class we do not have time to discuss the preparatory drawings and etchings, but I suggest to the interested students that they read the analysis of the painting by Malika Dorbani Bouabdellah.

[4]Dorbani Bouabdellah wonders if Delacroix visited a brothel instead (10–11).

[5]For a discussion of the paratexts of the 2002 edition of *Femmes d'Alger dans leur appartement*, see Bourget, "Réédition."

[6]Djebar herself wondered if this essay should rather be placed at the beginning, become the preface, and thus function as an overture to her collection of short stories (Zimra, Afterword [*Women*] 175).

[7]I use the translation by Marjolijn de Jager because it "is the first English translation of *Femmes d'Alger dans leur appartement* undertaken with her [Djebar's] consent and cooperation" (Zimra, Afterword [*Women*]162). It does not contain the short story added in 2002: "La nuit du récit de Fatima" ("The Night of Fatima's Story").

[8]Picasso made a separate portrait only of the servant and of the "Olympian" (9 Feb. 1954).

[9]The last part of "Ouverture" was added in the 2002 edition, together with "La nuit du récit de Fatima."

[10]This edition is no longer easy to find. In recent years, I brought my Fleuron Collection edition to class, but students use the paperback edition of GF Flammarion, whose

cover reproduces a study for the stabbed woman who appears on the foreground of *Death of Sardanapalus*.

[11] I put Pappas's article on reserve. In class we focus on the paintings by Delacroix that Balzac could have seen when he wrote his story: *Death of Sardanapalus*, *Women of Algiers in Their Apartment* from the Louvre, and several other paintings of his Moroccan journey.

APPENDIX

FORMAL GRID TO ANALYZE A VISUAL DOCUMENT

1. General impression = global response. How do you perceive the work in general? What kinds of emotions does the work arouse?
2. Description = objective description without value judgments, analysis, or interpretation
   - What does the work represent?
     - historical event, portrait, allegory, mythology
   - How is the subject matter represented?
     - Support: canvas, paper, etc.; flat, rough, or glossy surface
     - Tools: pencil, brush, crayon, knife
     - Material: oil painting, watercolor, ink
   - Size and scale of work: what relation do they create to the spectator?
3. Analysis = technical analysis. Which technique or method has the artist used to serve his/her objectives, to translate his/her ideas in the most appropriate way?
   - Composition: stable (triangle), repetitious, rhythmic, unified, symmetrical, harmonious, geometric, varied, chaotic, centrifugal, centripetal
   - Light: where does the light come from? Is it diffuse, direct, indirect? Chiaroscuro? Sfumato (or gradual blending of one tone into another like smoke)?
   - Perspective: treatment of space, foreground, background, middle ground. From what angle does the spectator see the image?
   - Lines: What lines dominate? Are they vertical, horizontal, oblique? Curves, arabesques? What rhythm is created by them?
   - Shapes: Are they realistic, simplified, geometric, blurred, abstract, incomprehensible? Are the scales accurate?
   - Colors: dominant colors, color scheme = palette. Is the general atmosphere somber or luminous? What do the colors evoke? Are they warm, cold? Do they represent reality in an accurate way? Do the colors create contrasts?
4. Interpretation
   - Analysis of the cultural and historical contexts
     - In what atmosphere was the work created?
     - In which part of the artist's career was the work created?
     - Which public is targeted?
   - Main idea, overall meaning of the work

5. Goals of the artist and the means to achieve them
    - What message does the artist want to transmit?
        - Personal ideas
    - Link between message and formal qualities of the work of art
6. Aesthetic reflection. Four elements should be considered:
    - Truth and/or authenticity of the message
    - Universality of the message
    - Concordance between expression and intended message
    - Unity and formal expression

Using Print, Film, and News Media to Teach Assia Djebar's *Oran, langue morte*

Christa Jones

Based on Assia Djebar's short story collection *Oran, langue morte* (*The Tongue's Blood Does Not Run Dry*), my upper-division undergraduate French-language literature class, Representations of the Algerian Civil War in Film and Literature, focuses on the Algerian civil war (1992–99), Algeria's *décennie noire* ("dark decade"). Discussions of Islam and of violent episodes of French-Algerian history—the Algerian War of Independence (1954–62) and the civil war with its many kidnappings and massacres, as well as current events—are useful to supplement Djebar's *littérature d'urgence* ("literature of urgency") and increase students' intercultural competency while fighting Islamophobia, given the widespread media-driven tendency to associate Islam with religious fundamentalism and terrorism.[1] To this end, students discuss *Oran* in conjunction with a mosaic of journalistic, historical, and literary materials—interviews, letters, world press photographs, newswire feeds, historical studies, literary criticism, literature, films, and documentaries—all of which serve to enhance critical thinking, in-class discussion, and student-teacher interaction.[2]

In conversations, some of my students have expressed reluctance to engage with literary texts, an attitude that underlines the continued crisis the humanities continue to suffer nationwide. Believing that an interdisciplinary approach to teaching can demonstrate the value and relevance of literature, I combine traditional teaching materials and methods—for example, a close reading of *Oran*—with an innovative recourse to journalistic, historical, and media sources to anchor the literary text in a sociohistorical context. By having a variety of audiovisual, virtual, and traditional texts echo and speak with one another, we as teachers or *passeurs de culture* ("transmitters of culture") can make literature tangible and relevant to students' lives, education, and careers; increase their intercultural competency; help them become global citizens; and counter Islamophobia. We can ensure that the present generation of students, infatuated with smartphones, *Twitter*, and social media, learns to appreciate, understand, and analyze francophone literature in its cultural and historical contexts and leaves the classroom better informed of international affairs. One of the challenges in teaching Djebar is to select appropriate secondary readings from the unabated flow of Djebarian literary criticism.[3] A thirty-minute France 2 interview with Djebar by Catherine Ceylac, "Thé ou café" ("Tea or Coffee"), which addresses Djebar's upbringing, education, and literary career, including her election to the Académie Française, provides an introduction to the person, scholar, and author. In the interview, Djebar says her texts are concerned with colonization, decolonization, and the ensuing question of immigration of North Africans to France (Ceylac and Djebar). Therefore students should be introduced to the history of postcolonial Algeria—the time period covered in *Oran*—by reading excerpts from *La guerre invisible: Algérie, années 90* ("The Invisible War: Algeria in the 1990s"), by the Algerian historian Benjamin Stora; the book centers on the post-1988 riot and the civil war decade and explains the rise of the Islamic Salvation Front (FIS, Front Islamique du Salut) and the emergence of various fundamentalist groups, including the Armed Islamic Group (GIA, Groupe Islamique Armé), the Movement for an Islamic State (MEI, Mouvement de l'État Islamique), and the Islamic Front for Armed Jihad (FIDA, Front Islamique du Djihad Armé). I also show excerpts from *Algérie(s)* and assign a student presentation on this eye-opening, investigative documentary.[4] Students are interested in the political background. To familiarize them with key figures and political leaders, such as Mohamed Boudiaf, Ahmed Ben Bella, Houari Boumediène, Chadli Bendjedid, Abdelaziz Bouteflika, and the FIS leaders Ali Ben Hadj and Abassi Madani; political events, such as the October 1988 revolts; and the rise of various fundamentalist groups, I use excerpts from the documentary *Algérie, 1998–2000: Autopsie d'une tragédie* ("Algeria, 1998–2000: Autopsy of a Tragedy"). A discussion of Djamila Sahraoui's documentary *La moitié du ciel d'Allah* (1995; "Half of Allah's Heaven"), which spans the Algerian War of Independence and the mid-1990s and features interviews with former مجاهدات (*mujahidat*, freedom fighters during the war of independence), helps students understand the challenges Algerian women continue to face, such as honor crimes, misogyny, and violence, after the implementation of the infamous Code de la Famille (1984; "Family Code").[5] Thus the female narrator in "Retours non Retours" ("Non-return returns") feels harassed by the male gaze and laments "les rues me chassent donc" (51; "So the streets would hunt me" [34]), a remark that I connect with a discussion on exile and immigration through excerpts from the documentary *Musulmans de France de 1904 à nos jours* ("Muslims of France from 1904 to Today"), which students find gripping.

On his visit to Algeria on 19 December 2012, which marked the fiftieth anniversary of Algerian independence from France, the French socialist president François Hollande, like his predecessor, Nicolas Sarkozy, did not formally apologize for the brutality of France's colonial past. But in a speech given before the Algerian parliament, he stressed the injustice of French colonization and conceded that suffering was caused by it: "Je reconnais ici les souffrances que la colonisation a infligées au peuple algérien . . . , pendant 132 ans, l'Algérie a été soumise à un système profondément injuste et brutal" ("À Alger"; "As I stand here, I acknowledge the suffering that colonization inflicted upon the Algerian people. . . . For 132 years, Algeria was subjected to a profoundly unjust and brutal system").

Lectures on the history of postcolonial Algeria—for instance, on the murder of President Boudiaf in 1992—will establish the setting of Djebar's short stories and convey the unspeakable violence that Algerians have suffered since independence. Students should also be introduced to key concepts of postcolonial criticism, through lectures and assigned readings and presentations based on

H. Adlai Murdoch and Anne Donadey's *Postcolonial Theory and Francophone Literary Studies* and Reina Lewis and Sara Mills's *Feminist Postcolonial Theory*. The topic of violence and terrorism is analyzed by Slavoj Žižek from historical, philosophical, and psychoanalytic perspectives (esp. chs. 2 and 3). Because excessive lecturing is perceived as tedious, students will view engaging, content-driven lectures about French-Algerian history, Islam, and literary theory as an opportunity to learn and hone their analytic and note-taking skills. They will have the opportunity to ask questions throughout the lectures and in the Q&A period. Subsequent clicker quizzes on historical events and postcolonial criticism are efficient and popular testing tools.

A list of guiding questions and topics distributed by the instructor allows students to discuss primary and secondary materials in the target language. To start out, an in-class reading of Jeff Humphries's "A Brief Conversation with Assia Djebar" stresses the collection's factual character:

> *Oran, langue morte* is the book I'm most personally attached to, because all seven of its [stories] are documentary. All of them, except the earlier story of Annie and Fatima, are about the violence, but they remain documentary in origin. Nearly all of the facts related in the [stories] are true. . . . They originated as first-hand retellings, then, from chance encounters during my stay in Paris in summer 1996.
>
> (Djebar qtd. in Humphries 15)

A discussion of excerpts from Stora's *La guerre invisible*, which stresses the lack of media coverage of the atrocities (both nationally, because of censorship by so-called reading committees, and internationally), and of excerpts from Philippe Bernard and Nathaniel Herzberg's *Lettres d'Algérie*, letters written by Algerians from Algeria to expatriate relatives in France and published in *Le Monde*, attest to the historical authenticity of Djebar's short stories and convey the impact of war on families in Algeria and in France.

In 1994, foreign nations, including France, closed their embassies in Algeria; major newswire services, including Thomson-Reuters, repatriated their reporters, no longer able to ensure their safety. As Stora writes, citing Thomas Ferenczi, a correspondent for *Le Monde*, by 1997 few visas were granted, resulting in a dearth of media coverage and making it impossible for reporters to do an in-depth analysis of the atrocities and to determine who had killed whom:

> "Il est impossible de connaître les circonstances exactes des tueries, impossible de saisir avec certitude qui sont les assassins et quelles sont leurs motivations, impossible de faire vraiment la part des manipulations, des règlements de compte, des manœuvres auxquelles se livrent les différentes factions en place." Les visas pour les journalistes étrangers sont délivrés au compte-gouttes. Et à l'intérieur du pays, une série de décrets et de lois restreint l'exercice du métier de journaliste. (*Guerre* 23–24)

> "It is impossible to find out the exact circumstances of the killings, impossible to determine with any certainty the identity of the murderers and their motivations, impossible to distinguish between manipulations, the settling of scores, and maneuvers carried out by the different groups in place." Visas for foreign journalists are issued very sparingly. And inside the country, a series of decrees and laws curtails the extent to which journalists can do their jobs.

Djebar's "Le discours de Francfort" ("The Frankfurt Speech"), which refers to *Oran* as a "chronique d'attentats, de peurs et d'alarmes rapportés par certains de mes proches, de mes amis perdus ou retrouvés" (245; "chronicle of attacks, fears, and alarms reported to me by close relatives, by lost or found friends"), underlines the importance of aesthetics, language, the female body, and of memory in writing—the significance of being an Arab woman writing in French, the *langue adverse* ("inimical language"), from a position of exile.

The first short story, "Oran, langue morte" ("Oran, Dead Language"), offers a retrospective analysis comparing the cycle of 1990s fundamentalist violence with the *plasticages* ("bombings") carried out in the 1960s by the OAS (Secret Armed Organization, Organisation de l'Armée Secrète), a terrorist organization made up of proponents of French Algeria. Excerpts from Stora and Gabriel Le Bomin's documentary *Guerre d'Algérie: La déchirure* ("Algerian War: The Tear") and historical sources from Stora and Tramor Quemeneur's *Algérie, 1954–1962* are useful to discuss key dates and figures of the Algerian War of Independence and the bombings carried out by proponents of French Algeria. They also help students visualize the complexity of the earlier war. We discuss French pacification (students watch the propaganda movie *Képis bleus*), the role of the FLN (National Liberation Front, Front de Libération Nationale) / ALN (National Liberation Army, Armée de Libération Nationale), the *harkis* (Algerian forces working for the French), the OAS, torture, the putsch of the generals, the fall of the French Fourth Republic, and so forth.

As the female narrator in "Oran, langue morte," puts it, recalling the brutal murder of her parents by the OAS, "La mort revient par cercles, Olivia!" (13; "Death comes in circles, Olivia!" [12]). The cyclical return of violence is also discussed in Stora's *La guerre invisible*.[6] To see the connection between the cyclical violence and intergenerational female solidarity, we view Sahraoui's feature *Barakat!* ("Enough!"), which addresses the thousands of kidnappings and disappearances of Algerian civilians in the 1990s. In the film, two women—a young medical doctor called Amel and her colleague, a hospital nurse called Khadidja, who is also a former *mujahida*—set off in search of Amel's abducted husband, a journalist. To visualize the civil war as lamented in Djebar's postscript, "Le sang ne sèche pas dans la langue" (367–78; "Afterword: The Tongue's Blood Does Not Run Dry" [209–15]), I show students world press photographs from *An Inquiry into the Algerian Massacres* (Bedjaoui et al.), depicting massacre victims and survivors, such as photograph 31, of a woman, titled "Why?"

(Blida, autumn 1997), or photograph 25, taken at Zmirli Hospital, 23 September 1997, after the Bentalha massacre and titled "A Woman Grieves the Loss of Dear Ones" (the famous *Madone de Bentalha* [Bentalha Madonna]). Press photographs, such as the iconic *Bentalha Madonna*, which Stora references in the opening paragraph of his *Guerre invisible*, underline the extent and collective trauma of massacres carried out in villages such as Sidi-Hamed (11 Jan. 1998, 350 dead), Raïs (29 Aug. 1997, over 300 dead), and Ouled Benaïssa (3 Oct. 1997, 38 dead).[7] I warn students about the cruelty of these images and am careful in my selection of them—in footage from the documentary *Algérie(s)* ("Algeria[s]"), for example, mass graves are shown, but the bodies are wrapped in shrouds. Viewing these photographs of victims, combined with reading Noam Chomsky's foreword in *An Inquiry into the Algerian Massacres*, fuels a discussion centering on the underlying reasons for this war and its estimated death toll of 150,000, largely made up of civilians.

"La fièvre dans des yeux d'enfant" ("Burning") illustrates the importance of writing in the face of or against death: writing to resurrect the past, lovers, and loved ones and as a rebellion against impending death.[8] Similarly, "L'attentat" ("The Attack") recounts how a journalist is gunned down by young terrorists on his way to submit an article feverishly written all night. In this context, I introduce the terms *littérature engagée* ("committed literature") and *littérature d'urgence* to highlight the importance of writing during the dark decade that lies at the heart of *Oran*. We discuss "L'attentat" in conjunction with an interview by Ghania Hammadou, an Algerian journalist turned novelist, which poignantly describes the consequences of death threats for journalists. A student presentation on the documentary *Algeria: The Life and Death of Algerian Journalists* reveals the increasingly tenuous position of Algerian journalists and their desperate attempts to maintain freedom of the press in the face of state censure, propaganda, and rising fundamentalism.

Discussing Djebar's short story "L'attentat" in parallel with "La femme en morceaux" ("The Woman in Pieces") makes sense, since in both texts the author (writer, narrator, *conteuse*, storyteller) assumes an activist stance, which is mirrored by the teacher-student relationship in the classroom. Both dissect political, textual, narratological, and bodily realities, and the classroom literally sets the stage for a theater of cruelty.[9] Students are captivated by discussions of trauma, revolt, and existential questions of survival under extreme circumstances. I talk about "La femme en morceaux" in connection with Yamina Bachir-Chouikh's film *Rachida*, which tells the story of a young Algerian teacher who survives a terrorist shooting in Algiers. Victimized by one of her own former students for refusing to place a bomb in the school where she teaches, she flees to a country village that is in the grip of terrorists who abduct and rape a young girl before carrying out a mass killing. A survivor of unspeakable brutality, Rachida ends up returning to the devastated school, where she resumes teaching, surrounded by the few students who survived the massacre and have the courage to come to class.

Considering the depressing content of Djebar's short stories, I provide relief by showing *Salut Cousin!* and *Bab el Oued City*, comedies by the Algerian filmmaker Merzak Allouache that are set in the 1990s. Students also welcome the opportunity to write a research paper comparing the beginning of the civil war, as detailed in *Bab el Oued City*, with Allouache's postwar sequel comedy, *Bab el Web*. To lighten up the class, we discuss songs from Rachid Taha's album *Tékitoi* ("Who're Ya?") and watch a video of Taha's return to Oran after twenty years in France. The video provides visual and cultural input about post–civil war Algeria and highlights the generation gap between older Algerians and the youth who do not necessarily speak French anymore but continue to dream of the West—France, Canada, and the United States—as havens of opportunity and wealth.

The second half of *Oran*, "Entre France et Algérie," ("Between France and Algeria") starts out with "Annie et Fatima" ("Annie and Fatima"), which tells the story of the French Algerian couple Annie and Idriss and their infant daughter, Fatima, who is kidnapped and brought to Algeria by her father after the couple's divorce. Annie travels to Algeria to meet her nine-year-old daughter, whom she has seen only in pictures sent annually, surrounded by a growing crowd of half brothers and half sisters. Excerpts from Tony Gatlif's powerful feature film *Exils* (2004; "Exiles") illustrate the complexities of cultural differences, nomadism, postcolonial identities, and the quest for the other. Both short story and film address those complexities and the need to discover the self embedded in the search for identity markers. Like Annie, who, dismayed to see her daughter dressed in a black chador, learns Berber to be able to communicate her love to her, Naïssa in Gatlif's film travels to Algeria with her French boyfriend, Zano, the orphaned son of pieds-noirs (European settlers in Algeria) emigrants, to discover her roots and undergoes a cathartic ceremony carried out by a marabout (religious healer), which is part of a longer journey of self-discovery.[10]

The short story "Le corps de Félicie" ("Félicie's Body") again showcases a cultural dichotomy through a mixed French-Algerian couple and their children, who are faced with religious, linguistic, and geographic differences. An introduction to the issue of immigration in France, based on Yamina Benguigui's popular miniseries *Aïcha*, is helpful here. The series deals with the problems faced by the children and grandchildren of Algerian immigrants and also provides much-needed comic relief. "Retours non retours" ("Non-Return Returns"), built on the metanarrative of changing complex mother-daughter relationships and the issue of immigrant Algerian miners in France, can be further investigated by a reading of the Moroccan novelist Tahar Ben Jelloun's "Entretien avec Monsieur Saïd Hammadi, ouvrier algérien" (*Fiancée* 63–76; "A Conversation with Mr. Saïd Hammadi, Algerian Worker"). Ben Jelloun's interview provides a male point of view on the hardships faced by immigrants in France. Similarly, a student presentation on Benguigui's film *Inch' Allah Dimanche* ("Inch'Allah Sunday") can illustrate the problems faced by female immigrants in France, addressing topics such as the hardships faced by cloistered women, female emancipation in the face of patriarchy, and the lack of communication in the Algerian immigrant couple in France.

The intertextual use of secondary and primary sources, in addition to references to specific historical and current events such as the Algerian government's brutal management of the hostage crisis in In Amenas in January 2013, provide additional perspectives on Djebar's texts and help explain the pervasiveness in them of violence. Students are asked to write one-page reflection papers after discussing each short story, stressing what they have learned and how the Djebarian text differs from other texts and films studied. Finally, as we read more and more short stories, students better appreciate Djebar's style and comment on the beauty of her language. They particularly enjoy reading and acting out loud the tale "La femme en morceaux."

NOTES

Unless otherwise indicated, all translations are mine.

[1]To introduce key concepts of Islam to non-Muslim students, I have found Michel Reber's concise *L'Islam* very useful. My students are fascinated by Islam and especially topics pertaining to Muslim women, such as marriage, divorce, repudiation, Islamic feminism, and the symbolism surrounding the headscarf or veil.

[2]This class could be taught in English, using *The Tongue's Blood Does Not Run Dry: Algerian Stories* (2006). All the teaching materials should be made available on *Blackboard*, *Canvas*, and library course reserves in either hard copy or digital form. Because of the difficulty of the original text, I supply students with the English-language version of the text. For homework, I give them worksheets featuring detailed comprehension and analysis questions for each text, to ensure that they are doing the required readings at home and come to class prepared for discussion.

[3]I recommend Calle-Gruber, *Assia Djebar, nomade*; Donadey, *Assia Djebar*; Erickson, *Islam*; Kelly, *Autobiography*; Mortimer, *Assia Djebar*; Murdoch; Ruhe; and Woodhull.

[4]The documentary is also available on *YouTube*.

[5]The Family Code legalized polygamy and made women dependent on male tutors for everyday decisions, de facto reducing them to second-rate citizens.

[6]Marie-Claire Chatelard's article provides a comprehensive summary of the atrocities committed by the OAS, as do a number of eyewitness accounts on *YouTube*—for instance, *Guerre d'Algérie, histoire de l'OAS*.

[7]For an in-depth discussion of this photograph, see Hanort.

[8]One student wrote a research paper analyzing the cathartic functions of writing in the face of death, comparing Djebar's *Oran* with her book *Le blanc de l'Algérie*, in which the narrator holds a posthumous monologue with the ghosts of murdered friends.

[9]Students were shocked to find out that this short story was based on a real event: a teacher in a small village located in the Jijel region was murdered in his classroom in front of his students on 13 February 1994 (Stora, *Guerre* 21).

[10]The themes of alterity and identity could be illustrated by reading excerpts from Kristeva's *Étrangers à nous-mêmes*.

Interdisciplinary Approaches to Teaching Documentary Genres in Assia Djebar's *La femme sans sépulture* and *La disparition de la langue française*

Dominique D. Fisher

Novels like Assia Djebar's *La femme sans sépulture* ("Woman without a Grave") and *La disparition de la langue française* ("The Disappearance of the French Language") are usually well received by students in French and francophone studies, in Franco-Arab studies, and by students who are in the process of completing a minor in history or cultural studies. Such students are particularly drawn to these novels because they facilitate discussions of colonization, the war of independence in Algeria, postindependence regimes, feminism and Islam, and Islam and globalization. Yet limiting the study of these novels to historical or sociocultural issues would frame them as ethnographic. The political dimension of Djebar's texts is not limited to their critique of history but is embedded in her writing practice. *La femme* and *La disparition* are complex, polyphonic, and hybrid, moving beyond national conventions, mixing and reworking Western and non-Western literary devices. Teaching them and stimulating the interest of students for literature may be challenging in the present academic climate, which does not promote the humanities. To what extent may literature courses attract students who need to fulfill North American college requirements for global issues? What sort of theoretical and pedagogical approaches might invigorate an interest in Djebar and for literature in general? This essay proposes an interdisciplinary framework that, by investigating her work, will show students the relevance of literature in today's world.

Djebar's fiction brings diverse arts and disciplines together and transforms them in a transverse fashion. It asks for modes of reading beyond Western binaries and beyond national, linguistic borders and across disciplines. It destabilizes the opposition between the real and the fictional and renders obsolete canonical definitions of factual and fictional narratives. One of the most distinctive aspects of her work is the conditions under which narratives are produced (see Fisher 131). Anne Donadey has demonstrated that narrative rupture, repetition, and *mise en abyme* are common features of anamnesis, trauma writing, and the aesthetic of detour in Djebar's works ("Expression" 78).

I discuss here how studying Djebar's references to documentary genres in novel and film in *La femme* and *La disparition* can illuminate the transnational dimension of her work and enhance readings of it.[1] These two novels are complementary from a formal and a thematic standpoint. One particularly helpful strategy is to analyze how the paratext introduces the notion of documentary genre in these novels.

La femme tells the story of the مجاهدة (mujahida; here a freedom fighter in the Algerian War of Independence) Yamina Oudaï, known as Zoulikha, who was arrested in 1956 during the war and tortured and whose body was discovered only in 2001.[2] Studying the notice to the reader about Zoulikha brings out various interesting comments in undergraduate and graduates classes on how Djebar conceives of "une approche documentaire" ("a documentary approach"):[3] on the one hand, she states that "tous les faits et détails de la vie et de la mort de Zoulikha . . . sont rapportés avec un souci de fidélité historique" ("all facts and details of Zoulikha's life and death . . . are reported with respect for historical accuracy"); on the other hand, she insists, "J'ai usé à volonté de ma liberté romanesque, justement pour que la vérité de Zoulikha soit éclairée davantage" (9; "I used my novelistic freedom at will, precisely to shed more light on Zoulikha's truth"). At first glance this paratext seems contradictory to students who have been taught that literature is fiction, but it is less of a problem for students who are familiar with the way in which Latin American literature deals with history and politics or with Fernando Ortiz's notion of transculturation.[4] Yet most students appear puzzled by the term *documentary*, which they traditionally associate with film.

I found it helpful to discuss with them what a documentary is. Students will give various examples of documentaries, such as the political documentary, the historical documentary, individual or collective nonfiction stories, or docufiction. All these subgenres point to the complex relation that documentaries establish with notions of truth and fiction. This complexity is characteristic of how Djebar articulates the real and the fictional in her work and refers to the documentary genre in *La femme* and *La disparition*. These novels lead us to the hypothesis that the documentary falls somewhere between André Bazin's statement that "every film is a social documentary" (40) and Christian Metz's statement that "[e]very film is a fiction film" (47).

La femme contains a direct critique of the historical documentary and makes use of the testimonial genre, which shares the following characteristics with neorealism: "[I]t is written and conceived collaboratively, outside the bounds of a singular consciousness, in its effort to produce a counterhegemonic rewriting of politics and history" (Khanna 112). In *La femme*, Hania, one of Zoulikha's daughters, says, "Je croyais . . . que la télévision avait besoin d'un documentaire, comme il y en avait eu tant sur les héros morts! . . . Zoulikha, vivante aujourd'hui, elle les aurait dérangés tous!" (90; "I thought . . . that TV needed a documentary like so many of those on dead heroes! Zoulikha, if she were alive today, would unsettle them all!"). Her comment leads us to examine why she dismisses the documentary. It brings us back to the origin of Djebar's novel, to the time when Djebar was making *La nouba des femmes du Mont Chenoua* ("The Nouba of Women from Mount Chenoua"). Hania's fear that the filmmaker is a spokesperson of the TVA (the Algerian TV) who will accommodate the nationalistic discourse of commemoration raises the question of the politics of representation of the documentary. Students point to the fact that the equivalency between documentary and truth is often compromised by the lack of neutrality of the filmmaker and by how the camera's gaze functions in power relationships and disciplinary systems. It is important to discuss also the position of Djebar as both a filmmaker and a writer who stands as an inquirer (79), a "visiteuse" (47; "visitor"), an "invitée" (90; "guest"), and an "étrangère, dans ces lieux, . . . pas du tout étrangère" (100; "stranger here . . . but not so much a stranger"). Being at the same time an outsider and a former neighbor of Zoulikha who wishes to have Zoulikha's story known, Djebar occupies an ambiguous position in the laws of hospitality. This position provides a springboard to discuss how documentary movies relate to the real and truth, and that discussion allows us to consider what gives *La femme* a documentary quality.

Most critics argue that the conditions of production of documentaries are similar to those of fiction films, since both transform the real by using cinematographic language and montage. Yet François Niney sees a difference between documentaries and fiction films in terms of contextualization and reception. A fiction film is always received as such, whereas a documentary can raise doubts about its factual nature, about its relation to the regimes of truth, and about the conditions under which it provides evidence. Hania's comment points to the invisibility of Zoulikha and consequently to the marginal place that women combatants occupy in official history. The way documentaries are read remains crucial since those films always respond to the desire to know, the "libido sciendi" (Lioult 131).

The questions of reception and *libido sciendi* help students discuss the relation between experience and the unveiling of truth in *La femme*. Djebar did not deliver the entire story of Zoulikha in her film *La nouba* but lets Zoulikha appear for about seven minutes in the middle of her film. Yet in *La femme*, she describes the film as "fiction et documentaire" (16; "fiction and documentary") because of its slow rhythm, the dialogues between women, its use of sound effects, traditional music (*nouba*), and Béla Bartók. The functioning of the real and of the reading codes in relation to the documentary are interesting aspects of both *La nouba* and *La femme*. Reading codes and the understanding of music and rhythm vary among cultures and students. Lila Abu-Lughod's observations on veiled sentiments in oral literature, whether poetry or song in Arab and Bedouin societies, are particularly relevant here. Poetry and songs are "a vehicle for personal expression and confidential communication" (26) but also part of daily life (27). As such they have a social and performative function. Veiled sentiments work as a "defiant discourse" that resists power structures in a Foucauldian sense, whether dealing with gender, family, social, or political issues (29). The veiling of sentiments thus makes the personal political. I use the term *veiling effect* to refer to an aesthetic that disrupts the structuring of narratives and uses the personal as a counterhegemonic tool in an oblique fashion.

In *La femme*, the truth about Zoulikha is mediated by the experience of the women who were close to her (her daughters, her sister-in-law, and Dame

Lionne) and by their oral narratives. I found that the notion of the veiling effect helped students understand the many ways in which Djebar's documentary approach uses fiction to claim the recognition of Zoulikha's memory. This notion facilitates discussions of the oblique unfolding of the women's narratives, of the links between those narratives and body language and rhythm. The veiling effect also elucidates the various facets of the aesthetic of detour in Djebar's writing, such as the intersection of poetry and song or the *nouba*-style telling and its relation to film, novel, and historiography. Students also see how Djebar reconstructs Zoulikha's voice as spectral. By making Zoulikha speak from the tomb, Djebar unearths repressed historical memory and denounces the politics of commemoration. She is thus writing a counterhistory and a "métacritique d'observation du processus dans lequel il s'agit de porter témoignage au processus de témoignage lui-même" (Donadey, "Expression" 80; "a metacritique of the process in which one can bear witness to the process of witnessing itself").

The dedication in *La disparition* brings out the veiling effect as well as the political dimension of Djebar's writing: "À Djaffar L. dont l'amour pour la Casbah m'a inspiré ce roman" ("To Djaffar L., whose love of the casbah inspired this novel"). Like most dedications, it establishes an ambiguous relation among the author, the dedicatee, and the work itself. The dedication blurs the boundary between the private and the public and between the fictional and the real. Who is Djaffar L.? Djebar's response maintains a veiling of meanings regarding both his identity and the book's genre:[5] "La personne dont le récit oral est le point de départ est adressée dans la dédicace du roman: 'À Djaffar L.'" (Schuchardt 371n1; "the person whose oral testimony is at the origin of this novel is addressed in its dedication"). The reference to oral literature inscribes this novel in "social historical reality" (Abu-Lughod 29). Like the notice to the reader in *La femme*, the dedication in *La disparition* invites us to discuss how this novel unfolds between fact and fiction.

Djaffar L. and the casbah are two referents that immediately trigger comparisons with Gillo Pontecorvo's *The Battle of Algiers*, even though the name of Djafar Lhadi—the code name of Yacef Saadi, a hero and a leader of the FLN (Front de Libération Nationale ["National Liberation Front']) who plays his own role in this film—is spelled differently. When I ask my students how Djebar's novel compares with this film, some invoke its neorealist style and agree that both Pontecorvo and Djebar mix facts with fiction and exploit "the experimental realization of the imaginative constitution of the political and the historical" (Khanna 111). Others mention *The Battle of Algiers*'s negative reception in France as a Third World film.

The question of reception opens to the many facets of *The Battle of Algiers* as a documentary-style film. Although a reconstruction of the battle of Algiers that does not use any newsreel footage and is shot in flashback, it is often mistaken for a documentary.[6] *Cahiers du Cinéma* reveals that it was at first denigrated by French film culture because of its style and vision of the Algerian Revolution: "[T]he autonomy of cinema as art coincides with the dismissal of an Italo-

Algerian production" (Caillé 377). Yet in 2004 the reception of the film moved beyond a "French problem" and was seen as a "conflict between Islam and 'the Western World'" (384). Besides opening debates on French denial versus the duty of memory, the reception of this film invites discussions on the multiplicity of codes of readings in documentary genres.

We have seen that in *La femme* the combination of fiction and documentary by means of the veiling effect produces a counterhegemonic discourse on the place of women in history. In contrast, students agree that in *The Battle of Algiers* the representation of women during the Algerian Revolution is "severely underplayed" (Amrane-Minne, "Women at War" 342) and that the role of the FLN is overemphasized. It is important at this point to introduce Ranjana Khanna's analysis of the famous sequence in which women unveil themselves in front of the mirror. Although Khanna speaks of this film as a documentary-style work, she identifies "'a zone of occult instability' of cultural representation" in the forging of national identity (117). In this sequence, the silence of the women, their gestures, and their gaze in the mirror contradict the efficiency of the use of the camera and the mirror as a weapon in Third World cinema: "Cutting through [the documentary] form, they pose questions concerning their role in the nation to come" (121–22). The mirror introduces a break in the representation and the moment in which it "reflects the drama of revolution and of filmmaking" (123).

What Khanna identifies as a dysfunction in the "documentary form" and the irruption of a "third space" (123) or "a symbolic space of political nonrepresentation" (124) has also been identified by students as the emergence of a veiled discourse on the place of women in the Algerian nation. In contrast, *La nouba*, which transmits the voices of women, was shown only once by the RTA (Radio-Télévision Algérienne), "because it was thought to give a disrespectful and limited view of male war veterans" (125). Yet this film mixes documentary genre with fiction by means of the veiling effect: the *nouba*-style fragmented structure, the brief insertion of images of war in black and white, the mobility of the women, and the oblique use of the voice-over (Lila "speaks directly only to her child" [Khanna 127]). *La femme* pushes the criticism of nationalistic ideology in postcolonial Algeria further by expanding the narrative space of Zoulikha's haunting voice.

Like *La femme*, *La disparition* delivers a critique of the representation of the Algerian Revolution. One strategy I found particularly useful is discussing how the mixing of fiction and the real in this novel demystifies the hegemony of the FLN as well as the cult of heroes. As in *La femme*, women are shown to be resistant to manipulation by French colonists and the patriarchy both. Although this novel focuses on Berkane's difficult return to Algeria after twenty years of exile in France because of the trauma of the revolution and torture and because of his ignorance of radical Islamism and the civil war in the nineties, it is helpful to draw attention to the role women play in his recovery of the foreclosed memory of these events. In his family, during the revolution, his mother was the only one who knew how to read and speak French. As a narrator Berkane underlines the power of her gaze and veiled discourse: "Ma mère surveillait, de ses yeux de chatte, le conseil de famille entre hommes" (47; "My mother with her cat's eyes was watching the family council between men"). She was also the guardian of the Algerian flag. The description of the general strike of December 1960, unlike in *The Battle of Algiers*, focuses on the patio as a site of resistance, a place where women exchanged and circulated information, made and hid the flag.

When Nadjia tells Berkane the story of the murder of her grandfather, Baba Sidi, by the FLN in 1957, she uses an oblique discourse: "mon introduction est trop longue" ("my introduction is too long"). She does not go "directement au fait" (88; "straight to the fact"), nor does she speak of the "dernier film" (89; "last movie"). She claims to remember the traumatic story of this murder, though she was only two years old and her grandmother told it to her. Yet her monologue, besides being the product of the painful work of anamnesis, crosses the borders of the *récit* ("narrative"), the polyphonic tale, and theater. This veiling effect ultimately draws striking parallels between the violence of the FLN and that of radical Islamists.

The mixing of fiction and the real leads us to discuss how *La disparition* and *La femme* exploit the veiling effect to denounce torture. In *La disparition*, Berkane shows Maryse his drawing of "l'offrande du sable fin" (165; "the offering of fine sand") but cannot explain it to her. In *La femme*, the spectral voice of Zoulikha also evokes torture obliquely. Speaking of torture and rape has long been taboo on both the French and the Algerian sides. But in the Islamic tradition, rape carries the meaning of a violation of the code of honor. In her last monologue Zoulikha utters the word "torture" (217) but never that of rape. She signifies rape by metaphors of tearing ("seule la douleur le long de mes cuisses me déchirait" [217; "only the pain between my legs was tearing me"]), metaphors of birth and death, and the threatening posture of the men standing next to her. The way Djebar uses Zoulikha's voice finally invites comparisons with the way in which Louisette Ighilahriz "describes the brutality of her torture but [cannot] speak of the rape" (Mortimer, "Tortured Bodies" 110).

An interdisciplinary approach to Djebar allows students to remove themselves from conventional readings of fiction and document and work with the ways in which the author calls hegemonic discourses into question beyond artistic and national borders.

NOTES

[1]By *transnational* I mean an expression of resistance against hegemonic discourses, whether of a national (e.g., the French or the FLN version of the Algerian Revolution) or religious nature (e.g., radical Islam).

[2] Mildred Mortimer notes that "although the martyr's remains had not been discovered when Djebar made the film and began the novel, they had been unearthed before the completion of the novel in 2001" ("Tortured Bodies" 111).

[3] All translations are mine unless otherwise indicated.

[4] Ortiz introduced the notion in 1940 to express the "complex transmutations of culture that have taken place" in Cuban society (98).

[5] On the ambiguity of dedications and their destination, see Genette, *Paratexts* 131–35.

[6] Even people in the Pentagon watched it after 9/11 to draw lessons from the French on how to win the war against terror.

"Gender, Mystery and Difference": The Treatment of Myth in Assia Djebar's *La disparition de la langue française*

Annica Schjött Vonèche

More than fifty years after the signing of the Évian Accords, which marked the end of French colonial power in Algeria, the two nations are still trying to come to terms with the legacy of their common past. The colonial depiction of the Orient as a foil for the West, the official French view of Algeria as an inseparable part of France during the French-Algerian war, and the postcolonial reluctance on the part of both countries to acknowledge the legacy of 130 years of common history are all examples of how myth has been instrumental in forging specific views of the Franco-Algerian relationship on both sides of the Mediterranean.

In my undergraduate French literature class on the role of the cultural other in French and francophone literature, I taught Assia Djebar's *La disparition de la langue française* ("The Disappearance of the French Language") with a focus on how Djebar simultaneously alludes to, subverts, and deconstructs some of the most widespread myths relating to the Franco-Algerian relationship, past and present.

In order to provide my students with a working definition of myth and its functions, I started the class with selected readings from Roland Barthes's *Mythologies*. Barthes's analysis of how myth can be used to promote specific, often politically motivated views of the past and present is particularly helpful for students unfamiliar with the concept of myth. The first essay we read was "Grammaire africaine" (128–34; "African Grammar"). The reading provided material for a discussion on the use of myth in political propaganda; it also lay the groundwork for an examination of the various ways in which the French and Algerian establishments have used myths to create and promote politically desirable views of the Franco-Algerian colonial and postcolonial relationship.

After this initial encounter with Barthes's definition of the workings of myth, we went on to read "Le mythe, aujourd'hui" (179–233; "Myth Today"), which helped students acquire an understanding of the theoretical underpinnings of myth as understood by Barthes. For students unfamiliar with semiotics, this text can be quite complex, but I found that succinct explanations of a few of its key terms, such as *metalanguage*, *signifier*, and *signified*, gave them a better grasp of his method. The essay that we had already read and discussed provided a concrete example of Barthes's method for cultural analysis. In order to further deepen the students' understanding of myth, I assigned short oral presentations in which the students were asked to use Barthes's method to analyze a modern myth of their choosing. The students demonstrated that they had grasped the main characteristics of Barthes's method by analyzing texts ranging from Super Bowl commercials to presidential electoral campaign speeches.

The next step was to link the general concept of myth to the specific myths that have governed Franco-Algerian relations. Here, Barthes's "Continent perdu" (152–54; "The Lost Continent") provided a fitting transition by addressing one of the myths that arguably has had the strongest influence on the French view of Algeria: the myth of the Orient. This text touches on some of the main components of the orientalist myth, such as the archetypal depiction of the Orient as monolithic, ahistorical, and exotic.[1] We then went on to read and discuss the introductory chapter to Edward Said's *Orientalism* ([1979] 1–28) together with the chapter on the myth of the casbah from Zeynep Çelik's *Urban Forms and Colonial Confrontations* (11–57). We also examined artistic renderings of the Orient from such French orientalist painters as Jean-Léon Gérôme and Eugène Delacroix, with whom Berkane, the main character in Djebar's novel, appears to identify on his return to Algeria after decades spent in France (71–72). Together, these texts and artistic expressions provided the students with an insight into the different components of the myth of the Orient.

Our examination of *La disparition de la langue française* began with a brainstorming session in which I asked the students to identify passages from the novel where the influence of the myth of the Orient on Berkane's Algerian childhood memories is apparent. This influence is particularly noticeable in his memories of growing up in the Casbah of Algiers (e.g., 53–56). I instructed the students to look at the three elements defined by Çelik as the main components of the casbah myth: "gender, mystery and difference" (21–22).

The students identified the novel's description of the chaotic and decidedly non-Western character of the casbah as an example of oriental difference and mystery. Berkane's casbah is a timeless, unchangeable universe; he believes that it has stayed the same through the ages thanks to "la permanence des pierres, des maisons à terrasses, des rues d'ombre et des escaliers en paliers, et des taches étroites de ciel qui vous suivent, surtout des ruelles avec la foule s'écoulant" (64; "the permanence of the stones, the terraced houses, the shadowy streets and leveled stairways and the narrow patches of sky that follow you, especially the alleys where the masses flow by").[2] Our discussion focused on the chaotic and mysterious aspects of the casbah in his memory, such as the exotic architecture and the constant movement of crowds of people living on the margin of society: "La Casbah de Berkane grouillait d'appellations, autant que de chômeurs, de drogués, de gars du milieu, de dockers et de mendiants, oui, tout bougeait, encombrait, s'entremêlait" (54; "Berkane's casbah was teeming with designations, as much as with the unemployed, drug addicts, gangsters, dockworkers, beggars, yes, everything was moving, crowding, entangling").

I asked the students to compare Berkane's descriptions of the casbah with the introductory scene to Julien Duvivier's 1937 film *Pépé le Moko*, which is used as an intertext in the novel (53). In the film's introductory scene, a local police officer presents the casbah in a way that reveals striking resemblances to the description of the casbah in Djebar's novel. Like Berkane's memories, this scene highlights the non-Western architecture of the casbah, described as "grouillante comme une fourmillière" ("teeming like an anthill") and its mysterious inhabitants defined by their exoticism, such as its "traditionalistes . . . mystérieux. Des Kabyles, des Chinois, des Gitans, des Aïmatlos" ("mysterious . . . traditionalists. Kabyles, Chinese people, Gypsies, stateless persons"). A detailed comparison between the passages from the novel describing Berkane's memories of the casbah and the film's introductory scene allowed the students to better see how Djebar inscribes Berkane's memories into the larger context of the myth of the Orient, in which *Pépé le Moko* plays an integral part (see Rolot and Ramirez 383; Vincendeau 53–64).

In order to better grasp the articulation of gender in the myth of the casbah and its influence on Berkane's memories, we went back to the introductory scene of *Pépé le Moko*. In the off-camera description of the women of the casbah they are described as sexualized, foreign, and threatening creatures: "des filles venues de tous les pays, de tous les formats . . . des sans âge, des sans forme, abîmes de graisse où nul n'ose se risquer" ("women from every country, of all sizes . . . ageless, shapeless, chasms of fat where no one dares to venture"), while the camera zooms in on partially undressed female bodies in the casbah. This scene allowed the students to identify a similar albeit more subtle influence of this element of the myth in Berkane's memories—for example, in the brief mention of the presence of "des filles pas honnêtes . . . de celles qui sortent quand elles veulent" (64; "bad girls . . . of the type who go out whenever they like"). We talked about how the feminization of the casbah can be seen as part of what Çelik calls "the broader project of the feminization of the Orient" (22), depicting the Orient as a whole as inherently feminine and sexual.[3]

A few students disagreed with the conclusion that the portrayal of the casbah in the film and in the novel are influenced, consciously or unconsciously, by myth. They pointed out that the description of the casbah in the novel is based on its actual physical appearance. Referring back to "Myth Today" allowed me to clarify that according to Barthes all myths take as their point of departure details actually present in the object. Myth manipulates our view of the object by presenting these details as the whole truth, while discarding any element that contradicts it (199–200).

I brought another passage in the novel where the influence of myth is apparent to the attention of my students. It is the scene describing Berkane's "vision obsédante" (61; "haunting vision"), which comes to him as he is standing outside the Djemaa El Djedid Mosque in the casbah. In this vision, the physical, present-day square, where shortly after the French conquest the traditional buildings were partially destroyed and the mosque turned into a cathedral, coexists with a mythical space from the precolonial era. Berkane wants to exhume the vestiges of that early Algiers in order to reconnect with a mythical place unspoiled by the French presence and the cultural and physical transformations it brought (61). Berkane's wish to reconnect with Algeria's authentic and homogeneous past is reminiscent of the view of an unadulterated Algerian mythical, national identity promoted by the ulema movement, responsible in large part for the attempts to create a postcolonial Algerian cultural identity (see Harbi 26). The students were quite surprised to realize that the core concepts conveyed by the myth of the Orient and by the ulema myth are strikingly similar on both sides of the Franco-Algerian colonial divide. Both see *algérité* ("Algerianness"), to use a neologism after Barthes's model (193–94), as a culture untouched by time and foreign influence, a culture radically different from, incompatible with, and untouched by French culture.

It is interesting that the novel also shows the influence of a myth that expresses values opposite to the orientalist and ulema myths. In France during the French-Algerian war, the myth of a deep and insurmountable difference between East and West was replaced by its opposite, the idea that Algeria was an integral part of the French nation (Pervillé 128–29) created through the denial of all differences between French subjects of European descent and those of Northern African descent, in theory if not practice. This idea is reflected in the reprimanding of a young Berkane by his schoolteacher for drawing the Algerian flag. It is perfectly in line with the French policy of cultural assimilation in Algeria that the teacher calls Berkane's action "[u]ne insulte à la République, à la mère patrie" (49; "an insult to the Republic, to the motherland").[4]

By encouraging my students to read *La disparition de la langue francaise* through the lens of myth, I helped them gain an understanding of how various myths have historically influenced the view of the Franco-Algerian relationship, as well as how Djebar alludes to them in the novel. But to limit an analysis of her novel to a mere tracing of allusions to myths in the text would be reductive, therefore the final part of the class was devoted to an exploration of how the novel questions and deconstructs these myths. The students compared and contrasted Berkane's memories of the casbah with the description of the physical casbah he encounters on his return to Algiers. Berkane in fact recognizes that his nostalgia has turned the casbah into a partially real and partially imagined site that both embodies and preserves his past: "tant de fois dans l'exil, ensuite, il s'est imaginé que le microcosme de cet univers passé garderait à jamais sa réalité" (55; "so many times in exile, he imagined that the microcosm of this past universe would forever continue to be a reality"). But when confronted with the present-day casbah, he is shocked to discover that the sites of his childhood have been transformed into "non-lieux de vie, en aires d'abandon et de dénuement, en un espace marqué par une dégradation funeste" (66; "nonlivable spaces, sites of abandonment and destitution, areas marked by a gruesome degradation"). He hoped that his inside knowledge and understanding of this neighborhood would allow him to reconnect with its *algérité*: "La Casbah va lui proposer ses venelles, ses ruelles en nœuds, en escaliers d'ombre . . . car [il] ne vien[t] ni en étranger ni en touriste attardé, simplement en . . . enfant du quartier" (53–54; "The casbah will offer him its passageways, its twisting alleys and shadowy stairways . . . because [he] come[s] neither as a foreigner, nor as a belated tourist . . . but simply as . . . a neighborhood kid"). To his surprise and disappointment, however, the inhabitants of the city treat him as an outsider (59), and the casbah that he remembered is nowhere to be found—if indeed it ever existed. The discrepancy between the real and the remembered casbah is so great that he is initially at a loss for words (67–68).

According to Barthes, in order to deconstruct myth and reveal it as an impostor, it is necessary to separate form from meaning (201). This separation happens in the novel when Berkane's memories of the casbah are confronted with its physical reality. The failure of the local population to recognize him as one of their own, along with the unexpected changes of the casbah, denaturalize the myth of an eternal *algérité*. The nostalgia that was at the heart of his childhood memories is lost, because nostalgia is possible only as long as there is a distance between the subject and the desired object. Susan Stewart explains:

> The nostalgic is enamored of distance, not of the referent itself. Nostalgia cannot be sustained without loss. For the nostalgic to reach his or her goal of closing the gap between resemblance and identity, lived experience would have to take place, an erasure of the gap between sign and signified which would cancel out the desire that is nostalgia's reason for existence. (145)

The exposure of the manipulation exercised through myth and fueled by nostalgia makes it impossible for Berkane to hold on to his view of the casbah. Thus he is forced to recognize the narrative construction underpinning his memories.

Djebar deconstructs Algerian myths relative to the Franco-Algerian relationship in a similar manner. As a case in point, I used the novel's treatment of the myth of the Algerian hero as a national independence fighter. My students, when asked to analyze the descriptions of Berkane's participation in the demonstrations against French rule and his arrest, quickly concluded that his behavior is anything but heroic. Berkane's first act of protest against the French colonizer quickly degenerates into an orgy of pillaging and destruction (144–45). His dreams of becoming a martyr in the independence struggle are revealed as a self-serving wish to "savourer, post mortem . . . [s]a propre gloire" (155; "enjoy [his] own glory post mortem") and the subsequent arrest is depicted as a moment of ridicule rather than heroism (156).

Going further than a criticism of the image of the nationalist hero, Djebar breaks up the interpretive monopoly of myth by endowing key terms with alternative meanings. The story of Berkane's drug-addicted Uncle Tchaida redefines the figure of the nationalist hero. When Tchaida was alive, he was considered "le dernier des derniers" ("the last of the last"), but his death at the hands of a French officer turns him into "un personnage exemplaire" (77; "an exemplary character") in the eyes of his neighbors. He is depicted not as a nationalist hero but as "le seul innocent . . . le héros absolu" (80; "the only innocent . . . the absolute hero"). Berkane's version of the Algerian hero is thus that of a marginalized person without a political agenda, one whose heroic quality is precisely that of being an antihero. This reinterpretation of the nationalist myth can be read as an implicit criticism of the postcolonial Algerian historiography, which promotes "l'image mythique d'un univers manichéen où les rôles sont clairement définis entre les héros et les traîtres, les libérateurs et les oppresseurs" (Stora, *Gangrène* 230; "the mythical image of a Manichaean universe where the roles are clearly defined between heroes and traitors, liberators and oppressors").

This black-and-white interpretation of the past, propagated by myth, helps us better understand why Berkane remembers the first time he saw the Algerian flag but not the lynching of a Spanish butcher, which took place at the same time (34–35). The existence of an Algerian flag, distinctly different from the French flag, makes perfect sense to Berkane because the division between theirs and ours fits neatly into the preconceived notion of fundamental difference between the colonizer and the colonized: "La logique semblait sans faille: chacun son drapeau" (35; "the logic seemed flawless—each had its own flag"). However, the gratuitous violence committed by his own people is incompatible with the myths of good versus evil, victim versus villain, and colonized versus colonizer and is therefore absent from his childhood memories when recalled through the prism of myth.

These are but a few examples of how Djebar treats and deconstructs the Franco-Algerian myths in *La disparition*. I found that encouraging students to find more examples helped them gain insight into both the specificity of her treatment of history and myth and the novel's general caution against allowing myth to monopolize and distort the interpretation of the past.

The final question I brought up in this class was about the novel's ending. When asked whether or not the novel has a happy ending, my students almost all argued that Berkane's unexplained disappearance, presumably at the hands of terrorists, signifies a failure for his quest to rearticulate the Franco-Algerian memory beyond the monopolizing influence of myth. However, when we did a close reading of the letters sent by Berkane's lover, Nadija, a few students noted that the passage where Nadija describes Algeria as a "tout petit passage entre l'Andalousie perdue et mythique et tout l'ailleurs possible" (214; "a very small passageway between the lost and mythical Andalusia and all other possible spaces") does offer a glimmer of hope. This quote, the students argued, indicates that embracing rather than denying Algeria's past connection to Europe might open up possibilities in the future.

I used this insightful observation as the introduction to a concluding exploration of how this novel fits into the larger corpus of Djebar's work, in particular her project of developing a nonexclusionary language capable of narrating the Franco-Algerian relationship past and present. In her previous work, Djebar repeatedly explored the possibility of creating "l'entre-deux-langues" (*Ces voix* 51; "an in-between language")—that is, a language reflecting two different cultures without belonging completely to one or the other. In *Les nuits de Strasbourg* (1997; "Strasbourg Nights"), for example, a French-Algerian couple invents an alternative language that contains the single word "Alsagérie," made up by combining the two words *Alsace* and *Algérie*. Similarly, in *Le blanc de l'Algérie* (1995; *Algerian White*), Djebar proposes a French language that is modified, infiltrated by other languages. This language is identified as the language of the dead, with whom the narrator conducts dialogues throughout the novel. It is only through the interaction between the living and the dead that language becomes complete. I offered the possibility of regarding this view of Algeria as the passageway between a lost mythical land and all other possible destinations as the concretization of Djebar's "in-between language." To conclude our investigation of Djebar's treatment of myth, I suggested that this passage can be read as the beginning of the creation of a new type of myth, one that does not aim to dictate a specific preset view of the Franco-Algerian relationship but that, on the contrary, opens up a world of possibilities beyond confining polarizations and limiting simplifications.

NOTES

[1]For an in-depth analysis of Barthes's treatment of this myth, see Knight.

[2]All translations from *La disparition de la langue française* and from *Pépé le Moko* are my own.

[3]On the association of the casbah with illicit and dangerous sexuality, see Taraud 131.

[4]This view of the Franco-Algerian relationship is clearly articulated in a speech given by Pierre Mendès France as a reaction to the bomb attacks perpetrated by the FLN in November 1954 (see Pervillé 128–29).

Teaching Assia Djebar's Work in an Age of Fundamentalism

Kathryn Lachman

The vibrant intertextuality of Assia Djebar's work is both one of its most remarkable features and the hardest to convey to students. Djebar cites texts from across a wide array of epochs, genres, languages, and national contexts, while also incessantly reworking motifs from her own literary production. Her writing is thus linked to an ongoing practice of reading and revising. This intertextuality can be difficult for undergraduate students to grasp if they encounter only one of Djebar's works during a semester, yet it is essential to understanding the performative and revolutionary aspects of her oeuvre—as one that enacts freedom, mobility, and feminist solidarity through the constant references that open her texts to difference.

In order to help students appreciate this dimension of Djebar's writing (and to allow them time to engage with her richly poetic language), I favor teaching several of her essays and short stories rather than one of her major novels. In the discussion below, I focus on an upper-level undergraduate seminar on francophone North African literature titled Literature, Film, and Fundamentalism. Pairing Djebar's two essays on Albert Camus with short novels by Camus and Kamel Daoud introduces students to ongoing debates about language and national identity in the Algerian context, about whose voices constitute Algerian literature, or as one critic put it, which *qalam* writes for Algeria.[1] Djebar's response to this question, of course, was to argue for the pluralism and heterogeneity of Algerian heritage and to advocate above all for the inclusion of Algerian women's voices. Assigning her story "La femme en morceaux" ("The Woman in Pieces") in juxtaposition to Tahar Djaout's unfinished novella *Le dernier été de la raison* (*The Last Summer of Reason*) and films by Merzak Allouache confronts students with another of the major preoccupations of Djebar's work throughout the 1990s, the relation between writing and mortality: be it death prescribed and forestalled daily through storytelling, as in the *Thousand and One Nights*; accidental death, as in the case of Camus, who died in an automobile crash accompanied by his editor and the unfinished manuscript of an autobiographical novel; or death by assassination, as with Djaout and other Algerian intellectuals, who were murdered by Islamist militants during the civil conflict of the 1990s. While every author confronts death as the ultimate sentence of silence and fixity, this pressing mortality was all the more intensely felt by Djebar and other Algerian writers who found themselves the unambiguous target of Islamist terror. Djebar's "La femme en morceaux" conveys the urgency of writing—and of translation, interpretation, and all forms of artistic creativity—as a means of resisting political efforts to silence public expression, and as a way of prolonging voice and movement. By engaging with several of Djebar's short works dialogically, students acquire a more complex sense of the author as both a reader and public intellectual.[2]

Literature, Film, and Fundamentalism[3] examines representations of Islamic fundamentalism across multiple genres and national settings in view of helping students make sense of the rise of Islamism in North Africa and the Middle East, the emergence of the Islamic State, the refugee crisis in Europe, the attacks in Paris of 7 January 2015 and 13 November 2015, the Cologne incident of December 2015,[4] and the ascent of far-right parties across Europe. As the media bombards students with information about these issues, the course seeks to equip them with the background and analytical tools to develop a more critical perspective. Djebar's work brings complexity to the discussion of fundamentalism through its nuanced treatment of Islam, advocacy for a pluralistic Algeria, and denunciation of both government and Islamist violence in the 1990s.

Algeria is a key place to begin a discussion on Islamic fundamentalism because the emergence of radical Islam there reveals much about the legacy of colonial violence and postcolonial politics. Our first class session includes a screening of Gillo Pontecorvo's *La battaglia di Algeri* (*Battle of Algiers*) in order to familiarize students with the Algerian anticolonial struggle and the tension between secular and religious ideologies at work in the constitution of postindependence Algeria.[5] In the second and third week, students read Camus's *L'étranger* alongside Djebar's essays on Camus and on Daoud's *Meursault contre-enquête* (*The Meursault Investigation*); these texts expose them to ongoing debates about ethnic, gender, and religious identity in Algeria. Through journal writing prompts and class discussion, I ask students to compare the approaches that Djebar and Daoud bring to Camus's work. Both writers establish Camus as an essential precursor to their own work and a major figure in Algeria's literary heritage, while each identifies and rehabilitates different subject positions marginalized in Camus's fiction. The fourth week of the course focuses on Djaout's powerful depiction of the devastating impact of Islamism on secular culture in Algeria in relation to Allouache's 1994 film *Madinat bab el-oued* (*Bab el-Oued City*), which recounts the tyranny of an Islamist group over a neighborhood in the heart of historic Algiers.[6] In the fifth and final week in the Algerian unit, students read Djebar's "La femme en morceaux" in conjunction with Allouache's 2012 film *El Taaib* (*The Repentant*), which addresses collective trauma as one of the enduring legacies of the civil war of 1992–99 and critiques the state policy of amnesty and reconciliation.[7] That the protagonist of "La femme en morceaux" is a teacher who has chosen to expose her students to multiple translations and variants of one of the stories from the *Thousand and One Nights* underscores once again the critical roles of reading, writing, translating, and interpreting in Djebar's vision of a pluralistic, multilingual, and democratic Algeria.

Strangers at the Crossroads: Camus, Djebar, and Daoud

In 1995, Djebar took the floor at the University of California, Berkeley, to claim Camus as an essential voice of Algerian literature. She later published the text of her lecture in essay form under the title "Camus, 'le premier homme,' le dernier livre." Students today need to consider the audacity of this gesture within its political and historical context. In the United States, Camus is still largely taught as a twentieth-century French writer; meanwhile, in North Africa, his work is absent from the curriculum. Despite recent claims by Alice Kaplan,[8] his legacy in the Maghreb remains fraught because of his identity as a pied-noir ("settler") of French expression, his opposition to Algerian independence, and his silence on the use of torture by the French military.[9] In the light of the wide international acclaim,[10] Daoud received in 2013 for *Meursault contre-enquête*, a rewriting of Camus's *L'étranger* some fifty years later from the perspective of Haroun, the surviving brother of the nameless Arab whom Meursault murdered, the position Djebar took on Camus nearly two decades earlier at the height of the Algerian civil war is worth reexamining. On one hand, it affirmed her conviction that North Africa belonged within a diverse Mediterranean world. Djebar vehemently opposed the narrow vision that the Algerian government had sought to impose on Algeria after independence of a single religion (Islam), one language (Arabic), and one party (the FLN). She argued that this policy had stunted the nation's capacity to develop as a pluralistic democracy and countered with her own expansive view of North Africa's cultural heritage, in which she included Saint Augustine and Apuleius,[11] nineteenth-century French historians, military generals and artists, pied-noir writers,[12] the women Amazigh writers Fadhma and Taos Amrouche,[13] along with the leading Algerian intellectuals Kateb Yacine, Mohammed Dib, and Djaout.

On the other hand, Djebar's vindication of Camus's *algérianité* ("Algerianness") acknowledged a common history of marginalization. The belated publication of Camus's final novel, *Le premier homme*, which had been found unfinished in the trunk of his car at the time of his fatal accident in 1960, gave Djebar the opportunity to reevaluate Camus. It exposed her to a very different image of the author as someone who had grown up in poverty, lost his father early in life, and appeared newly vulnerable in his unpolished prose. Djebar notes that a chapter from an abandoned early novel, *La mort heureuse* (*The Happy Death*), found its way into *L'étranger*, suggesting that Camus approached writing through a process of repetition and revision, much as she herself set about writing the autofictional Algerian Quartet, a series that remains incomplete, with only three of the four projected novels in print. She felt affinity with Camus because he had been excluded on the grounds of his identity: he had been marginalized in France because of his North African origins, just as she had been sidelined in postindependence Algeria as a francophone woman. If throughout the first three decades of her career, Djebar had done everything to avoid speaking of Camus, the unanticipated literary event of his posthumous novel made it impossible *not* to talk about him. She chose to do so in California, as far from Algeria as possible. Even then, she seemed to arm herself with critical theory, wielding a language influenced by the Deleuzian concept of lines of flight (*Ces voix* 225) and Maurice Blanchot's reflections on the artificial finality of any book in contrast to an author's ongoing oeuvre (229). Her reluctance was palpable in other ways as well. By articulating her desire to engage with Camus in the future tense, she both evoked and forestalled the encounter: "Y aura-t-il enfin rencontre? Peut-être pas vraiment encore, mais il n'y aura plus cet évitement . . ." (225; "Will there finally be an encounter? Maybe not quite yet, but there will no longer be avoidance . . ."). She deliberately wrestles with Camus's legacy in both essays, "Camus, 'le premier homme,' le dernier livre" and "L'absent et l'étranger." One year later, in *Le blanc de l'Algérie* (*Algerian White*), her elegy for Algerian writers who suffered violent or untimely deaths, she not only places Camus alongside such revered figures as Mouloud Mammeri, Djaout, Kateb Yacine, Frantz Fanon, and Jean Sénac but also cites him in the book's epigraph (see Erickson, "Translating" 95).[14]

Djebar's approach to Camus was pioneering in other ways as well. In 1997, influenced by the first wave of postcolonial studies[15] and alarmed at the violent implosion of the Algerian state and the relentless assassinations of intellectuals by FIS militants, Emily Apter asked why secular Algerian authors like Djebar had reappropriated Camus despite his systematic erasure of Arab subjectivity. Apter saw their embrace of Camus as

> part of a larger reaction-formation against the climate of anti-westernization and religious censorship. Rather than reject Camus as a traitorous proponent of French-Algeria . . . , many native Algerians today . . . prefer to

> lay claim to Camus as part of their own symbolic capital—a star in the firmament of an Algerian literary heritage inclusive of pied-noir writers. ("Out" 501–52)

Apter argued that Camus's reduction of Algerian subjects to a silent, impenetrable gaze signaled a troubling disregard for the other's language and history, in sum a "negation of a subject people at the time of colonial war" (504–05). She urged readers to attend to the markings of colonial power and French ethnocentrism in Camus's work and to be skeptical of the idealized Mediterranean subjectivity he evoked. In many ways, Djebar was already practicing this kind of reading. It informed her virtuosic engagement with the colonial archive in her novel *L'amour, la fantasia* (*Fantasia: An Algerian Cavalcade*). It is also apparent in the essay "L'absent et l'étranger," where she deliberately uncovers the traces of the Algerian women in Camus's work: "Derrière ces deux hommes [Fromentin et Camus], des ombres de femmes. . . . Et d'abord la mère de Camus, silencieuse; son mutisme, à l'orée même du génie de son fils, je le perçois aussi blanc, aussi lourd que le voile des femmes de ma famille" (*Ces voix* 219; "Behind these two men, shadows of women. . . . And first of all, Camus's silent mother; I perceive her muteness, at the very edge of her son's brilliance, as white, as heavy as the veil of the women of my family").[16] The self-reflective approach Djebar brings to Camus shows students how critical it is to examine their own positioning as readers. Discussing Camus as a North African writer allows them to debate what constitutes an "authentic" French, Algerian, Mediterranean, or world author.

In "Camus, 'Le premier homme,' le dernier livre," Djebar imagines what it would have been like to meet Camus: "Face-à-face donc sur un carrefour, une place de marché, n'importe quel lieu public d'un faubourg d'Alger" (*Ces voix* 225; "face to face at a crossroads, a marketplace, any public place in a neighborhood of Algiers"). This fictional encounter allows her to articulate her own position with respect to Algerian and French literary history.[17] She defines herself as "[é]trangère à l'Etranger" (224; "a stranger to *The Stranger*") in order to convey the paradoxical proximity and distance she feels between herself and Camus and vis-à-vis Algeria. She went into exile in 1980 when the government-led Arabicization of higher education made it impossible for her to hold an academic position in the field of history as a French speaker; the assassinations of intellectuals in the 1990s made return impossible. Throughout the 1990s, she struggled to gain recognition in France; meanwhile, many of her friends and colleagues in Algeria fell victim to Islamists, and several of her own works were banned. When she herself was listed as a target for assassination, she sought refuge in a teaching post at Louisiana State University. The very title of *Le premier homme* resonates with her own status as a first woman: she was the first Algerian woman to attend the prestigious École Normale Supérieure school in France. In 2005, she became the first woman of the African continent to be elected to the Académie Française. I ask students to work out possible translations for the opening of the essay, "Moi, étrangère à l'étranger," and we then discuss the challenges of rendering "étrangère" in English without losing its multiple valences: Djebar speaks as a foreign woman in a foreign land (the United States) *and* as an Algerian woman whose subjectivity is excluded from *The Stranger*.

Djebar saw her marginality as a source of mobility and freedom; in the preface to *Ces voix qui m'assiègent*, she describes her writing as both "en marge" ("on the margin") and "en marche' (7; "in motion").[18] Ironically, her North African origins made her highly marketable for a contemporary readership that celebrated women writers from the Global South, whereas some fifty years before, the French had rejected Camus because he was not from mainland France: "*Ce qu'ils n'aimaient pas en lui, c'était l'Algérien*. . . . [C]e qu'ils reconnaissent en moi, c'est l'Algérienne. Ce qu'ils reconnaissent? Rectifions: Ce qu'ils espèrent de moi, c'est l'Algérie-femme." (224; "*They did not like the Algerian in him*. . . . What they appreciate in me is the Algerian woman. What they appreciate? Let's revise: What they expect of me is Algeria-as-woman"). Students who have read Kateb Yacine's *Nedjma* will recognize the deeper critique implicit in Djebar's remarks: all too often, Algerian women have been objectified and aligned symbolically with the nation in ways that restrict their agency. Kateb's Nedjma is both the object of male desire and the archetypical image of the Algerian nation the protagonists yearn to bring into being; over the course of the novel, she is exploited, silenced, and constrained.

Djebar's imagined encounter with Camus provides an opportunity for students to engage in creative writing. I ask them to envision the conversation between the two authors and to work individually or in small groups to draft a scenario that they then share in class. In preparation for this exercise, they read the introductory chapter of Mireille Rosello's *France and the Maghreb*, in which Rosello analyzes how select works of fiction perform the work of conflict resolution by imagining meetings between individuals who come from opposite sides of conflicting histories and who engage in a dialogue that begins to disrupt and transform the terms of their collective relations. I ask students to think about how the works of literature they have encountered represent cross-cultural dialogue. What is the broader political and social impact of such works? We then enlarge the conversation to include Daoud's *Meursault contre-enquête*. I invite students to think about how Djebar might have rewritten *L'étranger* had she taken on the project. And how might she have responded to Daoud's representations of women? Students observe that women characters remain sidelined and auxiliary in Daoud's novel, despite the slightly broader range of possibilities he affords them. While Daoud expands on the feminine roles in Camus's novel (the mute mother figure and the sister-whore) to include a female doctoral student, all these figures remain phantasms for the narrator who defines them. The narrative unfolds at a bar in Oran where Harun, the brother of the unnamed Arab whom Meursault murdered, speaks to an unnamed interlocutor.[19] Harun's monopoly over the narrative is a striking contrast with the multiple narrators and perspectives that inform Djebar's work. I ask students to compare Daoud's revival of a murdered fictional Arab to Djebar's efforts to recuperate the severed hand of Haoua, a nineteenth-century Algerian woman who was struck down by her ex-husband in a cavalcade and whom Eugène Fromentin immortalized in his journal. The narrator of *L'amour, la fantasia* takes up the hand and gives it the pen in a remarkable act of affiliation and solidarity, illustrating how Djebar brings the female body into her writing—a body that is subject to fragmentation, dismemberment, and other forms of symbolic violence in the name of patriarchy and religion.[20] While students may not be familiar with *L'amour, la fantasia*, Djebar again takes up the image of Haoua's hand in the essay "L'absent et l'étranger," illustrating the patterns of repetition that mark her oeuvre: "C'est si longtemps après, me semble-t-il, je me saisis de cette main vivante, main de la mutilation, pour écrire cette mémoire du siècle passé; et que cette 'seconde main' se soumet à ma voix qui défaille..." (*Ces voix* 220; "I take up this living hand, a hand of mutilation, in order to write the memory of this past century; and . . . this 'second hand' submits to my failing voice. . . .")

The 1990s: Pedagogy and Storytelling in Crisis

Djebar's "La femme en morceaux" foregrounds an exemplary scene of teaching. The narrative unfolds in 1994 in Algiers in the midst of the violent civil war at a time when militants from the Islamic Salvation Front were attacking intellectuals with impunity. Although conscious of the threat she faces, a young teacher named Atyka guides her students through different French translations of "The Tale of Three Apples" from the *Thousand and One Nights*.[21] The *récit* shuttles between contemporary Algiers and thirteenth-century Baghdad, weaving alternately between Atyka's classroom and the story of a young wife who falls victim to her husband's jealous rage, is dismembered, enshrouded in white cloth, placed in a sealed wooden chest, and sunk into the Tigris River. Her body is discovered by a local fisherman, who retrieves it in exchange for a hundred piastres at the request of the caliph and his vizir on a nightly stroll through the city. The sight of the body moves the caliph to tears and fuels his desire for retributive justice; it also unleashes a chain of stories, none of which reveal anything about the subjectivity of the woman in pieces. This omission fascinates Atyka, who freely imagines the situation of the murdered woman, her relationship to her husband, and the pressures of motherhood. Djebar's narrative accompanies Atyka through four successive class sessions; it moves with the protagonist as she walks home through Algiers and reflects on her goals for the following lessons. We are made privy to the young teacher's more private musings on feminine desire, thoughts she does not share with her students but that fuel her own interest in the tale. On the fifth day, Islamist militants burst into Atyka's classroom and kill her in front of her students, leaving her dismembered and beheaded like the young woman in the *Arabian Nights*. As the story comes to a close, the perspective shifts to one of Atyka's students, Omar, who watches and listens in terror as the teacher's severed head continues to speak.

Djebar confessed that this story was one of her favorites (Zimra, "Sounding" 114); it is also popular among my students at the University of Massachusetts, Amherst. As Clarisse Zimra notes, the story features multiple layers of intertextuality: it engages with *The Arabian Nights* and the Qur'an, as well as with two of Djebar's earlier works, the story "La femme qui pleure" ("The Weeping Woman") and the novel *Ombre sultane* (*A Sister to Scheherazade*). While *Ombre sultane* affirmed the salutory power of feminine solidarity and writing, "La femme en morceaux" offers a darker view: no reprieve comes for the young protagonist, and her students endure the trauma of witnessing her murder. Zimra argues that the story foregrounds participation ("Sounding" 109). It also interrogates teaching and its legacy, questions very much in our minds as we reflect on pedagogical approaches to Djebar's work and mourn the author's death in February 2015. The orphic image of the beheaded woman who speaks beyond death has now become a figure for Assia Djebar, as her works continue to interpellate readers after her death.[22]

"La femme en morceaux" illustrates how Djebar positions her writing voice in relation to other women. The story sets up a frame in which Scheherazade, Atyka, and the author occupy parallel positions: each of these women takes on the role of storyteller at the risk of death. Although Djebar wrote the story outside Algeria, where the threat of an Islamist fatwa was less imminent than for those inside the country, she was profoundly shaken by the crisis and the loss of colleagues and friends, many of whom she eulogized in *Le blanc de l'Algérie*. When she accepted the Fonlon-Nichols Prize from the African Literature Association shortly after the story's publication, she underscored her solidarity with the story's young protagonist: "La porter en moi comme l'Algérienne du conte, tête coupée qui persiste à parler" (qtd. in Zimra, "Sounding" 116; "To carry her [Algeria] within me like the beheaded Algerian woman of the story who persists in speaking").[23] Djebar thus expressed her determination to maintain a connection with Algeria despite living in exile, and to sustain the idea of a free and pluralistic Algeria so that it might one day come into being. Through the comparative structure of the phrase, Djebar suggests that both exiled writer and martyred woman embody the nation despite attempts to marginalize them. Djebar deliberately prolongs the memory of Algerian women who, like Atyka, have fallen victim to Islamist violence. She is determined to go on speaking despite attempts to silence her. By moving between historic Baghdad and contemporary Algiers, the story connects women from the thirteenth and twentieth centuries who wield language (*la parole*) in defiance of a violent and oppressive authority. Yet at the very center of the story is a woman who does not speak, who is presented only as a mutilated body and whose untold subjectivity Atyka endeavors to imagine before falling victim to an eerily similar act of violence.

The text presents writing as a double bind: Djebar writes against the threat of silencing but at the same time is conscious of writing as silence.[24] From the very first novel of her Algerian Quartet, *L'amour, la fantasia*, she presents writing as an inevitable betrayal: the capacity to write endows a woman with movement and mobility, but the act of writing threatens to immobilize the subject. French, the language of the former colonial power, facilitates her self-expression, but her words remain at a distance from her intimate experience and desires. Thus every text must be reworked in the next, implying a constant need for repetition and variation. This tendency manifests itself across all three of the novels of Djebar's Algerian Quartet, as the author returns repeatedly to rewrite moments of her childhood.

The story invites reflection on the relation between writing and teaching. What is Djebar's relation, as a scholar who taught at the University of Algiers, Louisiana State University, and New York University, to the young protagonist of the story? What does the story convey about teaching in zones of conflict? Atyka's students come from diverse backgrounds; some of the female students wear the veil, while others are more secular. They respond to the various translations of the *Arabian Nights* with questions about politics, linguistic choices, religion, and gender equality. Atyka attempts to limit the discussion to literature: "*Nous ne sommes ni en sciences politiques, ni en cours de religion! Je vous rappelle que nous commentons des extraits traduits des* Mille et Une Nuits!" (*Oran* 198; "*This is neither a political science nor a religion class. Let me remind you we are discussing translated excerpts from* The Thousand and One Nights" [*Tongue's Blood* 116)]. Her pedagogical approach is highly textual and discussion-oriented; the readings she assigns provoke wide-ranging questions, but she does not intervene much to guide her students toward a particular view, except occasionally to put forward a feminist reading. For Zimra, "The tale comes to ethical meaning through a willing collaboration among the students, much as the sultana's had depended on her sister's" ("Sounding" 116). Although Atyka facilitates this collaboration, she does not discuss the aspects of the story that interest her most: the intimate relationship between the murdered woman and her husband. She imagines the young mother as overburdened with three small children and another on the way; she empathizes with her isolation and lack of access to birth control. She sees the husband as loving but blinded by desire, pride, and jealousy. Atyka's reflections are only given to readers: "*Atyka a gardé pour elle . . . les scènes de tendresse, de sensualité entre les époux . . . heureuse de s'imaginer presque parmi ce couple—cette inconnue alanguie de Bagdad, au temps d'Haroun el Rachid et de Djaffar*" (*Oran*

180; “Atyka kept the couple’s tenderness and sensuality for herself . . . happy to imagine herself almost in between this couple—to imagine this languorous stranger from Baghdad in the time of Haroun el Rachid and Djaffar” [*Tongue’s Blood* 106–07]). These unspoken thoughts go into the writing of the story; writing enables Djebar to break free of prohibitions and to reflect on what is most intimate and sensual.

Interestingly, Atyka’s approach to teaching reflects Djebar’s own classroom manner, particularly her informality, warmth, and conversational style. It recalls my experience as an auditor in Djebar’s seminar Egyptian Francophone Literature at New York University while a doctoral student at Princeton University. Because of her reputation as a somewhat erratic teacher, Djebar’s classes were often small; this particular semester, I was one of only two students. Djebar would invariably arrive breathless and late, wrapped in a glamorous shawl with Chanel sunglasses holding back her hair, to embark on an informal but generous discussion on the Egyptian authors Andrée Chedid and Edmond Jabès. She never lectured but rather facilitated a three-way discussion of the readings, posing pertinent questions and often digressing into stories about her own friendships with important artistic figures, such as the filmmaker Youssef Chahine.

On their first reading of “La femme en morceaux,” students may comment that the opening of the story is repetitive or even halting.[25] I ask them to specify what produces this effect, then show them how the disjointed prose mimics the literal dismemberment of the woman. Students can also be asked to identify the different influences on the story, which range from the classical myth of Orpheus to magical realism. The story’s denouement features one of the signature motifs in Djebar’s work: the idea of a writing that emerges from a cut, a writing that refuses to close wounds but instead allows them to speak. I assign excerpts from the opening chapter of Cathy Caruth’s *Unclaimed Experience* and Ranjana Khanna’s *Algeria Cuts: Women and Representation, 1830 to the Present* to show how the story addresses trauma and the limits of representation. Karima Bennoune’s *Your Fatwa Does Not Apply Here* (the chapter “Growing Roses in the Triangle of Death”) is helpful as optional supplementary reading: the testimonies Bennoune gathered from survivors and witnesses of Islamist violence in Algeria help further contextualize Djebar’s story. This juxtaposition of fiction and human rights journalism allows the class to consider issues of form and genre: What can a short story convey that journalistic reporting cannot? How does Djebar’s intertextual engagement with *The Arabian Nights* enhance the affect and power of the story?

The final section of “La femme en morceaux” lends particularly well to close analysis in class because of its striking formal elements and powerful representation of trauma and witnessing. After his teacher is brutally beheaded in front of him, Omar imagines he still hears her voice finishing the story of “The Three Apples.” His sudden obsession with the color white provides an opportunity for students to investigate the particular significance of white in the Algerian context. White is associated with Algiers, a city known for its exceptional luminosity; it is also the color of mourning, of the burial shroud, of martyred innocence, and of the blank page, the inverse image of writing. A remarkable feature of this closing is the abrupt typographical change that Djebar introduces: up to this point in the story, she had used two distinct fonts to distinguish the alternating narratives—the tale from the *Arabian Nights* was given in regular font, suggesting its primacy, while the story of Atyka in contemporary Algiers was placed in italics. This distinction abruptly collapses in the final section: the narrative set in contemporary Algiers is now in plain text, suggesting that present reality can no longer remain bracketed off from the fictional world of the *Thousand and One Nights*. Zimra argues that the breakdown of this distinction "cast[s] doubts as to the salvatory function of literature once so confidently reclaimed in *Ombre sultane*"; in fact, a young Algerian teacher who closely resembled the fictional Atyka was assassinated soon after the story's publication, further disrupting the boundary between fiction and reality in contemporary Algeria ("Sounding" 118). The uncontrolled slippage between the different frames of narration in Djebar's story recalls Djaout's *Le dernier été de la raison*, in which contemporary reality similarly blurs with fiction and madness, illustrating the traumatic violence of the Algerian conflict, the precarious situation of intellectuals, and the imperiled status of stories and storytelling.

Allouache's film *Le repenti* (2013) gives students an opportunity to debate the ways in which Islamists are represented in each of these works. The film focuses on the aftermath of the conflict and the problems with the government-imposed amnesty: in rural villages, former perpetrators and families of victims inevitably encounter one another and seek out informal means to achieve retribution. One of the film's achievements is its sensitive portrayal of Rachid, a former Islamist, whom it is difficult to dismiss as a thug or monster because of his youth, poverty, and vulnerability. Students can debate whether this is a blind spot in Djebar's story or whether Allouache's film benefits from a necessary temporal distance from the violence, which allows him such generosity of imagination.

The works discussed here demonstrate the stakes of writing for, from, or about Algeria in the 1990s. In the overture to *Femmes d'Alger dans leur appartment*, Djebar famously declares that the greatest responsibility of the woman writer is to position herself as close to other women as possible without assuming their place. She takes great care to articulate the terms of her relation as a writer to other Algerian women, seeking to establish proximity without laying claim to another's position (9). As witness to the violence of the colonial period, the anticolonial struggle, the postindependence state, and then militant Islamism, the question of a writer's responsibility preoccupied Djebar throughout her career. Following the tragic assassination of fellow intellectuals and friends, Djebar came to see writing as a dialogue that suspends the death sentence. When accepting the Frankfurt Prize for Peace in 2000, she declared, "[L]'écriture à laquelle je me vouais dans ce malheur algérien . . . est le dialogue suspendu avec l'ami sur lequel est tombée la hache, dans la tête de qui a sonné la balle, tandis que, vous, vous survivez . . ." ("Discours de Francfort" [Cairn.info]; "The writing to which I devoted myself amidst this Algerian tragedy . . . is the suspended dialogue with the friend on whom the ax fell, into whose head the bullet went, while you, you survive . . .").

The pronounced intertextuality of Djebar's work reflects her understanding of writing as a dialogue across time and space. When considered alongside works by Djaout, Allouache, Daoud, and others, Djebar's essays and short fiction convey the vibrant creative response that Islamism and one-party rule have met with in the Algerian context. As students engage with these works through creative writing, debate, close reading, and comparative analysis, they develop a more situated and complex understanding of Djebar's resistance to all oppressive doctrines and isms.

NOTES

[1]See Shaden Tageldin for a compelling discussion of linguistic politics in Djebar and Ahlam Mosteghanemi.

[2]Exposing students to the intertextuality of Djebar's work in dialogue with other texts introduces them to what Edward Said called a strategy of contrapuntal reading. When multiple perspectives—within and among texts—are brought into relation, preconceived notions of history and relations of power begin to shift. As I discuss more fully in *Borrowed Forms*, it is precisely this kind of rigorous, comparative approach that Djebar's work demands.

[3]The syllabus comprises works from Algeria, Morocco, Israel, Palestine, Mauritania, Syria, Afghanistan, Iran, and France. In addition to the texts discussed here, students read Michel Houellebecq's *Soumission* (*Submission*), Atiq Rahimi's *Syngué sabbour* (*The Patience Stone*), Faïza Guène's *Kiffe kiffe demain* (*Kiffe Kiffe Tomorrow*), Boualem Sansal's *Le village de l'Allemand: L'affaire des frères Schiller* (*The German Mujahid*), Mayanthi Fernando's *The Republic Unsettled: Muslim French and the Contradictions of Secularism*, Gilles Kepel's *Quatre-vingt-treize* (*Ninety-three*), Fadela Amara's *Ni putes, ni soumises* ("Breaking the Silence"), Abd al Malik's *Sufi Rapper: The Spiritual Journey of Abd al Malik*, Joann Sfar's *Le chat du rabbin* (*The Rabbi's Cat*), Riad Sattouf's *L'arabe du futur* (*The Arab of the Future*), and Marjane Satrapi's *Persepolis*. We also discuss the following films: Abderrahmane Sissako's *Timbuktu*, Ziad Doueiri's *The Attack*, and Nabil Ayouch's *Les chevaux de Dieu* (*God's Horses*).

[4]Mehammed Mack offers insightful analysis of the Cologne affair and the media frenzy it provoked.

[5]In presenting the film, I call attention to the active role Algerian women played in the struggle, the film's critical treatment of torture, the bankrupt moral currency of the French Resistance, and the strategies through which the FLN (National Liberation Front) began to consolidate its monopoly on power, setting itself up to dominate Algerian

politics for the next sixty years. We discuss the symbolic significance of the Algerian war for international revolutions and the Pentagon's use of the film in 2003 as a manual for fighting popular insurgencies in Iraq and Afghanistan.

[6]Shot under dangerous conditions in rapid takes, *Bab el-Oued City* conveys the pervasive anxiety and sense of entrapment among residents of Algiers.

[7]The government of President Abdelaziz Bouteflika imposed amnesty in 2005 with the Charter for Peace and National Reconciliation and Peace, shutting down the kind of truth-seeking initiatives that have been so important in postconflict situations like South Africa and Rwanda.

[8]In an interview of Daoud by Robert Siegel that aired on National Public Radio, Kaplan is quoted as asserting that "Algerian writers, whether or not they agreed with Camus, they've always loved this novel. And it's really part of the literary patrimony of Algeria" (Siegel).

[9]On the controversies surrounding Camus's legacy, see Beaumont; Apter, "Out of Character" 502–03.

[10]Kaplan hailed the novel "as the most important work to emerge from North Africa in recent years" (Siegel).

[11]In "Le triangle linguistique" ("The Linguistic Triangle"), Djebar calls into question the categories of "Western" and "Algerian" to emphasize how successive layers of migration and conquest in the Maghreb brought diverse linguistic traditions and cultural influences. "Le premier grand roman occidental—avec *Le Satiricon* de Pétrone—est *L'âne d'or* ou *Les métamorphoses*, écrit au milieu du IIe siècle en latin par Apulée, un Africain qu'on dirait aujourd'hui algérien, puisque né et élevé à Madaure, dans le Constantinois. . . . Ce chef-d'œuvre . . . serait donc le premier roman de la littérature algérienne!" (*Ces voix* 54); "The first great Western novel—with Petronius's *The Satyricon*—is *The Golden Ass* or the *Metamorphoses*. Written in Latin in the middle of the second century by Apuleius, an African whom one would call today Algerian, because he was born and raised in Madaure in the Constantine region. . . . This masterpiece . . . would thus be the first novel of Algerian literature!" Djebar rejects the notion that Arabic is the sole authentic language for contemporary Maghrebian literature and argues that original writing will emerge in Algeria only when the nation acknowledges its complex multilingual inheritance (Berber, Arabic, French). On this subject, see also Anne-Emmanuelle Berger's *Algeria in Others' Languages*. All translations in this essay are mine unless otherwise noted.

[12]In *Femmes d'Alger dans leur appartement* (1980) Djebar engages with Eugène Delacroix; in *L'amour, la fantasia* (1985; *Fantasia: An Algerian Cavalcade*), she takes up the memoirs of Eugène Fromentin, as well as the writings of the French general Aimable Jean Jacques Pélissier and others who participated in the nineteenth-century conquest of Algeria. In each instance, she brings Algerian voices into a dialogue hitherto dominated by Europeans.

[13]Djebar writes on Fadhma Aït Mansour-Amrouche in "D'un silence l'autre" (*Ces voix* 116–28; "From One Silence to Another") and on Taos Amrouche in "Taos ou le chant du phénix" (131–37; "Taos or the Song of the Phoenix").

[14]The Kabyle writer Mammeri died in 1989 in a car crash, as did Camus almost three decades earlier; Sénac, who famously broke with Camus over the Algerian question, was murdered in Algiers in 1973; Djaout was murdered by Islamists of the GIA faction in 1993, leaving behind his own unfinished novel, *Le dernier été de la raison*; Kateb died of

cancer in 1989; Fanon died of leukemia in 1961 and did not live to see Algeria's independence.

[15]I am thinking of the foundational texts of the late 1980s and early 90s, *The Empire Writes Back* by Bill Ashcroft, Gareth Griffiths, and Helen Tiffin, and *Culture and Imperialism*, by Edward Said.

[16]Djebar calls attention to the double marginalization of Algerian women in Camus's fiction. If Meursault's Arab victim is nameless, Arab women are absent and invisible. In order to recover the trace of these women, one must look "au-delà de la ruelle et de la médina, jusqu'aux places, jusqu'aux plages où l'autre société coloniale évoluait, vidée de nos hommes qu'elle avait exclus, tandis que nous, les femmes, les hommes nous excluaient à leur tour, ce qui nous enfermait tous davantage. Prisons dans l'immense prison" (*Ces voix* 222; "beyond the backstreet and the medina, right up to the squares and beaches where the other colonial society spent its days, emptied of our men whom it had excluded, all the while [Algerian] men excluded us women in turn, which confined us all the more. Prisons within the immense prison"). For an insightful discussion on how to read Camus against the grain, see Apter, "Out of Character"; Graebner.

[17]In "L'absent et l'étranger," Djebar critiques the Eurocentric and male solipsism in the writings of both Camus and Fromentin: "J'ai mis du temps pour reconnaître les personnages de ces deux grands écrivains, leurs ombres sœurs" (*Ces voix* 221; "It took me some time to acknowledge these two great writers' characters, their shadow sisters").

[18]This ambivalence corresponds to Susan Suleiman's notion of exile: "Is this distance a falling away from some original wholeness and source of creativity, or is it on the contrary a spur to creativity? Is exile a cause for optimism (celebration, even) or its opposite?" (1).

[19]Camus's confessional novel *La chute* (*The Fall*) similarly unfolds at a bar, but in Amsterdam.

[20]I address the symbolic violence found in *Nulle part dans la maison de mon père* ("No Place in My Father's House") in the essay "Echo's Legacy."

[21]The name Atyka means "pure, virginal, and affectionate."

[22]When *Le premier homme* was published some thirty-four years after the author's death, Camus also seemed to continue to speak beyond the grave, much like the orphic figure to which Djebar makes reference.

[23]Djebar had given Zimra a draft of her lecture for simultaneous translation.

[24]In response to an Italian journalist's query as to why she wrote, Djebar answered, "J'écris à force de me taire!" (*Ces voix* 25; "I write by virtue of remaining silent"). She saw herself as a "francophone voice" only in her activity as a professor and public intellectual; she insisted on qualifying her francophonie as one in "constant and irresistible displacement" outside the geographic limits of the dismantled former colonial empire (27). When it came to her writing, she rejected the notion of francophonie in favor of "franco-graphie," emphasizing the ambivalent relation between writing (in French) and the multilingual voices of Algeria: "Oui, faire réaffleurer les cultures traditionnelles mises au ban, maltraitées, longtemps méprisées, les inscrire, elles, dans un texte nouveau, dans une graphie qui devient 'mon' français" (29; "Yes, to make the traditional cultures that have been banned, mistreated, long disdained, brush up against one another, indeed to inscribe them in a new text, in a *graphie* that becomes 'my' French").

[25]"Là, au fond de ce fleuve, le Tigre, dort un corps de jeune femme. Un corps coupé en morceaux. Les morceaux soigneusement enveloppés d'un voile. D'un voile blanc de citadine. Un voile de lin à peine entaché. A peine ensanglanté" (*Oran*, 163; "Here, in the bottom of this wide river, the Tigris, rests a young woman's body. A body cut into pieces. The pieces are wrapped carefully in a veil, the white veil of a city woman. A linen veil, just barely soiled. Just barely bloodied" [*Tongue's Blood* 97]).

Reading Assia Djebar in Dialogue

Dana Strand

Over the years, teaching texts by Djebar in my undergraduate literature and culture classes has paid out in dividends that greatly surpassed my admittedly high expectations, which had been primed by my already profound appreciation for her writing. More specifically, I have discovered that her works, if read in dialogue with others, become in some sense polymorphous, as certain facets of her novels and short stories are thrown into higher relief when they are reflected in the light of complementary texts. Despite (or perhaps because of) the formal and philosophical complexity of her works, they lend themselves to alternative interpretations that emerge from their productive intersection with other pertinent historical, theoretical, or literary writings. For example, paired with texts that interrogate official history, a number of her novels vividly illustrate the deleterious consequences of mobilizing collective memory to promote a politically inspired narrative. Excerpts from Benjamin Stora's study *La gangrène et l'oubli: La mémoire de la Guerre d'Algérie* ("Gangrene and Forgetting: Memory and the Algerian War") or Robert Young's trenchant reevaluation of Western history through the lens of postcolonial theory, *White Mythologies: Writing History and the West*, thus set the stage for reading such novels as *L'amour, la fantasia* (*Fantasia: An Algerian Cavalcade*) and *La femme sans sépulture* ("Woman without a Grave"), in which Djebar calls on women's voices to recuperate the silenced history that has been all but excised from official accounts of the national past.

Although I have taught Djebar's works in a number of contexts, I confine my discussion here to two examples, the first drawn from a chronologically organized course that traces the relation between Algeria and France since 1830, the second drawn from a class on memory that focuses on the intersection between personal story and collective history. These are both advanced courses taught in French, with enrollments of between fifteen and twenty-five students who, in most cases, have lived or studied in a French-speaking country.

In the course on Algerian-French relations, we consider passages from Djebar's most overtly autobiographical work, *Nulle part dans la maison de mon père* ("No Place in My Father's House"), alongside works by Hélène Cixous. Pairing these readings enhances students' appreciation of the diverse voices that contribute to the Algerian cultural and historical scene at the same time that a better understanding of Djebar's place in that landscape emerges from considering her works in dialogue with those of her contemporaries. During the course on memory, Djebar's efforts to reconstruct the silenced past through a chorus of female voices in *La femme* and in her earlier film that explores the same subject, *La nouba des femmes du Mont Chenoua* ("The Nouba of Women from Mount Chenoa"), come into clearer focus when read in conjunction with *La mémoire et les jours* (*Days and Memory*), a work by Charlotte Delbo evoking the traumatic recollections of survivors of war and violence.

While the first course stresses the Algerian Djebar, introducing students to many fundamental concepts underlying current approaches to postcolonial theory, the second opens her works up to a more general consideration of the links among trauma, testimony, and memory.[1] In response to the recent debate in the field over the division between French and francophone literatures, I have made the pedagogical choice to incorporate works by a North African author into a class that principally explores literary (and cinematographic) responses to historical events in France.

Strong arguments for crossing these borders in our courses are put forth in a 2007 volume of collected essays entitled *Pour une littérature-monde* (Le Bris and Rouaud ; "For a World-Literature"). To cite just one example, the novelist Alain Mabanckou, in his contribution to the self-described manifesto, defines the francophone writer today as someone "[qui] brise les frontières, efface les races, amoindrit la distance des continents pour ne plus établir que la fraternité par la langue et l'univers" (56; "who breaks through boundaries, erases racial differences, lessens the distance between continents in order to establish a brotherhood based only on shared language within the same cosmos").

The course on Algeria includes a section entitled "Voix algériennes" ("Algerian Voices"), in which we read works by a number of authors, from Mouloud Feraoun to Maïssa Bey, whom we can locate at particular positions in the Algerian landscape by virtue of their differing experience, background, or historical moment. One of these voices belongs to Cixous, who, although born and raised in Algeria, is the daughter of an Austro-Hungarian Ashkenazi Jewish mother and a Sephardic Jewish father. As roughly contemporaneous women writers, raised in prerevolutionary Algeria and recognized as having a decidedly postmodern turn to their writing, Cixous and Djebar often pose similar questions, but careful reading of their texts can reveal that their struggles to come to terms with their Algerian roots take notably different turns.

In order to allow students to better understand the difference between Cixous and Djebar, we first read an autobiographical text entitled "Pieds nus" ("Bare Feet"), in which Cixous presents her childhood in Algeria as marked by exile and exclusion. Recounting an incident that occurred when at the age of five she came into possession of a secondhand pair of sandals, she describes how she brazenly flaunts her newly acquired possession before a six-year-old Arab shoeshine boy whom she encounters in the street. As she props her foot up on his box, she recoils in horror as the boy defaces her white sandal with a condemnatory streak of red polish. Aware of her own complicity in provoking the defiant gesture, she returns home, "du sang sur l'âme pour l'éternité" (63; "blood on my soul for eternity" [59]).

Much of "Pieds nus" reinforces the image of a fractured society, fraught with binary differences (Jews and Arabs, men and women, Europeans and North Africans), whose resulting inequalities color her otherwise carefree memories of the life that she and her family led, paradoxically during the World War II years, when the anti-Semitic policies of the Vichy regime stripped them of their French citizenship. Yet, the account begins with the evocation of her childhood in the Algerian countryside near the city of Oran, a sort of prelapsarian vision of her oneness with the land, as she walks barefoot in the footsteps of past generations inhabiting this ancient territory.

Despite the price her family paid when her father, as a Jew, lost his right to practice medicine, Cixous recalls their liberating sense of being "sans patrie, sans affreux héritage . . . incroyablement heureux comme des sauvages absous de pécher" (60; "without a homeland without a ghastly heritage . . . we were unbelievably happy, like savages absolved from sin" [56]). As we engage in a close reading of this story, we are careful to focus on how Cixous characterizes her relation to Algeria, because our conclusions will help us establish a useful contrast with Djebar's writing.

We next consider a passage from another autobiographical work by Cixous, *Rêveries de la femme sauvage* (2000; *Reveries of the Wild Woman*), where she expands on the themes and motifs introduced in "Pieds nus." Representing Algeria as a place marked by insurmountable physical and social barriers, she describes a horrifying scene that encapsulates the terrible reality of the country: at the age of seven she witnesses in Oran a fatal accident in which the veil of a young Algerian girl becomes entangled in the mechanism of an amusement park ride. Trapped as in a vise by the tightening cloth, the girl's body is torn in two. Describing her reaction to the scene, Cixous writes:

> La faute me prend, ici, dans ce wagonnet. La faute, son terrible mystère. Je n'ai rien fait. J'étais là. Je suis encore là. J'ai vu. J'ai vécu. Je ne suis pas morte. Il y a faute. Et c'est ma faute obscurément. . . . C'est une tragédie qui est aussi une Ville, un pays, une histoire, l'histoire de celle que je ne suis pas. (146)

> The fault grips me, here, in the little carriage. The fault, its terrible mystery. I did nothing. I was there. I am still there. I saw. I lived. I am not dead. There is a fault. And it is my fault, somehow. . . . It's a tragedy that is also a City, a country, a history, the history of the one I am not. (81–82)

The last sentence of the passage reveals its metaphoric implications, dominated by the image of an implacable mechanism and irrevocably intertwining the suffering of the innocent insider with the innocent guilt of the outsider. This passage is highly evocative, inviting diverse interpretations, for the purposes of the course, but we underscore two salient features it shares with Djebar's writing on Algeria. First, as an outsider who nevertheless identifies with the young female victim at the end of the passage, the narrator creates a constantly shifting subject position, thus calling into question the rigidly defined categories that contributed to the historical tragedy that the passage illustrates. Second, the mutilated female body, signaling both personal and communal tragedy, figures prominently in Djebar's work.

By contrasting this passage with one taken from Djebar's *Nulle part dans la maison de mon père* (2007), her most overtly autobiographical work, we arrive at a more complete understanding of how important the interplay is between the private and the public in her writing.[2] Djebar recounts how, at the age of seventeen, she becomes unofficially engaged to a young man, in defiance of societal and familial taboos. Troubled by an argument with her fiancé that flares up as they walk in the streets of Algiers, she is overcome by a paralyzing thought: "Si mon père le sait, je me tue!" (353; "If my father finds out, I'll kill myself!"). In a spontaneous response to this terrifying possibility, she runs blindly down a flight of steps leading to the sea, racing into the path of an oncoming tram:

> Parvenue tout en bas, résolue, gaie, tout désespoir dissipé, vais-je traverser l'avenue? Non, me coucher là, en diagonale, sur les rails!
>
> A l'ultime seconde, j'ai imaginé mon corps de jeune fille coupé . . . en trois! (358)

> When I make it to the bottom, my mind made up, carefree, all despair slipping away, will I cross the avenue? No, I'll lie down right there, across the tracks!
>
> At the last second, I imagined my girl's body cut . . . in three!

The image of her body cut in three provides a retrospective lens through which her particular position in relation to Algeria can be reconsidered. Expelled from the father's house (and her nation's history) through her refusal to submit to the place reserved for her under patriarchy, Djebar evokes here the anguish of powerlessness and exclusion she shares with other Algerian women. Placing Djebar's autobiographical anecdote in a broader cultural perspective, Jenny Murray notes, "The narrator's relationship with her father becomes a metaphor for her ambiguous attitude to Algerian culture and traditions" (*Remembering* 78).

When read in tandem, the two passages, with their powerful common central imagery rooted inexorably in history and in the female body, reinforce students' engagement with the compelling issues they raise. A careful comparison of all three passages—the two from Cixous, the one from Djebar—allows us to consider a number of questions thrown into relief by reading them in dialogue. For example, does Cixous's nostalgic memory of her almost pre-oedipal relation to Oran in "Pieds nus" bespeak a generalized colonial longing for the lost empire?[3] Are the two autobiographical characters in these passages implicated differently in the frightening scenes they recount? How does Cixous's position as an outsider distinguish her identification with the young Arab girl from Djebar's haunted vision of her own mutilated body, as the threat of an unbearable confrontation with her own patriarchy unleashes the specter of divided selfhood?

In my course on memory, the question of personal and official recollection is often intertwined with the issues of trauma and testimony. We read *La femme*, Djebar's account of Zoulikha, a female freedom fighter during the Algerian War of Independence, in conjunction with Delbo's *La mémoire et les jours*, but Delbo's hauntingly understated passages about women's war experiences may at first appear to test the geographic and historical boundaries of an undergraduate course. Other works included on the syllabus have already drawn our attention to the unavoidable interconnectedness of colonial and hexagonal events and their aftermaths.[4] As it turns out, twentieth-century French history (as well as the literature that both reflects and interrogates its influence on France and on the former colonies of France) provides ready examples of the uncanny crossovers between traumatic events seemingly separated by time and place. For example, the plot of Didier Daeninckx's *Meurtres pour mémoire* (*Murder in Memoriam*), turns on the nefarious real-life role played by Maurice Papon, first in persecuting Jews as a Vichy official in the Bordeaux region during the Occupation and then in the massacre of Algerians during the October 1961 demonstration in Paris, where he was chief of police.

We consider the Delbo text first, since it is considerably more accessible than Djebar's novel, and we pay particular attention to its formal features: the disparate passages expressing a wide array of voices, the stylistic and generic diversity, and the muted approach to the unspeakable pain and suffering of primarily female victims of concentration camps or other wartime atrocities. Students are quick to recognize that Delbo succeeds in creating a sense of collective testimony, as her loosely fashioned narratives and free-verse poems oscillate between the "I" and "we" of shared trauma. After students read an article in which Nicole Thatcher explores the challenge that Delbo's work posed to the patriotic stories of (male) resistance and heroism that dominated official history in France for the two decades following the war, they are primed to discover how Djebar goes about rewriting the historical myths of the Algerian war in *La femme*.

Our discussion of Delbo's work has prepared us for Djebar's approach to Zoulikha's story: students find that they must piece together the details of Zoulikha's capture, torture, and murder at the hands of the French colonial forces from the collected voices of women who have become the present-day guardians of the story, just as the composite picture of suffering and a different sort of courage from that normally celebrated in conventional war accounts emerged from the voices of Delbo's witnesses taken in concert. As students work through the Djebar novel, it is particularly rewarding to discover how attuned they have become to reading, in the words of Stacey Weber-Fève, "against the grain of two gazes" (11): they are ready to dismantle stereotypes and received ideas promoted by both the alarmingly persistent French colonial discourse as well as by postindependence militant nationalist agendas.

We devote a good deal of time to Djebar's notice to the reader, in which Djebar declares her intention to rewrite the truth of Zoulikha's story by placing it in the center of "une large fresque féminine" (9; "a large female fresco"), modeled after ancient mosaics found in her native city of Césarée (Cherchell). In the short papers that students write undertaking a close reading of this passage, they often stress how the notion of truth she proposes escapes narrowly defined limits imposed by time and place. And they recognize that, like Delbo, Djebar shies away from claiming authority over a piece of history, seeking rather to evoke it through the intervention of multiple female narrators, including Zoulikha herself, whose monologues echo, throughout the narrative, from beyond her unmarked grave.

Djebar parcels out the story to a collection of female voices representing different social classes and generations, taking care to emphasize the intersection of languages, dialects, and subject positions that characterizes the communication of those voices. As the story unfolds in overlapping, discontinuous, and distinctly nonchronological oral exchanges among women, the students arrive at a keen understanding of the political significance of her project.

Once we have discussed the ways in which *La femme* offers a contrapuntal historical account of testimonies of war, we view relevant scenes from Djebar's film *La nouba*. Occupying a space between fiction film and documentary, *La nouba*, which lacks a clearly defined story line or dominant central character, does not provide easy access to its universe. As Reda Bensmaia's perceptive reading suggests, its world "is not a totality that preexists the elements that constitute it; rather it is an apparently chance juxtaposition or dissemination of fragments (of [hi]stories and events) in search of a unity to come (or to be created)" (877). Yet by focusing on what Bensmaia calls "the esthetic of the fragment" (880), we can explore the common ground the film shares with Djebar's quest for anamnesis in *La femme* and Delbo's pluralized remembrances in *La mémoire et les jours*.

Although only a small part of the film deals with Zoulikha's story, Djebar's goals in the novel come into clearer focus when students can visualize the integration of its accounts of Zoulikha's exploits into the rhythms of women's daily lives in present-day Algeria. As Weber-Fève notes, in these sequences that meld contemporary voice-overs with both archival images and the loosely articulated memories of women, "it is not enough to just watch what takes place on the screen. One must also listen to the dialogue, music, and sounds recorded in the sound track and question how it connects to the images projected" (12).

Although the structure of *La femme* actively encourages readers to imagine a comparable spatialization of the narrative, students may not initially be attuned to this important feature of the novel, which can be masked by the linear nature of written texts. Their appreciation of the work is thus enhanced by their viewing experience, as they evaluate, through group analyses of short selected sequences, what the interrelations among dialogue, music, sounds, and images contribute to their understanding of Djebar's project.

It is my hope that these few examples will suggest to readers of this collection other productive pairings of Djebar's texts that help students discover the multifaceted nature of her works. Whether your course stresses life writing, postcolonial analysis, feminist theory, or the uncertain boundaries between history and memory, reading her texts in dialogue will open up exciting new ways of addressing the provocative questions they raise.

NOTES

In this essay, the translations from the French are mine, unless otherwise indicated.

[1]For a discussion of an approach to teaching postcolonial theory through Djebar's novel, see Strand.

[2]Struck when I first read *Nulle part dans la maison de mon père* by the common ground it shared with Cixous's *Rêveries de la femme sauvage*, I sought to exploit the pedagogical potential of the comparison. Since then, Alison Rice, in her *Polygraphies*, has explored at length the many synergies between Djebar's work and that of Cixous, citing among her examples the passages I have been using in my course. Situating these texts in an excellent theoretical discussion of the relation between testimony and fiction, Rice's invaluable analysis should be required reading for anyone considering teaching Djebar in context.

[3]In writing about French women's postcolonial films from the late 1980s and early 1990s, Alison Murray suggests that, despite these filmmakers' efforts to destabilize the colonial gaze, their memories of childhood in the colonies can drift into nostalgia for a "lost authenticity" (236).

[4]Using *hexagonal* to refer to continental France is common in French studies. In this context, the term avoids the political pitfalls of a distinction between the mainland and the colonies.

Unraveling the Limits of Narrative and "The Blood of Writing": Teaching Assia Djebar's *So Vast the Prison* in Comparative Contexts

Vlatka Velčić

Literary critics frequently compare Assia Djebar's novels and stories with the texts of other women writers, especially French and postcolonial women writers (either francophone or from other linguistic backgrounds).[1] However, teaching Djebar exclusively as a woman writer or her texts solely in the francophone postcolonial literary tradition not only could reinforce gender stereotypes and linguistic and national boundaries but also does not do justice to the multiple linguistic and cultural layers present in her work. It also marks her texts as separate from world literature or easily relegated to its margins and as such removed from established classics.[2]

Classroom practice confirms that Djebar is best read and analyzed in comparative contexts—transcultural, transhistorical, and transnational—which include a wide spectrum of world literature. Such contexts reveal her work as exemplary of world literature in David Damrosch's sense.[3] Damrosch first posits that "*World literature is an elliptical refraction of national literatures*" (201), and indeed Djebar not only refracts Algerian national literature but also problematizes and exposes both the concept of national literatures and the very idea of "elliptical" refractions of world literature. Even students new to literary studies quickly notice that she negotiates not only national—in the sense of statehood—literatures (such as Algerian and French) but also several cultural traditions, some of which span centuries (Berber, Arabic, Andalusian, and even Roman in *So Vast the Prison*). When Djebar's texts are taught in translation, in an American classroom, the multiplicity of literary traditions foregrounded in them confronts a complex host culture that itself, especially in Los Angeles, where I teach, has a heightened awareness of its own distinctive and various cultural traditions—Chicano-Latino-Spanish, Native American, African American, Anglo-American, and an array of other world cultures mingling in a global metropolis.[4] The elliptical nature of "source culture" and "host culture" (Damrosch 201) therefore becomes multiple in both its foci, and texts such as Djebar's in fact reframe the very concept of world literature in the twenty-first century.

A second characteristic of world literature, according to Damrosch, is that "*writing . . . gains in translation*" (201). Djebar's texts easily lend themselves to a discussion of issues of translation. If one reads Damrosch's gain in a broad metaphoric sense, every reading and, indeed, every translation, viewed as an interpretation, necessarily adds new contexts and meanings to a text. When one reads and teaches the world literature canon, whether Homer, Dante, Cervantes, or more modern writers, such as Flaubert, Dostoevsky, and Kafka, one always encounters the question of how any work of literature, inevitably rooted in its own specific linguistic and historical contexts, resonates for students immersed in the multiplicities and complexities of contemporary global mass culture. Damrosch's definition of world literature allows us to reverse the question: What new meanings do different linguistic, cultural, and historical contexts bring to both canonical and contemporary works of world literature? Djebar's writing displays a keen awareness of all these issues. On the linguistic level, Anne Donadey carefully charts the many ways in which Djebar's French prose incorporates Arabic ("Multilingual Strategies"), and Mai Al-Nakib compares her use of French with Kafka's use of German, which ultimately results in the creation of a "minor literature," as framed by Gilles Deleuze and Félix Guattari (Al-Nakib 274). In fact, reading Djebar in an English-speaking classroom continues to underscore her never quite completed search for meaningful expression; it adds further linguistic and semantic layers to her palimpsest.

Pedagogically, Djebar's deterritorialization of French compares well not only with Kafka but also with Chinua Achebe's strategy of inserting Igbo names, words, proverbs, and cultural contexts in the English text of, for example, the widely read *Things Fall Apart*. Of course, English translation of Djebar undoubtedly glosses over some important puns obvious in French. Joyce Lazarus points out the connection in *Vaste est la prison* between *j'écris* ("I write") and *je crie* ("I scream") and between *amère* ("bitter") and *la mère* ("the mother") (92). These puns become exceptionally meaningful at the end of the novel, when the narrator responds to the violence perpetuated by radical Islamists during the 1990s civil conflicts in Algeria. Despite some unavoidable losses, Djebar in English translation gains a global audience, and her writing immediately enters many conversations about global postcoloniality as well as the wider conversation about what literary expression can and cannot transmit across cultures and history.

Damrosch's third characterization of world literature is as "*a mode of reading: a form of detached engagement with worlds beyond our own place and time*" (201). Djebar's texts explicitly relate the difficulties of disengagement as they continually address, expose, and require multiple modes of reading and writing as part of their narrative. Different critics read this characteristic of her prose in terms of Edward Said's contrapuntal narratives (Mortimer, "Edward Said") or visual and aural ekphrasis (Al-Nakib). Regardless of which terminology and underlying methodology one feels most comfortable utilizing in the classroom, Djebar's texts undeniably comment on their own creation. Her narrators repeatedly address issues of not only who speaks and who does not, how and under which conditions one speaks, but also what kind of speech is used. Her prose employs narrators and characters that use verbal (oral or written), visual (painting), musical, and even corporeal language.

Damrosch's definitions position Djebar's *So Vast the Prison* in particular for the comparative and world literature classroom. The novel allows readings that, while rooted in a specific postcolonial Algerian situation and keenly engaged with issues of contemporary feminism or feminisms, express concerns that mark the world literature canon: the universal themes of love, death, violence, self, and community. But the novel's main contribution to contemporary engagements in world literature is its unrelenting questioning of its own abilities to fashion relevant meaning through written or even spoken language.

So Vast the Prison employs autobiography, Algerian history, and women's history to repeatedly call into question the ways in which such histories are reported and thought about, and it ultimately questions the value of narrative itself.[5] Like the authors of many classics of twentieth-century world literature (e.g., Proust, Joyce, Musil, and Beckett), Djebar continuously experiments with novelistic structures. *So Vast the Prison* moves from the personal story of an infatuation, to a historical narrative of Roman and Napoleonic conquests of areas surrounding ancient Carthage, to a collection of stories about the narrator's family interspersed with scenes describing the narrator's shooting of a film.[6] The changes in voice and perspective, obvious even in translation, parallel changes in the structure of the novel. What emerges finally is a unique unraveling of narrative, because traditional novelistic structure cannot encompass the full range of issues related to contemporary women, postcoloniality, and subaltern subjects. Narrative must be refashioned to be more inclusive and global. In this construction or reconstruction, the novel becomes increasingly aware of its own limitations—for example, it exposes the narrator's dependence on a language or languages and on closed patriarchal power structures. For Djebar, this struggle reveals itself in the novel's attempts to inscribe different languages (French, Arabic, Berber) and different narrative forms, only to find them inadequate. *So Vast the Prison*, in making the novelistic form global, finds that form insufficient; at the same time, the novel narrates universal global issues such as identity formation and freedom of expression, only to find that they evade novelization.[7]

For Djebar, narrative and language cannot adequately record the dynamic human condition—in particular, the violence of our postmodern, postcolonial world—so she redefines the literary project in general, its scope and its purpose. I have taught her in juxtaposition with postcolonial women writers whose texts work under many of the same constraints and contexts, such as Arundhati Roy (India), Etel Adnan (Lebanon), Ama Ata Aidoo (Ghana), and Dubravka Ugrešić (Croatia). Her sociocultural perspective and aesthetic sensibility also resonate with such ethnic women writers in the United States as Gloria Anzaldúa, Octavia Butler, and Toni Morrison.[8] What many of these writers have in common is that their exploration of feminist or postcolonial issues has led them to a willingness to experiment and to attempt ways out of "the prison-house of language."[9]

Each section of *So Vast the Prison* offers different challenges for students, and an instructor can connect ideas from each section to other readings and critical contexts in a world literature classroom. For example, from the opening section, "The Silence of Writing" (11; "Le silence de l'écriture" [11]), Djebar focuses on issues of language and the two forms in which language commonly manifests itself: writing and speech. With this focus, her writing immediately inserts itself into contemporary theoretical conversations crucial for literary studies. Semiotics, deconstruction, and psychoanalysis are all rooted in a particular interpretation of the complex and ambiguous relation between the language we use and the world we live in. Advanced students, who have been exposed to literary theory—since many undergraduate programs do not shy away from literary theory—quickly recognize connections to Jacques Derrida, Jacques Lacan, and perhaps even Fredric Jameson in the initial struggles of Djebar's narrator to use "the father's language" in order to exit the "the silence of writing" and stop the dissipation of the "living trace" (11; "la trace vive se dilue" [11]). Toward the end of the opening section, which functions like a prologue to the novel, the narrator overhears the "secret" language of traditional women in Algiers who use an Arabic word, "l'e'dou," meaning "enemy" (13; "l'ennemi" [13]), to refer to their husbands. Informed students recognize the relevance of contemporary feminist theorists, from Hélène Cixous to Sara Suleri, who analyze how women use language and other cultural practices, even in a relatively repressive patriarchal society, to resist and undermine the language of the father.

In the first part of the novel, "What Is Erased in the Heart" (17; "L'effacement dans le cœur" [17]), the first-person narrator, named Isma later in the novel, ponders her attraction for "The Beloved" ("L'aimé"), a man other than her husband. She continues the exploration of female versus male language through the most traditional linguistic device available: the language of love. Isma attempts to embrace the language of passion, obsession, in the hope that her communication with her lover—their "secret bond," their "mutual attraction" (92; "notre lien secret, notre attirance mutuelle" [91])—will counteract the public, patriarchal language that she shares with her husband. At first it might seem that Isma is using the same language of love, expressing a "capricious desire" (32; "une envie qui s'avouait caprice" [32]), that has been exploited by popular romance fiction, but this same strategy has been used by many postcolonial women writers. From Isabel Allende's *The House of the Spirits* to Roy's *The God of Small Things*, they use the language of love and passion to inscribe their heroines' drive to transgression, their heroines' attempt to find their own voice and to resist constraining social norms. Feelings for the Beloved allow Isma to search for her own voice for the first time; she promises herself that she will "tell the truth; without mincing words she would explain [her] real motivation" (31; "faire semblant d'avouer le vrai, éclairer sans la moindre atténuation la motivation réelle" [31]).

But when Isma succumbs to her urge for confession, what results is not liberation but a night of violence. Her husband beats her, enforcing a muteness from which she attempts to emerge in the course of the novel's narrative. Whereas in Djebar's novel the impulse to speak and the violence that follows speech are connected to passion, twentieth-century world fiction abounds with examples in which language in its intention to create meaning succumbs to silence in the face of violence in the real world, as in Marguerite Duras's *Hiroshima, Mon Amour*, which questions the ability to speak and to love in a world after the atom bomb.

Although Isma recounts her relationship with her Beloved, it soon becomes clear that the language of passion, the language of the senses, is inextricably connected with the language or languages that one speaks and all the traditions and history transmitted by language. Isma constantly informs the reader that she moves almost seamlessly between two languages, Arabic and French. For her generation, the generation of Algerians who fought the war of liberation from the French colonial empire, Arabic is a language of resistance, and Isma is proud to speak it. French was the language of power and the official discourse, while for Isma, Arabic, at least spoken Arabic, is the language of the private realm. But to her dismay, the Beloved speaks not Arabic but French. She partially excuses him: because his mother is Berber, he did not learn Arabic at home. The real reason, she quickly realizes, is that "[w]hen I was fifteen I lived in a country at war! Arabic was the language of flames—not of governmental power, as it is now" (41; "À quinze ans, moi, je vivais dans un pays en guerre! L'arabe était la langue du feu, pas comme à présent celle du pouvoir" [42]). The novel develops the idea not only that the impulse to speak can lead to ambivalent results but also that it is not clear which language one should speak, which language can lead one to understand oneself and others.

The issue of language is explored not just in terms of gender—such as male versus female discourse—but also in terms of the postcolonial context. As that context becomes the focus of the second part, "Erased in the Stone" (121; "L'effacement sur la pierre" [119]), we are introduced to events of Algerian history that place the issue of language in a diachronic perspective. In many ways, this historical section is the most difficult for students, who generally do not have the needed background to follow the novel's tale of discovery and translation of the inscription on the stele from Dougga, which confirms that Arabic and French are both languages of the conquest of the Berber people. The narrator offers a long list of the traces that the Berber language and culture left through thousands of years as vehicles and symbols of resistance from vast prisons. The nineteenth-century scholars' supposition that "this strange writing came alive, was a voice in the present, was spoken loud, was sung" (147; "cette écriture étrange s'animait, se chargeait d'une voix au présent, s'épelait à voix haute, se chantait" [145]) was not only correct—"the writing was alive" (148; "l'écriture vivait" [146])—but also was transmitted "for endogamic use (mainly with their mothers, their wives, and their daughters)" (147; "pour un usage endogamique [avec leurs mères, leurs épouses et leurs filles essentiellement]" [145]). Students in the American world literature classroom, reminded of the suppressed but significant influence of Native American languages, histories, and cultures (including the matrilineality of some Native American cultures) in the Americas, will understand the influence of the Berbers in Algeria and North Africa. Berber complicates the issue of the Arabic versus French debate—that is, both Arabic and French are languages of the colonizers who roamed the Algerian landscape over centuries and violently silenced all whom they conquered. Students will recognize Djebar's echoes of the crucial discussions about language in postcolonial studies started by Achebe ("African Writer") and Ngũgĩ wa Thiong'o, especially since the debate is frequently anthologized and read in the classroom.[10]

Djebar's novel explores the limits of language further in its third section, "A Silent Desire" (169; "Un silencieux désir" [165]). Both spoken and written forms of language become too limited for Isma to talk about herself, Algerian women, men, and their history. Students in our classrooms might not relate to the specific musical idioms that preoccupy Isma—at the beginning of the novel, she works as a musicologist—but they certainly understand the role that music plays in the formation of a person's identity.[11] They understand her preoccupation with music and her realization that words are inadequate and distort reality, no matter what language one speaks. When Isma attempts to exit the prison of her marriage, she already knows that words either mask the truth or are unable to express it. Music is part of her inheritance and identity. Her mother's family brought sheet music from Andalusia, which they fled centuries before, and the old scores are part of Isma's childhood. Isma describes how French soldiers destroy these Andalusian pages during the Algerian war because they cannot recognize the music notation and fear that it transmits subversive messages. Music leads her to find liberation in dance. From early childhood, dancing in the circle of women is part of her heritage, but she also dances alone in the Western nightclubs that have sprung up along the Algerian coast, and she finds that liberating. But her most sustained attempt to transcend the limitation of language is through visual representation.

Students are already aware of the importance of film as a medium, but they need help in understanding the specific historical and cultural background that allows Isma to turn her film about women from her tribe in the Chenoua mountains into an attempt to subvert and reframe both the colonial and the male gaze, which is the conventional way to inscribe voiceless postcolonial women. Djebar's own film, *La nouba des femmes du Mont Chenoua*, on which Isma's fictional film is based, is of limited help to students.[12] Seeing it, they can better visualize Isma's attempts to surpass the constraints of language by becoming a film director, a role unusual for a woman in her country, and by harnessing the power of the camera on mostly female subjects. But the pace of the film, its long artistic shots, and the lack of clear story line present difficulties for students, who are used to quick-paced and plot-driven Hollywood productions. A teacher needs to point out Isma's attempts to construct parallels between the constricted vision of the camera's aperture and the restricted vision of Arabic women who wear a veil. The gaze of Arabic women becomes the piercing eye of the camera: "All of us from the world of the shadow women, reversing the process: We are the ones finally who are looking, who are beginning" (180; "Nous toutes, du monde des femmes de l'ombre, renversant la démarche: nous enfin qui regardons, nous qui commençons" [175]). The liberating gesture represented by film is subverted as well: Isma cannot shoot everything or reveal all Algerian cultural and historical complexities, and ultimately "the camera takes nothing" (256; "la caméra ne prend rien" [251]). Film, as another import from the West, can easily be used to orientalize women, just as nineteenth-century paintings did. So many subjects that Isma considers the most interesting, such as the woman of uncommon beauty nicknamed the Madonna ("la Madone"), must remain outside her camera's gaze, because Isma, as opposed to Western colonizers, refuses to film the woman without her and her family's permission and therefore preserves the woman's right to decide whether or not to participate in the process of representation and resistance.

Finally, neither music nor film offers a successful path for expression and resistance. Music provides only fragments; the camera's gaze is too confined. Djebar's novel struggles with the inadequacy of words and other forms of expression, such as music, dance, and film, to fashion the unique, intense reality of an individual in a particular sociohistorical and political global moment. Classroom discussion, addressing the complex framework and the dialogical qualities of the novel, can explore the relation between the local and the global, the individual and the national, repression and expression. To attempt expression and to search for meaning inevitably mean breaking out of a prison, but often there are unexpected consequences. The vast prisons in the novel are primarily women's and postcolonial prisons, but they also constitute a global modernity project, which an individual human consciousness must fight in order to make sense of an alienated, repressive, and chaotic world. Mariano Siskind points out that the project of modernity, which lies at the core of the concept of world literature, is at the same time liberating and limiting in its promise of universal freedom.

The forms of expression Isma employs to speak of her own, her people's, and human liberation not only reveal multiple slippages and lacunae but also always invite violence. In the course of the novel, it becomes painfully clear that prisoners who escape their prison experience not freedom but another round of violence. The moment Isma attempts to express her feelings toward her Beloved, her husband beats her. The novel traces this same cycle repeated throughout history, from the second century BC warrior Jugurtha, whose love for his country led to his imprisonment, to the violence during the war for independence in twentieth-century Algeria.

Regrettably, Algerian independence does not end the cycle, as in the representations (and the realities) of Achebe's independent Nigeria, Ngũgĩ's independent Kenya, or Ugrešić's socialist Yugoslavia. The novel ends with a gruesome description of the murder of a young Algerian female journalist by radical Islamist rebels. Ironically the woman, who is a friend of Isma's daughter, is executed because she protects a friend who is a foreigner.

In its discussion of language, the novel moves away from choosing between different linguistic codes, such as Arabic, French, or Berber, and becomes concerned instead with the form of the expression. It wedges itself in the narrow space between violence and silence. Expressing oneself, breaking out of one's prison, and exiting the silence are strong gestures. Expression produces wounds, pain, and in turn it is frequently blocked by violence. This uncomfortable narrative space is also a familiar space of much fiction—not only postcolonial but also modern and postmodern—that attempts to answer the question of how to speak in a global world that seems unable to control destructive impulses. For Djebar, any abandoning of silence, any escape from prison, while necessary, is fraught with peril and can easily lead to violence. Blood and writing, inextricably connected, underlie all human language and expression, and this message resonates in a world literature classroom.

NOTES

The expression "The Blood of Writing" (351; "Le sang de l'écriture" [341]) comes from the title of the fourth part of Djebar's *So Vast the Prison*. Since I teach Djebar's novel in translation, quotations in this essay are first presented from Betsy Wing's English translation of *Vaste est la prison*. Quotations in the French original follow.

[1]For an influential book-length discussion of Djebar as a female postcolonial writer, see Donadey's *Recasting Postcolonialism*. For Djebar's own discussion of her attempt to represent Algerian women and their voices, see her "Forbidden Gaze, Severed Sound" and Clarisse Zimra's afterword to *Women of Algiers in Their Apartment*.

[2]By comparing Djebar's *Fantasia: An Algerian Cavalcade* with the works of great autobiographers such as Augustine and Ibn Khaldun, Spivak in her "Acting Bits / Identity Talk" offers an early recognition of Djebar as a world literature author beyond francophone and postcolonial contexts. Nine years later, Apter, in "On Translation in a Global Market," situates Djebar as a perennial on "the roster of non-Western literature" in "'global-lit' courses" (2).

[3]Damrosch's "What Is World Literature?" is an influential text defining world literature in the twenty-first century.

[4]One could also argue that, despite the apparent lack of American students' interest in formal foreign language instruction, as evidenced in many universities, no classroom in the United States in this global and Internet age can be truly monolingual.

[5]This questioning is obvious to readers familiar with French, which does not distinguish between *l'histoire* ("history") and *l'histoire* ("story").

[6]Note that Djebar's narrator, later named Isma, is quite autobiographical. The film shooting described in the novel is a direct reference to *La nouba des femmes du Mont Chenoua* (1978), which Djebar made when she took a decade-long break from publishing fiction.

[7]See Siskind on the "globalization of the novel" and the "novelization of the global" and how they relate to his questioning of world literature.

[8]For a comparison of three female writers from different cultural and linguistic traditions—Djebar, Dangarembga, and Anzaldúa—see Donadey's "Overlapping and Interlocking Frames."

[9]I am loosely using the concept of Fredric Jameson, whose *Prison-House of Language* advocates always exploring historical and cultural context in addition to analyzing linguistic utterances and language features.

[10]Zimra's interview reveals Djebar's awareness of and views on the debate, as well as her recognition of classical Arabic, as opposed to spoken Arabic, as a patriarchal language ("Afterword" [*Women*]).

[11]Djebar's film *La zerda et les chants de l'oubli* (1982), the first half of which is now readily available on *YouTube*, in a mostly Arabic version with no subtitles, can offer students a glimpse into the music and dance described in the novel.

[12]The film is currently available from Women Make Movies, but it is expensive. A more available alternative, which I often use in the classroom, is Gillo Pontecorvo's well-known *Battle of Algiers* (1966); the film does not focus on Algerian women but still offers a context for understanding Algerian anticolonial resistance and includes some examples of women's participation in the war of independence from the French.

Teaching Assia Djebar, Islam, and Islamic Feminism in the Post-9/11 World

Carine Bourget

Teaching anything related to Muslim women in a Western context entails engaging the orientalist tradition and its enduring clichés and specifically views of Islam as inherently oppressive to women. The challenges posed by the looming specter of orientalism that instructors face when teaching works by Muslim women writers have been exacerbated by events at the beginning of the twenty-first century. Teaching about Islam entails facing several challenges, from the "deeply imbedded skepticism and even contempt of religion in academe" noted by a religious studies scholar (Kassam 209) to the post-9/11 wave of Islamophobia.

Assia Djebar's work can help bring about a nuanced picture of the Muslim world through her rendering of the culture of her native Algeria, a Muslim-majority country, as well as of gender issues that are relevant to the entire Muslim world. Having students pay attention to Islam in a broad sense allows me to point out that postcolonial countries in general and Algeria in particular have a history that predates colonialism and that, while colonialism is a key moment with lasting consequences, it is not the only defining factor. It is also crucial to highlight the specificity of Algeria and Djebar's situations to counter students' tendency to lump all things Muslim into one monolithic and stagnant whole.

When teaching about Islam in general and Muslim women in particular, one must first emphasize to students a distinction between two meanings of the word *Islam*—Islam as a sociological and historical reality (the Muslim world), and Islam as a faith and a theology—keeping in mind that they shape each other. Djebar's work explores both aspects through her creative rendering of Muslim women's experiences and through her engagement with Islamic sources that are used to codify gender roles and expectations. I first address teaching some of her work as a window into the Muslim world through her rendering of Algerian women's experience. I then turn to the Djebarian texts that specifically address Islam as a faith and its legal and social ramifications.

My experience teaching Djebar is limited to advanced undergraduate and graduate literature, film, and culture courses, for the most part taught in French. Different course levels and configurations dictate different choices, as students' needs and abilities differ, whether one teaches undergraduates still struggling with the French language in a francophone course or a course in women's studies in English, or whether one teaches Djebar as part of a general education requirement on world literature or in a graduate seminar on Islam in African literature. The activities and strategies suggested in this essay to guide students to read Djebar's works critically and the optional companion readings and films can be customized depending on a particular instructor's goals as well as students' interests and backgrounds.

Teaching about Muslim and Algerian Women through Femmes d'Alger dans leur appartement *and the Quartet*

Because of the prominence of the orientalist tradition in Djebar's intertext, students must be introduced to the concept of orientalism. Thanks to its visuals and interview form, excerpts from a video of an interview of Edward Said engage undergraduates much more than would the reading of *Orientalism*'s introduction (Said, Jhally, and Talreja). For the purpose of teaching *Femmes d'Alger dans leur appartement* (*Women of Algiers in Their Apartment*), I recommend the video's introduction as well as the segments entitled "The Repertory of Orientalism" and "Orientalism and Empire." The three segments together last about ten minutes only; they provide a definition of orientalism and show sample orientalist paintings, including Eugène Delacroix's *Femmes d'Alger dans leur appartement*. Assigning these segments as homework provides an essential foundation to read Djebar's work without taking up class time.

I have taught the first edition of *Femmes d'Alger dans leur appartement* in French to fourth-year undergraduate students and graduate students in francophone literature courses and *L'amour, la fantasia* (*Fantasia*) in a graduate course. *Femmes* was the most challenging text for the undergraduate students, in part because Djebar's prose, which makes for such delightful reading, is one additional difficulty for students who are still grappling with the intricacies (and sometimes, let's face it, the basics) of the French language. In my experience, the title story in *Femmes d'Alger dans leur appartement*; that volume's postface, "Regard interdit, son coupé" ("Forbidden Gaze, Severed Sound"); and *L'amour, la fantasia* have been well received and led to fruitful discussions on the roles played by women in Algerian history and on the intersection of colonialism, religion, and feminism.

The following activities, conducted at the undergraduate level for *Femmes d'Alger dans leur appartement*, can be replicated with several of Djebar's novels, in particular *L'amour, la fantasia, Ombre sultane*, and *La femme sans sépulture*, given their range of characters or contrasts involved. Starting with a simple prereading activity to raise students' awareness about stereotypes of Muslim women, the whole class brainstorms associations that first come to mind on hearing the words "Muslim women." I write the associations on the board (scarf or veil predictably being number one), then divide students into small groups to elaborate on why these terms came to mind and what they evoke. The whole class then recapitulates the results of the group discussions.

Students are assigned the short stories with the following questions to keep in mind: Does the text reinforce or challenge the stereotypes discussed? What role does religion play in women's lives? The first question leads students to pay attention to the wide spectrum of Muslim women portrayed in Djebar's fiction and points beyond the dichotomy of the traditional versus modern woman. Students also note the role of women in the Algerian War of Independence, which takes center stage in Djebar's work. The second question leads students to examine the role of religion in women's lives, ranging from the use of set religious phrases that mark some characters' devoutness (such as "Allah est grand, généreux!" [*Femmes* 99; "Allah is great and generous!" (*Women* 30)]), to a cultural frame of reference (such as when Sarah refers to Ishmael [128–29; 51]).

Although Djebar's novels are replete with examples of women's oppression, there are several episodes that problematize and subvert a simplistic reading of Islam as an oppressive patriarchal religion. More often than not, students need to be guided through close readings of key passages. In *Femmes d'Alger*, for instance, the *hazab*, who embodies tradition (being the Qur'an reciter at the mosque), has educated daughters, including two who play sports (68–69; 10–11). The longing of the *hazab* for tradition is evident in his unease with his daughters' athletic aspirations (as well as with the circumcision of his son being carried out by a medical doctor), but he does not resist the changes, nor does he interfere in his daughters' choices. In the postface, Djebar underlines the gap between some values promoted by the Prophet's saying "le Paradis se trouve aux pieds des mères" ("Paradise is found at the feet of mothers") and the culture that values above all the mother, because she is, as Djebar interprets it, a "femme sans jouissance" (250; "woman without pleasure" [142]).

Other examples are the association of the Qur'an with the feminine in *L'amour* (255–58; *Fantasia* 181–84), a description of the prayer ritual that alludes to women's liberation through spirituality from the gendered role dictated by their body,[1] and invoking the Prophet as a model to condemn domestic violence in *Ombre sultane*.[2] When her drunken husband hits her and threatens to blind her, Hajila follows her mother's advice to protect herself. She recalls conversations she heard as a child between her mother, who praised her husband for his gentleness, and the neighbors who were victims of domestic abuse: "Invoquez le Prophète qui a condamné sans recours la force des mâles!" (*Ombre* 123; "Call on the Prophet who said all men of violence would be damned and no mercy would be shown to them!" [*Sister* 87]).

In another part of *Ombre sultane*, a woman claims her right to interpret and understand religion differently from what a local saint has preached: "L'islam est un, l'islam est nu et pur! Il te laisse loisir de te réjouir! Sa loi ne peut changer, elle est semblable de notre ville jusqu'à Médine, je n'ai besoin d'aucun *fqih* ou docteur de la zitouna pour me l'expliquer!" (164; "Islam is one, Islam is pure and unadorned! It allows you leisure for rejoicing! The law cannot change, it is the same, everywhere from our town to faraway Medina; I don't need any *fqih* or learned doctor from the *Zitouna* to explain it to me!" [122]). While this passage refers to a specific disagreement regarding wedding festivities that were forbidden by a saint followed by some villagers, it can be connected to Leila Ahmed's findings in a different context that they are talking about "two different Islams," one that is "establishment Islam (institutional and legal Islam), . . . which is authoritarian, implacably androcentric, and hostile to women" and one that is "the ethical message that the layperson justifiably hears or reads in the Quran" (*Women* 225–26). This passage from *Ombre sultane* and the novel as a whole can be read in conjunction with the chapter "The Struggle for the Future" in Ahmed's *Women and Gender* or with her *Quiet Revolution*. These texts emphasize the complexity of the phenomenon of reveiling and the similarities of opinion between veiled and unveiled women regarding certain gender issues. For instance, after recapitulating the numbers in a study that demonstrated that veiled women were more conservative than unveiled women, Ahmed points out that (1) the difference in the numbers are in many cases insignificant and (2) the majority of veiled women, while more conservative than their unveiled counterparts, support women's rights (*Women* 226–27).

To return to the question of the orientalist tradition, intertextual references, including mentions of paintings, abound in Djebar's work. For any meaningful analysis of the title of *Femmes d'Alger dans leur appartement* and its postface, we must consider images.[3] I have my students take a close look at one of Delacroix's paintings, as well as one of Pablo Picasso's,[4] to which I added Delacroix's *Odalisque allongée sur un divan* (*Odalisque Reclining on a Divan*) in order to problematize Djebar's laudatory interpretation of Picasso's *Les femmes d'Alger*. As a prereading activity for the postface, the class is divided up in groups and charged with comparing these paintings and describing how they fit Said's characterization of one of the images of the repertory of orientalism, "the sensual woman who is there to be sort of used by the man" (Said, Jhally, and Talreja). Doing this as a pre- rather than a postreading activity better highlights Djebar's problematic assumption that unveiling equals progress. Because her celebration of the liberation of the body by Picasso's rendering of Delacroix's painting is very much influenced by 1970s French feminism, she does not account for the enduring legacy of the colonizer's discourse on Muslim women (see Bourget, "Réédition"). For honors and graduate students, one could assign Frantz Fanon's "L'Algérie se dévoile" ("Algeria Unveiled") to point out the necessity to contextualize and historicize veiling and unveiling practices. To put some of the issues raised in a wider perspective, theoretical texts such as Chandra Mohanty's classic "Under Western Eyes" (in *Third World Women*) as well as Ahmed's chapter "The Discourse of the Veil" in *Women and Gender in Islam* are essential to highlight the long-lasting effects of the role played by colonialism in tainting feminism in the Muslim world.

If one is teaching the 2002 second edition of *Femmes d'Alger dans leur appartement* in a class on women's studies or feminism, one can compare the changes to the preface and postface and lead students to discuss what these updates bring to the 1980 work and how we read that text. I would pair the second edition with Mohanty's update of her groundbreaking article, "'Under Western Eyes' Revisited," to contrast how Djebar's and Mohanty's outlooks on women's issues have evolved—for example, an emphasis on intergenerational solidarity in Djebar versus class-crossing women's solidarity in Mohanty.

Teaching Islamic Feminism: Loin de Médine *and* La beauté de Joseph

Two of Djebar's works are particularly well suited to introduce students to the global phenomenon of Islamic feminism: *Loin de Médine* and *La beauté de Joseph*, two narratives in which Djebar engages directly with religious materials. Students need some background information about the context that prompted her to deal with Islamic scriptures: the rise of Islamic fundamentalism on the global scene (pre-9/11) and, more specifically, the 1990s Algerian civil war and its well-publicized atrocities, some of which targeted women who did not abide by certain Qur'anic precepts, such as covering their hair. Students need some basic outline of postcolonial Algerian history so as not to read the civil war through the prism of 9/11.

In *Loin de Médine*, Djebar revisits the beginnings of Islam in a creative way: most of the characters of her novel are historical, and most of the events are episodes from the time of the Prophet Muhammad, some well known by most Muslims, others not. In my experience, *Loin de Médine* is the most challenging of Djebar's texts to teach because most (Western) students lack basic knowledge about early Islamic history. I failed to make it an enjoyable reading for French graduate students (save one, who happened to have a Muslim background) in a seminar on Islam in francophone literature. On the basis of an invited lecture I gave in a Near Eastern studies graduate course, Gender Issues in Middle Eastern Studies, I surmise that *Loin de Médine* would be better suited to students in Middle Eastern studies, as they are better acquainted with the background knowledge needed to appreciate the book. Instructors teaching the English translation should bring to their students' attention the analysis of Rim Hassen, who demonstrated that the choice to render or not the feminine gender in the translation of some feminine words follows orientalist stereotypes and sabotages some of the subversive nature of the original text.[5]

As a compromise, one can assign excerpts,[6] because one of the main complaints from my students was that *Loin de Médine* has too many characters and events to keep track of. I am generally reluctant to do that, particularly for Djebar, because the structure of her books and system of epigraphs are important.[7] But in *Loin de Médine* one could concentrate on the two best-known feminine figures of early Islamic history, who are featured in the novel: Aisha and Fatima. Djebar unearths forgotten episodes involving them, as when they spoke up and resisted the powers in place. The chapters on Fatima, "La fille aimée" ("The Beloved Daughter") and "Celle qui dit non à Médine" ("The Woman Who Said No in Madina"), in which Djebar provocatively qualifies the Islamic inheritance law as a "révolution féministe de l'Islam" (79; "feminist revolution of Islam" [68]), should lead to a lively discussion on historicizing and contextualizing feminism in a variety of courses, specifically in gender and women's studies. The entry on Aisha in the *Encyclopaedia of Islam* (Watt) can help lay the groundwork for reading the relevant sections in *Loin de Médine*.

One of my most successful attempts at teaching a Djebarian text was with *La beauté de Joseph*. Unfortunately that text is out of print and has yet to be translated into English, but since it is very short, it can be distributed to students easily. Because it is a text that in part compares the biblical and Qur'anic renderings of the story of the prophet Joseph, the material is more familiar to students. That the narrative as well as the relevant sections of its two main intertexts are short makes it easier for students to assess Djebar's analyses and evaluate her take on the scriptures. I first assigned students the reading of the relevant biblical and Qur'anic verses[8] so they could better appreciate Djebar's interpretation of them.

La beauté de Joseph is a complex narrative that engages with the various texts in a literary way: for example, the banquet episode is staged as a play (34), and Djebar aestheticizes and engages in free associations in some passages (e.g., with the color red when the women cut their hands [36]). As she points out, the banquet scene is not in the Bible (36), but Thomas Mann included it in *Joseph and His Brothers*, demonstrating how the Qur'an inspired a Western artist (35). This cross-cultural fertilization should be pointed out to students as one example of Islamic culture's influence on Western literature.

Depending on the course's focus and the students' background, *Loin de Médine* and *La beauté de Joseph* can be paired with works by other francophone women as well as by feminist theorists. Djebar's creative approach might be contrasted with Fatima Mernissi's revisionist approach in *Le harem politique* (trans. as *The Veil and the Male Elite*), whose introduction and third chapter fit well with *Loin de Médine*, or with Amina Wadud's revisionist reading of some Qur'anic verses, particularly in the fourth chapter of her book *Qur'an and Woman: Rereading the Sacred Text from a Woman's Perspective*, "Rights and Roles of Women" (62–93). The film *Ruses de femmes*, by Farida Benlyazid, a Moroccan director, is a great follow-up to *La beauté de Joseph* in a unit on Islamic feminism, for Benlyazid's title alludes to one of the Qur'anic verses from Joseph's story (see Bourget, "*Kaidakunna 'adhimoun* Revisited"). Scholarly pieces dealing with Islamic feminisn include Miriam Cooke's "Multiple Critique" (*Postcolonialism*; a concise overview of Islamic feminism), Anouar Majid's provocative though lengthy "The Politics of Feminism in Islam," and Valentine Moghadam's critique grounded in the Iranian context in "Islamic Feminism and Its Discontents."[9]

The video *Women and Islam* is well suited to introduce some of these issues in general education courses; it is a brief (thirty minutes) and accessible interview with Ahmed, in which she argues for reinterpretation of the Qur'an and gives examples on hot-button issues such as polygamy and the veil (Interview). A newer and more comprehensive video, *Rights and Wrongs*, also featuring Ahmed and other well-known scholars, such as Wadud and Khaled Abou El Fadl, could be assigned in a specialized course (overall it represents a good introduction to early Islamic history and some Muslim women's rights issues, but it does run over two hours).[10] These excerpts from *Rights and Wrongs* could be used: the chapter "Imperialism," about how imperialism derailed feminist advances in the Muslim world; the chapter "Verses of the Curtain," about the hijab; and the chapters from "The Trouble with Medinan Women" to "Al-Nisaa," which situate the verse on polygyny in the historical context of the care of orphans.

Introducing Islam through Djebar's "Les nuits de Ramadan" in the Language Classroom

Although in most of my experience teaching Djebar, in advanced undergraduate and graduate literature and culture courses, the emphasis was on content, I also successfully integrated one of Djebar's short texts in a third-year advanced composition course. Djebar wrote a short preface to a photography book about Ramadan rites in various Muslim countries. In that four-page text, she recalls her experience and desire as a six-year-old child to participate in the fasting rituals. From a formal point of view, it can be incorporated into a unit about narrating past events, as it is a great illustration of the use of the habitual *imparfait*. The brevity of this text, focused on a self-contained childhood memory, makes it accessible, while the long, elegant sentences and refined vocabulary characteristic of Djebar's prose are sure to pose a challenge for that level. From a cultural aspect, this preface introduces students to Algerian Ramadan customs through a Muslim child's point of view and her desire to fast.

Here are several prereading activities that one can choose from to both activate students' background knowledge relevant to the text and present information that will facilitate the reading. One activity is to have students brainstorm what they know about Ramadan. It is also an opportunity to introduce some of the vocabulary (in particular words such as *carême*, *jeûne* ["Lent, fasting"]) and customs that students might not be familiar with.[11] One can show clips to help them understand what the author means when she talks about "la voix du muezzin" (10; "the muezzin's voice" [my trans.]) and show, on recent calendars, how the dates for Ramadan change every year. Unfortunately none of the pictures in the book illustrate Ramadan customs in Algeria or the Maghreb. After students read the text and answer basic comprehension questions, the instructor can guide the class to study the stylistic features of the text, paying particular attention to the recurring brackets, parentheses, and exclamation marks. A follow-up creative assignment might be to ask students to write their own narrative, using past tenses in French, about childhood memories linked to a specific holiday or family ritual.

Djebar's work can be included in courses in a variety of disciplines and topics. Her Islamic fiction in particular will prod students, Muslim and non-Muslim alike, to reassess their view of the Islamic other (for some) and take a fresh look at some well-trodden Islamic material and traditions (for others).

NOTES

[1]"Le corps devant Allah et son Prophète s'allège loin des hommes, loin de l'homme" (*Ombre* 172; "Prostrate in front of Allah and his Prophet, the body finds ease, far from men, far from the man" [*Sister* 128]).

[2]For more on this, see Bourget, *Coran* 61–63.

[3]Mary Vogl's article is a treasure mine of ideas on how to incorporate paintings, photographs, music, and film to teach *Femmes d'Alger dans leur appartement*.

[4]I recommend version O, but H, K, M, and N are also fine.

[5]See also Hanan Elsayed's article "'Silence' and Historical Tradition," which examines how Djebar's limited engagement with the historical Arabic sources leads her to paint a portrait of Tabari the historian that is in keeping with orientalist stereotypes, contrary to what his work actually suggests.

[6]I assigned excerpts when I was limited in the number of pages of reading I could require of students in the Near Eastern studies seminar.

[7]Spending time on the table of contents helps students see the architectural features of Djebar's texts.

[8]In the Bible, see Genesis 37, 39 (for the episode with Potiphar's wife), 40–50. In the Qur'an, see sura 12 "Joseph" (verses 23–53 for the incident with Zouleikha).

[9]Because Moghadam's article is focused on Iran, I would assign only the second half, starting with the section entitled "Islamic Feminism: An Assessment and Alternative View" (32).

[10]Its most original part is a snippet at the beginning in which Ahmed sarcastically remarks that she never gets calls asking her to explain why Islam has produced so many female heads of states.

[11]One should point out to students that the word *carême* is linked to Catholic practices.

Teaching Assia Djebar to Second- and Third-Year Students of French and Francophone Studies

Valérie J. Budig-Markin

Assia Djebar was one of a cadre of key francophone authors invited by James Gaasch and me to participate in a project to widen the cultural exposure and understanding of budding French majors to the world of francophone studies in Africa, Europe, Canada, the Caribbean, and Asia. This project, resulting in the French-language anthology *Diversité: La nouvelle francophone à travers le monde* ("Diversity: The Francophone Short Story around the World"), was intended to help make complete short works of francophone literature accessible to second- and third-year American students (Gaasch and Budig-Markin). *Diversité* was also purchased in Canada, Europe, and the Caribbean to teach French speakers about francophone literature and culture, and its editors and story authors were increasingly invited as visiting lecturers to American and African universities. One of Djebar's memorable lectures at Humboldt State University, for instance, was "The Arab Woman as Historian," a vision of the critical role of women in the transmission of oral history in the Maghreb.

If it seems that this level of critical thinking skills is a far reach for lower-division university undergraduates, teaching complexity is almost always rewarded with a surprisingly complex student response. A third-year student with the intermediate B2.1–1 level, as determined by the Common European Framework for Reference for Languages (CEFR), can "develop a clear argument, expanding and supporting his/her points of view at some length with subsidiary points and relative examples."[1] With a language proficiency of Intermediate High level on the American Council on the Teaching of Foreign Languages (ACTFL) scale, a third-year student can understand description and narration, describe and narrate orally and in writing, in different time frames.[2]

Second-year, intermediate-level university students can generally comprehend, process, and discuss the questions posed by selected short Djebar stories, not only because her stories about families are often accessible in terms of language, characters, concept, and situation but also because the students have similar questions about their own families and lives. Djebar's anecdotal stories deal with the language and issues of the family at home: dialogues between generations, in which religious and patriotic sayings punctuate the elders' talk of family, God, war, shopping, food, and death, in juxtaposition with the issues of school, lifestyles, acquaintances, and future prospects, which add a modern touch to the language of the younger generation.

Before students consider a story about a culture unfamiliar to them, they need an overview of the country's location, demographics, government, and history, all of which they have enough reading skill to understand in French, if the reading is limited to a one-page summary with subject titles. The author's biobibliography, however, which gives the story's intellectual, cultural, and historical context, may better be read in English and then discussed in class in French.

Other aids to comprehension include extensive glossing of the story itself, in French when possible, and prereading preparatory group conversations that lead classmates to discuss the events and concerns of their own lives and families that will find resonance in the story. More frequently in the past few years, students have been sharing their stories about family members in war zones and in exile and personal concerns about war and its consequences. These themes are particularly relevant to many of Djebar's stories, which therefore work well in classrooms with a diverse student body. Stories featuring exile, families split by national borders, and multiple identities and languages are especially significant for many Mexican American students, for example. There is a continual reference in prereading activities to the overlapping space between the Arab family, culture, and conversations and those of the students.

Students also need to learn to read for key vocabulary and for particular cultural expressions that will characterize the dialogues of the story. After they practice comparing common exchanges, cultural sayings, nationalistic slogans, and religious formulas, the professor can explicitly ask, "Do you use similar expressions? Do you often hear certain expressions at home? Are they religious or other gems of wisdom? Are they words of encouragement in times of uncertainty? Would you share some of them with your classmates?"

The story "Il n'y a pas d'exil" ("There Is No Exile"), selected from the section "Yesterday" in Djebar's *Femmes d'Alger dans leur appartement*, is a dramatic narrative that gives students a firsthand look at Arab culture in a family, country, and religion that may be new to them. The story is linguistically straightforward and invites its readers into a key moment of transition in Algerian culture. They have an opportunity to listen in on the daily conversations, the songs, and the religious sayings shared by Muslim women. The structure of the story—its space, time, characters, language, and dramatic parallels of rhythm and plot—is easy to interpret on multiple levels identifiable by the students. The story raises issues that both elucidate Algerian history and culture and distinguishes them from those of Tunisia, where the story takes place during the Algerian war. The story's presentation of Islam includes daily practices of the faithful men and women as well as broader issues: the paradox of war, with its prevalence of death in the midst of life, and the daily lives of women and young adults in exile. Djebar herself, who was only twenty-three years old when she wrote the story she postscripted "Tunis, mars 1959" (160; "Tunis, March 1959" [73]), can serve as a youthful role model for these students; her history is juxtaposed with the fiction at hand. "Il n'y a pas d'exil" is clearly a good choice for teaching Djebar to this public.

The greatest challenge posed by the story is its length. To stay engaged, students need to be actively involved throughout their study of the story. Possible interpretive activities for them are class presentations of the map and of the demographics of Algeria, Algiers, Cherchell, and perhaps Tunisia and Tunis. Having learned to distinguish and interpret habitual, repeated remarks before reading the story, they also enjoy role-play dialogues that help them better understand the many characters in the story. After they read the story, they can act out four or five different scenes in groups. They can bring in recipes for the pastries described or even make the pastries themselves and share them along with coffee or a mint green tea. They will be projecting themselves into a culture and learning through active experience.

The instructor's role is to pay careful attention to vocabulary and realia and to be prepared to add historical and cultural information when students ask questions. Every prereading activity, every term in the story selected for glossing, every interpretive exercise, and then the gradually widening perspective provided by postreading experiences should enable students to discuss Djebar's story and the Algerian exile community it portrays and finally to produce a thoughtful culminating written essay.

Without having to present the idea explicitly, the instructor can use a biographical comment to encourage students to respect the different cultural perspectives of the characters of the story they are about to read (see Gaasch and Budig-Markin 191). A vocabulary exercise, similarly, can teach much more than the meaning and use of the verb *soupirer* ("to sigh"), which students must conjugate and insert in the blank space in the sentence "Ayant vécu une vie pleine de tragédies, elle [Mère] ____ souvent devant ceux qui l'entouraient" (193; "Having lived a life full of tragedy, she [Mother] often ____ in front of those around her"). The sentence not only places a vocabulary word in context (and in a situation requiring the use of the imperfect indicative tense) but also proposes a fairly sophisticated conclusion about the character of Mère, whose tendency to sigh is a response to the cumulative tragedies of her life, not a sign of a weak character or of age.

Dividing "Il n'y a pas d'exil," a long story, into two or three sections, according to the story's rhythm and themes, helps students sort out, together, the identity and role of the ten characters and to highlight the discussion of death in one section and the marriage proposal in another. Seeing the first section as a scene in a play, students begin to appreciate the theatrical qualities of Djebar's prose. If the instructor uses the words *space* and *stage* as prompts, students quickly respond with comments about the window, the inside space occupied by the women, and the outside space from which the men enter. Students relate the singing of those who weep for the dead child to the chorus in classical Greek drama and to the all-pervasive presence of death in this story's theater of life.

In the second part of the story, the fiancé's mother and two other women, who resemble each other, come to obtain the consent of the bride's mother to the marriage of her daughter. Four conversations overlap in different rooms of the apartment as the women think and speak of marriage and of death in different ways, according to their social roles and ages. Formulaic speech pervades the entire visit, which is described as scripted by the narrator-bride. Students see the extensive oral quality of this written text, to which the offstage, outside sound of the crying mourners adds its own, wordless story. The instructor might introduce the concept of the funeral *thrène* ("mourning chant") in this context.

If students ask about the larger issues addressed by the story, the instructor can present an encapsulated history of the Algerian war and touch on religion, women's rights, and the cultural-religious importance of the family, or students can do some basic research and give such presentations to the class themselves. They can also present gender statistics of students and faculty members in Algerian, Moroccan, and Tunisian universities, as these reflect on the character Hafça, who comes to the home to give private language lessons. Research and class discussions help make students aware of women's educational opportunities and in some cases the statistical predominance of women in institutions of higher education and in many fields in the public sector today. Students might also be interested in the mix of languages in university teaching in North Africa, especially French, Arabic, and English, and in Djebar's experience as an Algerian professor and her response to the Algerian government's decision to require all university courses to be taught in Arabic, beginning in the 1990s.

The best way to make the opening discussion of the complete story comfortable for students is to introduce scenes—"La narratrice entre dans le salon où les invitées l'attendent" (Gaasch and Budig-Markin 204; "The narrator enters the living room where the guests are waiting for her")—and have them tell what happened in each one. Increasingly conceptual postreading activities begin with open-framed questions, such as, What is the role of Hafça in the traditional family's life? Should the narrator remarry or not? What is the meaning of the opening and closing of the windows? What roles do the different members of the family play? Later, as the students' understanding and confidence level increase, the focus might shift to more subtle qualities of Hafça's character, such as her hesitation to respond fully to a comment by the grief-stricken narrator.

It is interesting that discussion of the title of the story, "Il n'y a pas d'exil," which is explained by Hafça with reference to the narrator's father, requires substantial preparative class analysis of the religious perspectives of the different characters and should thus be postponed. It might be assigned as a final essay. Other important issues, such as Arabic speakers' learning the French language, life as an exile, and the struggle between life and death, are better presented or discussed in class before any writing assignment is given. If students are offered choices in their essays, they can better respond to the subject they select in ways that are thoughtful, appropriate, and original. They might choose to define a theatrical theme themselves like several examples of fifth-semester student paper topics: "Le théâtre de la vie," "Le théâtre de l'absurde," and "Le jour d'une tragédie" ("The Theater of Life," "The Theater of the Absurd," and "The Day of a Tragedy").

For less-experienced readers of French, the teaching of Djebar's stories should encourage active, participatory, respectful, and safe class discourse. Lead these students just enough to help them deal with the text's complexity. Narratives should be short, structurally complete, with dialogue easy to understand and repeat and with characters to whom students can relate. Topoi such as the window of the soul, solidarity in mourning, the woman's voice, and the presence of death in life are best presented as confirmations of student input.

Students should become aware of the wide gap between American and Algerian cultures and between the 1950s, when the story was written, and today. An interesting use of intertextuality that encourages this awareness is to play examples, from Djebar's films, of women crying and singing. From *La zerda et les chants de l'oubli* ("Zerda and the Songs of Forgetting") I have selected both the recurring image of the veiled woman in white with the trill of a woman's outcry in descending notes in the background and a series of individual camera shots of women and girls, accompanied by musical commentary in Arabic. In both scenes, silent women counter the camera's eye with their own. I also show one or two scenes in *La nouba des femmes du Mont Chenoua* ("The Nouba of Women from Mount Chenoua"), the first of women singing and dancing with a young girl in a candlelit cave, the second of women singing and dancing in a field. Second-year students can speculate about the different narrative and historical contexts of these scenes.

When women's rights in Algeria are discussed with respect to a short story by Djebar, students can learn, by summarizing the narrative in class, how fiction is a way to write history.[3] If time permits, or if the class is less mature, I show a short scene from Kamal Dehane's documentary *Assia Djebar: Entre ombre et soleil* ("Assia Djebar: Between Shadow and Sun"), in which Djebar walks down city streets with women and men of different ages and attire. Another scene from this documentary shows the author when she goes to her old French school in Blida and shoots a couple of baskets on the empty court. We talk about dress and tradition and living away from home for the first time, a change in lifestyle that many of our students are experiencing in their first year or two at the university.

Often discussions center on women and girls in different domains. Students can appreciate female characters who preserve tenderness despite harsh realities. That discretion and modesty are seen as cultural strengths makes Algerian feminism different from feminism in the United States. I weave these themes and aspects of Djebar's works into class discussions, especially as encouraging follow-ups to student comments.

Three Djebar quotes—and a Djebar title—I share with students to give them insight into her character, concerns, lyricism, and intellect:

> Le français m'est langue marâtre (*L'amour* 298; "French is my 'stepmother' tongue" [*Fantasia* 214])[4]
>
> [J]'apprenais que le regard sur le dehors est en même temps retour à la mémoire, . . . à l'œil intérieur (*Vaste* 298; "I learned that looking at the

outside in this way is simultaneously a return to memory, . . . to the inner eye" [*So Vast* 306])

"[D]errière le voile de cette réalité exposée se sont réveillées des voix anonymes, recueillies ou ré-imaginées, l'âme d'un MAGHREB unifié et de notre passé." (*Zerda*; "Behind the veil of this exposed reality awoke anonymous voices, gathered or reimagined, the soul of a unified MAGHREB and of our past")

Ces voix qui m'assiègent: En marge de ma francophonie ("The Voices That Besiege Me: From the Margins of My *Francophonie*")

I make certain that students leave the discussion with a sense of the diversity of experience among Algerian women. I remind them to consider women and family at home, different responses to the challenges of war, changing lifestyles, opportunities, and new roles to play on the global stage, as reflected in Djebar's educational and professional background, her languages, her experiences abroad, and her return to her homeland.

We summarize many elements of Djebar's oeuvre, some of them nuanced, along the two axes of literary and conceptual analysis. On the literary axis, students quickly recognize and respond to the following: multiple points of view among the characters, aspects of drama, the importance of music to the story and Djebar's oeuvre, oral elements captured by written narrative, culturally centered dialogue, Arabic-language elements in a predominantly French text (an example of interlanguage),[5] and interacting discourses and rhythms. Students find important or symbolic objects, spaces, and individuals who may or may not be representative of a group or type. After discussing the story, they learn to recognize smaller stories within the larger story frame and recognize questions that, unanswered, are intended to provoke reader discussion, in the spirit of the oral tradition.

Djebarian concepts that are summarized in class include both constant and changing social roles of Algerian women and men; different roles of members of the family, which may change according to social and political circumstances; Islamic practices in daily life; the coexistence of the traditional and the modern; and the personal and cultural consequences of living in exile. Students notice and are able to discuss how individual and collective values, culture, religion, education, and language are revealed in everyday occurrences. They learn to see how Algerian national history and the future proposed by Djebar's text determine the options open, or not open, to her young characters.

Student learner outcome assessment may be conducted in terms of any important theme or aspect of the story touched on but not thoroughly discussed in class. I have assessed student learning from process writing and from final essays of two to three pages in French, giving the students a choice of two themes. A successful theme prompts different students' readings of the story, creates academic and personal interests and challenges, and promotes intellectual maturity. Students set the tone for their essay, write a first draft, and share it with peers in a small group, and the group then collectively recommends one essay to be read to the whole class. The essays that are selected to be read aloud provide both ideas and models for the weaker writers and critical thinkers. Throughout this process the professor facilitates, commenting on the student arguments as needed.

Professorial feedback is given, in writing, for both oral and written work: corrections or indications of language errors and of any misunderstandings of the story line or characters, praise for interesting analyses or statements. The final revised essay (I offer third-year students two revisions to perfect their language and presentation) is assessed for language and literary techniques and cultural and conceptual comprehension.

Students who consider the theme of theater in Djebar's story have recourse to several class discussion topics, such as inside and outside spaces, the symbol of the window, and the many oral elements. Students who select the themes of voice, identity, or theater in Djebar's story have recourse to the discussion topics of inside/outside spaces and the window, and to such oral elements as dialogue, cultural sayings, mourning cries and chants, and the performance[6] enacted by the *fiançailles* ("engagement") ritual negotiations. The engagement performance illustrates the concept of the speech act: the hour-long of discussion, religious and cultural sayings, alternating discursive feints and retreats, and coffee and pastries all lead in graceful order to the final promise by the mother of her daughter's hand in marriage. This script is well known to the narrator-protagonist, who lived through it once before, even though those who reenact it now have never met before.

Assessment of the student learner outcome assignment should be based on a demonstrated understanding of at least three characteristics of the narrative and their role in the story. A paper marked excellent would contain an introduction that presents the thesis, a clear argument, sufficient information about the story's literary and cultural context to support that argument, and a conclusion. It would include ideas beyond those discussed in class. It would be thoughtfully organized and carefully written. A paper marked good would have the elements of the excellent paper but show no original critical thinking. A satisfactory paper would demonstrate an understanding of the characters, plot, and framework of the story and give three examples of theater in the story without explaining them well.

An important long-term objective of teaching Djebar at this early stage in the academic career of students is to give them a glimpse of what French and francophone studies can offer. Students, beginning to see how far they have yet to go in their lives and in their education, have in Djebar the perfect linguistic and intellectual model. They should also take pride in having made an important first step by analyzing a difficult literary text in French by a world-famous author who provides access to the history, culture, and languages of Algeria and Arab women. And this step was made both far from Medina and far from Paris.

NOTES

Translations from the French are mine unless otherwise indicated.

[1]Schneider and Lenz 11. At the B1 level, students can distinguish between statements in the past, present, and future; tell stories; describe personal experiences, hopes, and ambitions; speculate about possible situations and consequences; and write straightforward, connected texts (5, 7, 16).

[2]*ACTFL Proficiency Guidelines* 7, 13, 23. At the Intermediate Mid level, students can understand short texts with high-frequency vocabulary dealing with personal and social topics to which they can relate, and from connected descriptions and narration can write basic sentences with control in the present tense, with reference to other time frames.

[3]If the class is particularly interested in women's rights, I present the Family Code in Algeria (1984, 2005) and Personal Status Code (1956, 1997) and Nationality Code in Tunisia (1993) to show the difference in cultures and levels of religiosity in the two countries. I add another perspective by discussing the Personal Status Code of Morocco (1957, 2004). Recent changes in all these codes give increased rights to women in the context of their central role in the family and in Muslim law and culture. But Algeria was not yet independent at the time Djebar's story was written, and a Family Code was not instituted until 1984 (it was revised in 2005). On women's rights in Tunisia and Morocco, a good reference is Charrad.

[4]This quote is also available in Joubert 376–77.

[5]*Interlanguage* is defined by the *American Heritage Dictionary of the English Language* as "a lingua franca" and by *The Free Dictionary* as "a common language used by speakers of different languages."

[6]If the class members are mature enough for linguistic theory, they may be interested in this narrative event as an example of speech act theory, according to which an utterance, like a promise, may be a performative speech act in itself (Austin; Searle, *Speech Acts*). The subsequent debate over speech act theory decades later between Derrida (*Limited*) and Searle ("Reiterating") also interests mature or graduate students learning French. After learning about this concept, several students chose to write a subsequent, unsolicited revision of their essay incorporating the notions of performance and speech act theory.

Writing in *Bi-langue*

Maya Boutaghou

This essay analyzes Assia Djebar's writings in the light of her position as a francophone author located between several cultures and as a bilingual writer who produces bilingual texts. Much has been written about her familiarity with French and her complex ties to her intimate enemy, France. Her relation to Arabness, which is no less complex, has also been analyzed. Because her writings exemplify what Abdelkebir Khatibi calls "la bi-langue,"[1] an untranslatable term that is discussed below, I intend to analyze the poetics of the particular *bi-langue* at work in several Djebarian novels. My purpose is to investigate, through the lens of Arabic, the interactions between French and Arabic. I explore how dialectal Arabic and classical Arabic inform Djebar's French and how their visibility to the bilingual reader allows a double mode of interpretation. This field has already been studied on the lexical and narratological levels;[2] I extend this work to show how Arabic is concealed by a specific, distorted form of French syntax. The francophone reader could interpret this distortion as either Djebar's personal style or as a kind of bilingual poetic at work. Excerpts have been selected from different texts to show how Arabic is present not only through the explicit use of transliterated terms such as *hannouni* (حنوني), ʿ*amti* (عمتي), *hammam* (حمام), and *imam* (إمام) but also as a form of hidden translation, particularly in dialogic narrative sections.

There is a metaphoric relation between language and the female subject, who has to be partly silenced in order to be present in the Algerian context. The hidden presence of Arabic could be seen to mirror the condition of Algerian women, whose Arabness had to be concealed in order for them to travel, unveiled, the streets of the city. A large number of studies and books have analyzed the female subject in colonial and postcolonial situations,[3] but in this essay I explore in depth how the structures of groups of languages can coexist in the same textual space. Djebar consciously uses French to translate Arabic (e.g., see *Ces voix* 29). The French syntax of her writing mirrors her multilingualism. My translinguistic approach helps mark the distinctions between the languages.[4] I begin with a discussion of *bi-langue*, introduce the languages employed by Djebar, then demonstrate, with excerpts, how Arabic syntax transforms French syntax and gives Djebar's style its uniqueness.

Bi-langue

The concept of *bi-langue* was developed by Khatibi, a Moroccan author, to describe the linguistic reality of francophone Maghrebian writers. Francophone Maghrebian literature is informed by a multiplicity of languages that share the same cultural and textual space. Khatibi states something that readers from other cultural backgrounds, especially monolingual readers, should consider carefully when speaking, thinking, or writing about francophone writers, particularly francophone writers from the Maghreb:

> Tant que la théorie de la traduction, de la bi-langue et de la pluri-langue n'aura pas avancé, certains textes maghrébins resteront imprenables selon une approche formelle et fonctionnelle. La langue "maternelle" est à l'œuvre dans la langue étrangère. De l'une à l'autre se déroulent une traduction permanente et un entretien en abyme, extrêmement difficile à mettre au jour. . . . (*Maghreb* 179)

> As long as bilingual and multilingual translation theory is not developed, some Maghrebian texts cannot be analyzed using a formal and functional approach. The "mother" tongue is at play in the foreign language. A permanent translation and *mise en abyme*–style conversation unfolds between them, and it is extremely difficult to uncover.

To elucidate this conversation *en abyme*, my argument is rooted in the belief that the reader cannot sufficiently explore Djebar's poetics (in the etymological sense of "making") without taking into account the multiplicity of languages at work in her texts or without focusing on her internalized struggle between Arabic—itself double, as فصحى (fusha; "classical") and دارجة (darija; "dialectal")—and French. Her poetics is in fact determined by the metaphoric life and death of languages,[5] that is, their visibility and invisibility, and by the interactions between them vis-à-vis the complex political power structures of Algeria. Djebar explains in detail how the concept of *bi-langue* functions in her writing:

> Les multiples voix qui m'assiègent—celles de mes personnages dans mes textes de fiction—, je les entends, pour la plupart, en arabe, un arabe dialectal, ou même un berbère que je comprends mal, mais dont la respiration rauque et le souffle m'habitent d'une façon immémoriale. (*Ces voix* 29)

> Multiple voices besiege me—those of my characters in my fictional texts—, I hear them, most of them, in Arabic, in dialectal Arabic, or even in Berber, which I do not understand very well, but whose hoarse respiration and breath dwell in me in an age-old way.

At the time her first novel, *La soif* (*The Mischief*) was published, French was taught in schools, but Berber and Arabic were not.[6] Djebar's relation to Arabic and French has its origin in her experience of the educational system during colonial times, as the following excerpt from her inaugural speech to the French Academy demonstrates:

> Passionnée, étais-je à vingt ans, par la stature d'Averroes . . . mais alors que j'avais appris au collège l'anglais, le latin et le grec, comme je demandais en vain à perfectionner mon arabe classique, j'ai dû restreindre mon ambition en me résignant à devenir historienne. (413)
>
> As a twenty-year-old, I was passionate about the mighty Averroes . . . but while I learned English, Latin, and Greek at school, I would ask in vain to improve my classical Arabic and had to temper my ambition and resign myself to becoming a historian.

Indeed, when French education was established in Algeria in the 1880s (Tlatli 298), French was the only language taught.[7] When political nationalist movements started to emerge during the 1930s, classical Arabic was chosen[8]—for example, in the political party led by Ibn Badis, the Algerian ulema,[9] whose slogan was "Islam is our religion, Algeria our country, Arabic our language" (Kashani-Sabet 267). Arabic was considered as a symbol of the future nation, as a weapon to be used against the French, and as a response to the silencing of Algerian culture. There is an easy and understandable slippage between French language and French colonization, but before making any judgments regarding linguistic choice, we should remember that, during the rise of Algerian nationalism, most intellectuals used French to build a critical discourse against France—the best examples of such independence proponents were Messali Hadj and Ferhat Abbas. My purpose here is not to discuss the political situation of languages in Algeria but to show how, even when Algerian writers use French, their French is informed internally by a silenced Arabic, much as it was during the French colonial period in Algeria. Djebar, like many Algerian writers, is a victim of a linguistic genocide that was carried out by a blind system of oppression. I study how the "langue 'maternelle' est à l'œuvre dans la langue étrangère" (Khatibi, *Maghreb* 179; "the mother tongue is at work in the foreign language").

Djebar's Languages

The issue of Djebar's languages, developed in many ways throughout her novels and essays, particularly the essays in *Ces voix qui m'assiègent*, has received much attention from scholars.[10] Djebar grew up in a culture where many languages competed (Berber, dialectal Arabic, classical Arabic, French). She explores in depth the interface between affect and languages. In her volume of short stories *Femmes d'Alger dans leur appartement*, first published in 1980, she reflects on the plurality of voices in her writing. This aspect was developed in the first volume of the quartet, *L'amour, la fantasia*, her fifth novel. The concept of the subject in translation (Boutaghou 226) is at play in *Femmes d'Alger*, where she italicizes some terms to highlight the polyphony at work in her text (Donadey, "Multilingual Strategies" 30).[11] This plurality reveals another dimension of language: its gendered nature. Readers of *L'amour* remember her thoughtful and precise description of four languages (Arabic, Berber, French, and the language of the body) and their cultural coexistence (254; *Fantasia* 180). Mireille Calle-Gruber summarizes what becomes a leitmotiv in Djebar's work as Djebar attempts to make her languages visible even in translation:

> [F]emme, berbérophone par les grands-parents, arabophone par les parents, elle écrit dans la langue française qui fut celle de la colonisation au Maghreb, celle du père instituteur de la France dans un village du Sahel algérien. (*Assia Djebar* [2006] 17)

> [A] woman, a Berber speaker from her grandparents, an Arabic speaker from her parents, she writes in French, the language of colonization in the Maghreb, the language of her father, a primary school teacher for France in a village in the Algerian Sahel.

Djebar uses French to poetically translate the affective dimensions associated with each language.[12] The language of writing, the dry tongue, is inspired and nurtured by other languages: Berber (*libyco-berbère*), dialectal Arabic, and classical Arabic. A striking example of *bi-langue* is Djebar's discussion of the use of the term *hannouni*, whose pronunciation is informed by her dialectal Arabic:

> Comment traduire ce "hannouni," par un "tendre," un "tendrelou"? Ni "mon chéri," ni "mon cœur." Pour dire "mon cœur," nous, les femmes, nous préférons "mon petit foie," ou "pupille de mon œil." . . . Ce "tendrelou" semble un cœur de laitue caché et frais. (*L'amour* 117)

> How can you translate this *hannouni* by a word like "tender-hearted" or "*tendrelou*"? Or by "my darling" or "my precious heart." Instead of saying "precious heart," we women prefer the expression "my little liver," or "the apple of my eye." . . . This word "*tendrelou*" seems like the hidden heart of a fresh lettuce. (*Fantasia* 80–81)

Hannouni encompasses in its pronunciation the landscape and the stories of her childhood in Cherchell. Her attempt to translate it by using the circumlocution "un cœur de laitue caché et frais" conveys a sense of the untranslatable and of the distance between *hannouni* and whatever equivalent is proposed; the musicality is lost even if the French text offers tentative translations and tries to get closer to the meaning and the affect of the word (Donadey, "Multilingual Strategies" 32). Djebar chooses expressions in order to render the effects of dialectal Arabic in French, emphasizing the connotative more than the denotative elements of the words.

Readers can detect the gendered dimension of language in Djebar's discussion of Arabic in the reference to dialectal Arabic (*darija*) and the way it was specifically used by women in *Vaste est la prison*. This gendered use of *darija* is explicit in her writings, as in the passage about how her mother kept notes of traditional Andalusian songs:

> [M]a mère tenait surtout . . . à ses cahiers de musique: elle qui n'écrivait pas le français . . . elle ouvrait ces feuillets où, adolescente, elle avait noté la poésie des *noubas* andalouses. Elle en savait par cœur les couplets, mais relire les vers inscrits en arabe la préservait, dans notre cercle, du statut d'analphabète qui aurait pu être le sien. (170–71)

> [M]y mother set the greatest store by her books of music. Though she could not write French . . . she would open these notebooks where, as an adolescent, she had written down the poetry of the *noubas* of Andalusia. She knew the couplets by heart, and could read and write them in Arabic, so she could not be classified as illiterate, though otherwise she might have been so in our circle. (*So Vast* 175)

The language described is the written *darija*. It is often forgotten that *darija* has a written tradition. *Dialect* is in general

> [a] language or manner of speaking peculiar to an individual or class or region. Usually it belongs to a region, like the West Riding or East Anglia. A dialect differs from the standard language of a country, in some cases very considerably. Greek, German and Sicilian dialects, for instance, show great variations from the standard. A good deal of literature is in dialect, especially that created in the earlier stages of a country's civilization. (Cuddon 217)

What is known as dialectal Arabic has its own literature, songs, and recipes, but, relegated to popular culture, it lost its cultural value. Another factor, quite specific to Algeria, was the process of Arabicization. In order to give credence to the standardized version of Arabic, commonly termed classical (Kashani-Sabet; Tlatli), dialectal Arabic was considered to be impure. But the most prestigious institution for oriental languages in France, the Institut National des Langues et Civilisations Orientales (INALCO), offers a degree in each regionalized form of Arabic. It is now commonplace to consider Arabic in all its various forms. Someone from an Arabic-speaking region will know immediately that the dialectal Arabic of Oran is not the dialectal Arabic of Algiers or the M'zab. Djebar uses the expression "les Algéries" ("Algerias") (Calle-Gruber, *Assia Djebar* [2006] 19) to translate this linguistic situation.

Mimetic Arabic Syntax and Tropes

Djebar's style presents some syntactic constructions informed by dialectal and classical Arabic. Dialectal Arabic follows classical Arabic syntax; the difference between the two languages is mainly in vocabulary. Arabic syntactic structures can be split into two groups depending on the first element of the sentence: a verbal construction (or verbal sentence) starts with a verb, and the order is verb-subject-object; a nominal construction (or nominal sentence) starts with a noun, and the order is noun-syntagm, the syntagm a linguistic unit that can be nominal or verbal. Djebar's style is more a transposition than a translation[13] of Arabic vis-à-vis the perception of normalized French syntax. An effect of her style is *un écart* ("distance"), which could also be seen as the result of the poetic process of putting Arabic into French. The style is informed by Arabic syntax: the repetitive use of short nominal sentences, which in fact is the construction equating French and English sentences (with *être* and *to be*)—an example can be *lawnu al sama' azraq* compared with "la couleur du ciel est bleue" and "the color of the sky is blue"—because of the absence of an auxiliary *être* in Arabic; the use of anaphora and cataphora to supplement the pronoun in Arabic syntactic structures; and, finally, the use of metaphors and circumlocutions to render specific meanings, with attempts at paronomasia to mimic the music of the native language.

Arabic syntactic structures are common in passages that involve dialogue or first-person narratives. The dialogic parts are signaled by typographic signs such as italics or punctuation—what Veronika Thiel calls "linguistic didascalies" (*Assia Djebar* 54). Dialogue in the Djebarian narrative introduces the context of enunciation and language. The presence of a nominal sentence, transgressing the basic French grammatical construction, which is subject-verb-object, thus sounds strange in French. It gives a twist to the text, a mimicking of French orality as it masks Arabic orality.

In "Oran, langue morte," the first short story from *Oran, langue morte* (translated into English as *The Tongue's Blood Does Not Run Dry*), readers experience the translinguistic aspects of Djebar's writing. The female character, writing to Olivia, her French friend and colleague, narrates the death of her parents, Habiba and Abbas, who were involved in the anticolonial struggle as unionists. Here are two nominal sentences:

> J'ai embarqué enfin, et pour la France. À dix-huit ans, après mon baccalauréat. Pour mes études, a cru ma mère, enfin ma tante maternelle. Pour toujours, ai-je décidé. Contre le reniement des gens, des lieux, des choses elles-mêmes. Ma mère et mon père, enterrés là-bas, derrière une colline. (16)

> I finally embarked for France at eighteen, after getting my baccalauréat. My mother—well, my maternal aunt—believed that it was for my

> studies. I'm going away forever, I had decided. As a negation of people, of places, of things. My mother and my father, buried down below, behind a hill. (14)

In French, three sentences are nominal, having no verb. "À dix-huit ans, après mon baccalauréat" ("At eighteen, after my baccalaureate") juxtaposes two prepositional phrases and elides the verb: "après *avoir passé* mon baccalauréat" ("after having received my baccalaureate"). In the last sentence, the implicit verbal construction in French is "Ma mère et mon père sont enterrés là-bas" ("My mother and my father are buried there"). French readers notice a departure from the grammatical norm but consider it to be a creative shift that is particular to the author's style, a form of poetic license. For Algerian readers, however, the whole passage can be perceived as a form of dialectal Arabic.

In the nominal sentence, the verb is in second position. It can be constructed using an affix (a prefix or suffix), thus telling us whether the subject is in the first, second, or third person; singular, dual, or plural; female or male. In Arabic, if the verb contains information about the subject, then the subject does not need to be explicit. Moreover, there is no infinitive in Arabic; a verb always indicates a subject. If the subject is explicitly mentioned in a verbal sentence, it repeats the information given by the affix. Readers in French will note the insistent and repetitive use of personal pronouns: "Ma tante," "elle-même," "elle qui" in "*Ma tante elle-même—elle qui* m'a élevée après que 'ce' soit arrivé—s'est remise . . . à fredonner . . ." (*Oran* 15; emphasis added; "Even my aunt, who brought me up after 'it' happened, started to hum . . ." [*Tongue's Blood* 13]).

The following example illustrates the cataphoric use of personal pronouns, transposing an Arabic structure that could be verb-suffix without explicit reference to the subject: "J'avais dix ans, en 1962. *Ils* vous ont inhumés, un 5 février, à trois heures du matin. *Ils* n'avaient pas voulu nous rendre les deux corps" (16; emphasis added; "In 1962, I was ten years old. You were both interred on February 5 at three o'clock in the morning. They hadn't wanted to send us your bodies" [14]). It begins like a testimony or journal entry: "J'avais dix ans, en 1962" ("In 1962, I was ten years old"). The narrator addresses her parents with "Ils *vous* ont inhumés" ("You were both interred"), and the cataphoric use of the third-plural person *ils* ("they") leaves the door open for interpretation. In French, *ils* could be viewed as a form of oral discourse, where the referent is unclear, yet this structure is quite common in Arabic (classical and dialectal). If a sentence starts with a verb, the meaning is built cataphorically and the referent is often given later. Readers or listeners must ask, "Who are *they*?" This uncertainty could be intended as a way of maintaining the audience's attention, a device used in oral narratives.

The Arabic verb-subject structure, often built as prefix-verb-subject, is transposed into French: "Ma tante, de retour, m'a portée dans ses bras. *M'a déshabillée. M'a mis une chemise. . . . Elle* gémissait, *elle*, croyant que je ne l'entendais pas: 'Au nom de Dieu! . . . Au nom de Dieu!'" (17; emphasis added; "When she returned, my aunt took me up in her arms. Undressed me. Put me in my nightshirt. . . . Thinking that I couldn't hear her, she sighed, 'In the name of God! . . . In the name of God!' " [14]). If I were to translate the italicized parts into dialectal Arabic, the result might be close to خالتي, كي رجعت, رفدتني, بدلتلي, لبستلي (khalti, ki rej'at, refdetni. Bedletli. Lebsetli). The two sentences, with the elided subject, "m'a déshabillée" and "m'a mis une chemise," are asyntactic in French. They feature the transposition of a verbal sentence, starting with a verb and suffix, as an indication of the subject and the pronoun object, both signaled with a suffix: ت (t) indicates that the subject is third-person, singular, and female, and ي/ني (ni/i) indicates that the object is in the first-person singular. This structure is obviously Arabic transposed into French.

The repetition of the third-person "she" in the next passage also points to Arabic syntax. Since the subject of the verb is indicated by the affix, any mention of the subject pronouns constitutes an insistence in Arabic. The insistence is easily transposed into French by the anaphoric use of the pronoun *elle* ("she"):

> *Elle*! *Elle*, son visage de lune, dans sa grâce intacte et son charme. *Elle*, l'orpheline dès l'enfance, la fille de ma mère chérie: Habiba! Yeux fermés, n'importe, elle me regarde; oh oui, je le sais.
>
> (*Oran* 22–23; emphasis added)

> It was she! My sister, her moon face, in its grace and its charm. Orphaned as a child, the daughter of my dear mother. Habiba! Her eyes are closed, but I know—oh yes!—that she's looking at me." (*Tongue's Blood* 17)

Dialectal Arabic is again visible in the repetition of the pronoun (not always rendered in the published English translation) and in the nominal structure—there is only one verb, "elle me regarde" ("she's looking at me"). Other hints of dialectal Arabic are the use of metaphors such as "son visage de lune" (وجهها كي لقمر; wejeha ki leqmer; "her moon face") and circumlocution to designate Habiba, "la fille de ma mère chérie" ("the daughter of my dear mother"). These structures create a feeling of the *unheimlich* ("uncanny") in French, but in Arabic a circumlocution is a way of expressing the multiple existences of the beloved: Habiba is not only Habiba but also all the realities that her being expresses. The repetition of *elle* is juxtaposed with other expressions that signify the individual: "l'orpheline dès l'enfance" ("[o]rphaned as a child") and "la fille de ma mère chérie." It is as if the repeated invocation of her first name, "Habiba," will make her come back to life. Note that the vocative is still used in Arabic and is a strong indication of oral culture.

The use of *bi-langue* in Djebar distinguishes between the transcription of oral stories and the transmission of written narratives, such as the military archives of the conquest of Algiers. "Oran, langue morte" involves the transcription of an oral narrative, and this form is employed also in *Femmes d'Alger dans leur appartment*. An example of this oral, often lyrical, narrative is the section "Pour un divan de la porteuse d'eau" ("For a Diwan of the Water Carrier") in the title story, where repetition produces alliteration. It also forms part of the popular elegiac prayers performed by women in North African culture to the saints of the region. The prayers are common among the كياسة (kiyassa; "the women who perform massages and scrub") in the *hammam* ("public baths"). In the next passage, the vocative is used, and anaphora: "Endormie, je suis l'endormie," "on m'emporte, qui m'emporte." That the repetitions and expressions do not sound idiomatic in French indicates that *bi-langue* is at work:

> Endormie, je suis l'endormie et l'on m'emporte, qui m'emporte. . . .
>
> . . . .
>
> C'est moi—moi?—C'est moi qu'ils ont exclue, moi sur laquelle ils ont lancé l'interdit
> C'est moi—moi?—moi qu'ils ont humiliée
> Moi qu'ils ont encagée
> Moi qu'ils ont cherché à ployer, leurs poings sur ma tête, pour me faire couler droit, . . . moi dans les rocs du silence de voile blanc. . . .
> (*Femmes d'Alger* 108, 111)

> Asleep, I am the one asleep and they are carrying me off, who is carrying me off. . . .
>
> . . . .
>
> It is me—me?—It is me they have excluded, me whom they have barred
> It is me—me?—me they have humiliated
> Me whom they have caged in
> Me whom they've sought to subdue, their fists on my head, to make me drown while standing straight . . . me inside the rocks of silence of the white veil. . . . (*Women* 37, 39)

The anaphoric use of the first person, the absence of punctuation and the repetition of *moi* and *moi qui* all give the passage a lyrical effect. The alliterations (sounds such as [m], [wa], [ã]) and anaphors (*moi*, *moi qui*, *moi dans*, *voile blanc*) remind us of سجع (saj'), the rhymed prose that is frequent in Arabic.

Similarly, in *Ombre sultane* (*A Sister to Scheherazade*), the connotations surrounding the term "l'Homme" (9; "the Man" [7]) on the first page suggest Arabic phrasing. The presence of "il" and "l'homme" refers to الراجل (el-rajel), which in Arabic means "the husband." The article ال (*el*), translated by *le* in French, can be both specific and general, whereas the French *l'homme* means "man" more than "husband." With *el-rajel* the narrator indicates a whole gendered culture: "'[I]l' s'est éloigné. Ses souliers crissent régulièrement sur les dalles. 'Il' tousse; 'il' ouvre des portes; 'il' est parti" (*Ombre* 17; "'[H]e' has gone. You hear the regular squeak of his shoes on the tiled floor. 'He' coughs; 'he' opens doors; 'he' has gone" [*Sister* 8]). In this sentence, the narrative represents him as a stranger and an enemy. The series of short phrases separated by commas could well be an indicator of Arabic. Historically speaking, punctuation appeared late in written texts, having been introduced as part of النهضة (al-Nahda; "the awakening," the nineteenth-century renaissance) reforms; commas and periods then became the most common form of punctuation.

Djebar uses metaphors to produce semantic equivalents for Arabic expressions:

> . . . toi au soleil désormais exposée, moi tentée de m'enfoncer dans la nuit resurgie. . . . Ton rire désespéré à l'aube, ô Hajila, après que ma fillette t'a hélée, par-dessus la rampe. Sur la ligne d'horizon noyée, l'œil de l'aurore darde sur nous sa menace. (*Ombre* 11)

> . . . one who is . . . exposed henceforth to the sunlight, while I am tempted to plunge back into the night. . . . Your hopeless laughter at dawn, Hajila, after my daughter had called your name over the balustrade. On the blurred horizon, dawn darts its threatening eye at us. (*Sister* 3)

The vocative "ô Hajila" translates a common form in dialectal Arabic; يا هجيلة (ya Hajila) occurs frequently in oral narratives, once again showing dialectal Arabic at work—dialectal, because the vocative is a sign of orality. The first pages of *Ombre sultane* offer the reader a style replete with metaphors that mimic the elaborate Arabic style, in which all that is said about intimacy, marriage, love, and sexuality is expressed metaphorically. "[T]oi au soleil désormais exposée," "moi tentée de m'enfoncer dans la nuit resurgie," "Sur la ligne d'horizon noyée, l'œil de l'aurore darde sur nous sa menace"—these metaphors allude to Scheherazade and her sister. The tension between day and night reflects that Scheherazade was condemned to live by night in order to perpetuate her days. In the language on this theme, a creativity and newness result from the need to transpose the Arabic poetic imaginary into French.

The distance inherent in Djebar's style, *l'écart*, marks the distance internalized by the subject in translation. Wordplay and sound play appear even in the critical scholarship on Djebar,[14] because critics themselves occupy the position of subject in translation, looking for closer interpretations of our emotions. That Djebar is imitating and reproducing several voices (Donadey, "Multilingual Strategies"; Thiel, *Assia Djebar*) results in different narrative forms that have different values. Through her complex use of syntax, in which oral and written cultures intermingle, she represents both قلم (qalam; "pen") and كلام (kalaam; "speech"). Her French, transformed by Arabic, encompasses the variations and plurality of Algeria's voices, "les Algéries" ("the Algerias"; Calle-Gruber, *Assia Djebar* [2006] 19). It signals a multitude of discourses without hierarchies, operating at the same level, on the same page, all the while affirming the singularity of each language.

NOTES

All translations are mine, unless otherwise indicated. I thank Lucy Brisley for her careful and thoughtful help in editing this essay.

[1] *Bi-langue* is a term Khatibi uses to designate the multilingual situation from which francophone Maghrebian authors are writing (*Maghreb*). This situation is complex because writers in the Maghreb, at least those belonging to the postcolonial period, wrote in one language, French or classical Arabic. *Bi-langue* refers to the hidden interactions between two or more languages. The term can be extended to designate multilingual situations ("pluri-langue" is mentioned by Khatibi [179]), not just bilingual. Maghrebian literature, even when written in French, is produced in a multilingual context, in which classical Arabic, dialectal Arabic, and Tamazigh (Berber languages) are distinct. In Djebar's writing, it is particularly relevant to use *bi-langue*, as the term points to the problematic binary divisions between French and Arabic and between classical Arabic and dialectal Arabic.

[2] See Donadey, "Multilingual Strategies" and *Recasting Postcolonialism*; Kouchkar Ferchouli; Thiel, *Assia Djebar*; Boutaghou.

[3] To mention only a few scholars in the field of francophone women writers: Mortimer, Lionnet (*Autobiographical Voices* and *Postcolonial Representations*), Donadey (esp. her *Recasting Postcolonialism*), and Chikhi (esp. her *Romans*).

[4] I define the translinguistic approach as a back-and-forth movement between the written text in French and the imagined subtext in (mainly Algerian) Arabic. The prefix *trans-* signals this movement.

[5] This metaphor is particularly striking in the titles *La disparition de la langue française* and *Oran, langue morte*.

[6] See Kashani-Sabet's excellent article for a better understanding of the intricate history of languages and politics in Algeria.

[7] "Before the French conquest, the educational system consisted of Islamic institutions of learning such as the kataba, or elementary schools, the madrasa, or secondary schools, and the zawiya, or schools of higher education. The French, however, altered the existing [educational] institutions to accommodate the needs of the *colons*, or settlers. In the meantime, the education of indigenous Algerians was largely excluded until 1895, when a school was founded for the offspring of the workers of the French colonial bureaucracy" (Kashani-Sabet 266).

[8] In Algeria, Arabic is the official language. Algeria is a multilingual country where different Berber languages coexist alongside Arabic—both the rich and popular dialectal Arabic and the classical Arabic that is now mainly associated with the state. It must be understood that dialectal Arabic is a language, not just a colloquial version of classical Arabic. The syntax is similar, but the vocabulary mixes Arabic with other Mediterranean languages. Dictionaries of dialectal Algerian Arabic exist. Finally, there is a traditional culture in dialectal Arabic that includes songs, literature, proverbs, and so on.

[9] Kashani-Sabet reminds us how Ibn Badis and the ulema gathered in 1936 for the Islamic Congress in Algiers. Ibn Badis "requested further reforms such as the recognition of Arabic, in addition to French, as the Algerian national language." The same went for members of the Front de Libération Nationale (FLN) who did not impose a specific language and for whom "[l]anguage was not the overarching concern . . . during the years of revolt that led to Algerian independence." She explains the position of one of the "neuf historiques" (nine recognized leaders of the Algerian independence movement),

Hocine Aït Ahmed, who wrote in his memoirs that "the French language has been the principal, if not, exclusive vehicle, on a certain level of abstraction, of communication, oral or written, in the hearts of the leading organs of our district and of the party" (268).

[10]The image of the palimpsest can help illustrate the internal complexity of Djebar's multilingualism (the term *palimpsest* is mainly used by Donadey ["Multilingual Strategies"]). The palimpsest serves as a metaphor to explain how languages are not hidden but coexist. Djebar's rendition of multilingualism aligns with that of other multilingual authors who choose a dominant language. Anyone who practices several languages can feel the need to code-switch. In Djebar, translation from Arabic into French, both hidden and open, is the only tool allowing her to code-switch without disturbing her readers. The process imposes a double bind on the writer: the need to hide Arabic (dialectal and classical) and the impossibility of preventing Arabic from being intimately linked to French. It is as if readers were bearing witness to the powerful internalization of the rule at school that the students were allowed to speak only French.

[11]The subject in translation, as far as literature is concerned, deals with the writing process that results from the author's self-translation from a silenced language; it results from a position of speech informed by the back-and-forth movement between languages.

[12]Sofiane Laghouati shows how diglossia functions in four novels by Djebar. He analyzes her French-language imitations, in *L'amour*, of Arabic forms that use alliteration and play poetical games (105).

[13]Veronika Thiel suggests that, in Djebar's dialogues and first-person narratives, there are both translations from Arabic and transpositions of Arabic syntactic structures into French (*Assia Djebar* 54).

[14]Critics use titles that mimic Djebar's wordplay. For example, Gauvin's "Assia au pays du langage," Rice's "Algerrance: Envois et envols," and Lionnet's "Ces voix au fil de soi(e)" (in Asholt, Calle-Gruber, and Combe) all have a double meaning in French.

Tangled Tongues: Teasing Out Multiple Meanings in Translation

Alison Rice

Assia Djebar's writings have reached many American university students in English translation, thanks to the efforts of Dorothy Blair, Marjolijn de Jager, Tegan Raleigh, and Betsy Wing. Teaching these rich texts in a language other than the original presents a particular challenge to professors whose students may have little experience with reading literary works in translation. My pedagogical tactics inevitably involve focusing on linguistic reflections—on metacommentary—in Djebar's works, in an effort to sensitize my interlocutors to the author's awareness of language, not only of the primary language of composition but also of the multiple tongues that are more or less subtly present in the text.

I begin by making sure my students are aware of the deep significance of writing in French for an author born in Algeria nearly twenty-five years before the country gained independence from French rule. I provide them with some historical context and call attention to some salient quotations in Djebar's work, such as the following straightforward statement found in her afterword to the English edition of *Women of Algiers in Their Apartment*: "The French language, for me, is the language of those people coming onto my land with the colonial conquest" (184). To underscore the terribly painful—and deadly—past that Djebar the historian cannot help but confront when she uses French as her language of written expression, and to awaken students to the danger inherent in writing the self for a woman of Algerian origin, I turn to this much-quoted passage from *L'amour, la fantasia*, translated as *Fantasia: An Algerian Cavalcade*:

> Cette langue était autrefois sarcophage des miens; je la porte aujourd'hui comme un messager transporterait le pli fermé ordonnant sa condamnation au silence, ou au cachot.
>
> Me mettre à nu dans cette langue me fait entretenir un danger permanent de déflagration. De l'exercice de l'autobiographie dans la langue de l'adversaire d'hier. . . . (300)

> This language was formerly used to entomb my people; when I write it today I feel like the messenger of old, who bore a sealed missive which might sentence him to death or to the dungeon.
>
> By laying myself bare in this language I start a fire which may consume me. For attempting an autobiography in the former enemy's language. . . . (215)

Regardless of the level of their proficiency in French, I expose students to the original text in order to examine these powerful phrases in a detailed close reading. Not only do I hope students will be moved by these inimitable turns of phrase, but I also invite them to seek English equivalents with me.

Teaching Djebar's works in the English-language classroom calls for this initial move toward translation, in my experience. Turning students into translators from the moment they approach her writing makes them aware of the multiple possibilities that the original text contains and heightens their ability to analyze the translated text as its own literary creation. When I introduce the aforementioned passage from *L'amour* to my students, I like to divide them into small groups of four, in which three are unfamiliar with French and one has had some experience with the language. I ask them to focus on the words in the original that have obvious equivalents in English and create a list. The students typically discern the following cognates without any trouble: *sarcophage* ("sarcophagus"), *messager* ("messenger"), *transporterait* ("transport"), *condamnation* ("condemnation"), *silence* ("silence"), *danger* ("danger"), *permanent* ("permanent"), *déflagration* ("deflagration"), *exercice* ("exercise"), *autobiographie* ("autobiography"), *adversaire* ("adversary"). They examine this lexicon and discuss the meanings of the various words they have isolated from the rest of the text. Once they have had a chance to explore the connotations and implications of these terms one by one, I ask them to start to imagine the significance of the passage as a whole. I ask them to create two translations in English, the first as literal as possible, as close a rendition of the original as they can come up with, and the second as literary as possible, as elegant and inventive as they can imagine. With the help of the student in each small group who has had some exposure to French, they fill in the blanks, creating a flow from one of their isolated words to the next. If they cannot figure out what a more complicated word like *autrefois* or *cachot* means, I invite them to make an educated guess. Students often stumble over the expression *faire entretenir*, and they find it challenging to know exactly how to interpret the final phrase, which is not a complete sentence and seems to trail off, in their analysis, with the insertion of an ellipsis at its close. Observations like these in a discussion involving the entire class after students have finished their translations give me an opportunity to address the particular attributes that characterize Djebar's writing.

The prevalence of ellipses is one attribute that I underscore, and I have students reflect on the possible interpretations of the three contiguous dots that occupy a prominent place in Djebar's text. Students inevitably bring up the fact that an ellipsis implies that something is missing, that there has been an omission of some sort that this form of punctuation hints at. They also address the sense of interruption, the idea that something has been cut off, that a continuation or perhaps an elaboration of the writer's thought was truncated and therefore left her—and us, her readers—hanging. This sense of interruption is communicated through the French term for it: suspension points. I invite my students to speculate on why this author often opts to use ellipses. They come up with compelling ideas about the power of the written word to suggest but not to say, to point toward various truths instead of communicating them fully.

Some students find the ellipses to be unusual, even frustrating, but most come to accept them, understanding that this text is neither exhaustive nor definitive. Many see this form of punctuation as allowing the inexpressible to occupy an important place in the literary text, much as silence is a theme in this passage from *L'amour*.

During my discussion of this dense quotation with the class, I ask students to make note of two expressions in French, the first found in the verb *porter*, the second in the term *me mettre à nu*. I encourage them to suggest English equivalents, then ask them to ponder the implications of these terms, both in this passage and in the larger Algerian context. The terms open up to a conversation on the importance of family and propriety, including questions of childbearing, caring for the elderly, wearing the veil, and the roles of women in colonial and postcolonial Algeria. When American students start to understand the immense significance of these terms in dialectal Arabic, they often observe that their own language cannot translate them. Such comments find an echo in works by Djebar, and when students come across textual affirmations of the untranslatability of expressions from the different tongues of her homeland in their subsequent reading assignments, they quickly relate to this concept.

Once students have had a chance to share with the class their translations of the passage from *L'amour*, I present them with the published translation of it in *Fantasia*. The close analyses they have done of the original enable them to identify how this version differs from it and to appreciate translation's interpretation.[1] This in-class exercise is an important first step in making students aware of the "task of the translator," to quote Walter Benjamin's famous phrase. By involving them in this very task, I hope to help them understand in a personal way why Gayatri Spivak asserts that "translation is the most intimate act of reading" ("Politics" 400). Although I do not ask them to tackle translations at great length, their attempt to decipher a key passage from the original text provides them with the opportunity to see what kind of reading Djebar's texts call for in any language: close analysis that takes into account not only the words the author puts together in an idiosyncratic fashion but also the syntax that contributes to a style that is uniquely hers.

After we have completed the in-class translation exercise, the first-year university students in my seminars turn to Djebar's collection of short stories *Oran, langue morte*, which is *The Tongue's Blood Does Not Run Dry* in the English translation (on the title page, all the words of the title are lowercased). When we approach this text, I ask students to analyze the title of the translation for content as well as style: I ask them what reasons there might be for the decision not to capitalize any of its words. I show them the original French title and ask them if they think the English is more appropriate for an anglophone readership. Students tend to find this title intriguing—though for some its image is shockingly graphic—and think that with the subtitle"Algerian Stories" it holds greater appeal for them than "Oran, Dead Language." We consider the two meanings of the word *tongue*: the organ in the mouth and the speech that this organ produces.[2] I urge students to begin their reading of Djebar's text with the afterword, which paradoxically serves as an introduction. It is in these pensive pages that we find self-reflexive commentary:

> Je me dis parfois: "Tu les saisis de loin, écris-les en te glissant au plus près de leur corps, de leur cœur! . . ." A quoi bon les inscrire, peu leur importe, elles—celle qui va mourir, celle qui va s'abriter, se recroqueviller ou celle qui se tait, yeux baissés, pour survivre?
>
> Après tout, quelle que soit l'approche tentée pour les écrire frémissantes, le sang—leur sang—ne sèche pas dans la langue, quelle que soit cette langue, ou le rythme, ou les mots finalement choisis. (372)

> Sometimes I tell myself, "You grasp them from afar, write them by placing yourself somewhere that is closest to their bodies—their hearts! . . ." What good is it to write them down—she who will die, she who will take refuge, she who will close in on herself, or she who will keep quiet, with downcast eyes, in order to survive?
>
> After all, whatever approach is used to write their shuddering, the blood of the tongue—their own blood—does not run dry, no matter what tongue it is, nor what rhythm nor what words are finally chosen. (212)

In this passage Djebar is contemplating her writing project in a textual gesture that she has adopted in many of her works, most notably in *L'amour*. When students encounter a paragraph like this one for the first time, they often need some guidance to fully appreciate the depth of its message. I invite them to read these words aloud, paying attention to cadence, intonation, and accentuation. I continue our discussion of the two meanings of *tongue* and suggest that we expand our understanding of the book's title to include the plurality of languages that have an influence on Djebar's writing in French. When Djebar questions the use of writing the stories of her countrywomen while she is far from her homeland during the dark decade of civil war in Algeria, she is also questioning her ability to accomplish the task of the translator, and students are quick to pick up on this doubt in her work.[3] I ask them to remain attuned, when they read, to the presence of what critic Anne Donadey has referred to as "multilingual strategies." I caution them that they will have to be on the alert, for these strategies are not limited to an occasional term in italics; the polyphonic nature of Djebar's writing reflects innovation in phrasing and syntax that is connected to her familiarity with other forms of communication.

The short stories that make up *Tongue's Blood* draw the students' attention to language in ways that are thematic as well as stylistic. For instance, "Annie and Fatima" recounts a French mother's attempt to connect with a daughter she has not seen in years. In order to properly communicate with her daughter, Fatima, Annie studies the Berber language in Paris, trying to become proficient in " 'la langue de la fille'! Une langue non plus de l'origine, mais de son avenir" (228; "'the language of the daughter'! The language not of her origins, but of her future" [134]). When she finally reunites with her daughter in Algeria, she not only speaks to her in this language but also provides her with written comments, in Latin and Tifinagh (a Berber language). In "The Attack," Arabic terms such as *chouyoukh* are explained in the text, and a number of French expressions are encased in quotation marks, including "main tendue" ("reaching out"), "responsable" ("responsible"), and "portes" ("carries") (144–45; 86). Placing words in quotes heightens our awareness of how they are being employed; it calls attention to the fact that these are loaded terms, that they may be euphemisms, and that they signal other ways of speaking—and thinking. The term *carry* is explained later, in the short story "Félicie's Body." Students find this tale of a French mother's passing away to be compelling, and when I invite them to compare the treatment of elderly people in their own society with the familial fidelity depicted in this short story, they focus on this word, which communicates a tradition: "elle, ta fille, elle 'te porte'—comme on dit en arabe dialectal pour les soins du corps de l'autre, du corps souffrant: non pas assister, mais 'porter' un vieux père ou une mère" (279–80; "she, your daughter, she 'carries you'—as one says in [dialectal] Arabic about someone taking care of another's suffering body. Not helping, but 'carrying' an old father or mother" [163]). This passage sheds light on connotations of the word *porter*, which are significant in the first passage my students encounter, the one from *L'amour* that they study in depth and translate themselves.

In "Félicie's Body," students come to an untranslatable notion that impresses them and often appears in their essays. The women of Oran respect the Frenchwoman of the story's title so much that they attribute a "qualité spécifiquement musulmane" ("specifically Muslim quality") to her: "*Nya*, c'est la *nya* que possède cette *roumia*!" (255; "*Nya*, this *roumia* has *nya*!" [150]). Félicie, though she is a foreigner with different beliefs, is seen as possessing "cette bonne foi qui est la bienveillance, ou l'attention silencieuse aux autres, à tous les gens simples" (333; "this good faith which is a kind of benevolence, or a silent respect for others, for all people" [191]). I ask students to create a list of new vocabulary words for each of the short stories in this volume, and the list for "Félicie's Body" has not only *nya* and *roumia* but also *pieds-noirs* and *harkis*. Definitions can sometimes be found in the text itself, as in the explanatory phrases that attempt to capture the essence of *nya*, but some terms are not paraphrased or glossed in any way. I take advantage of our classroom discussions to address the words that are unfamiliar to American students but not to French readers.

What most impresses my students in *Tongue's Blood* is the text's attention throughout to names and their meanings in Algeria and to their ultimate untranslatability, because in this country what one is called is intimately tied to what one believes. Students analyze the names that are bestowed on Félicie's children: born to a French mother and an Arab father, they all bear both a

French name and an Algerian one. Students are fascinated by the children's choice to create a similar second name for their mother when she dies and the concomitant decision to make her Muslim so that her body may be transferred from Paris to Oran and buried beside her husband. In their study of "Oran, Dead Language," students understand the importance of names and their consequences. Thomas Dugan, one of the students, writes:

> Djebar depicts the narrator's troublesome situation particularly well when she discusses the different roles that French and Arabic played in her identification of "mother." While terming her birth mother the French "Maman" and her aunt, who fills the void of the mother role, the Oranian Arabic "Mma," the author plays on the idea of the battle between the two cultures in the immigrant individual. Though she always accepts her mother as "Maman," this Francophone identification is a particularly ironic title for the adult narrator, considering her mother's death at the hands of Frenchmen. This sentiment is felt in her graveside declaration "'Maman!' I called her by the French 'Maman'—she who was assassinated by the French." . . . It is of particular note that it is difficult for the narrator to identify which mother is her true mother, much as it is difficult for her to decide whether France or Algeria is her true homeland.

Dugan's comments were written after two class sessions devoted to the short story "Oran, Dead Language," during which students responded to sets of questions about the oral epistolary form; terms of endearment and their translatability or untranslatability; official terminology; the use of French in the English-language text during the crucial altercation between the young girl and the Frenchwoman in the hospital; the title; the writing project and its relation to memory. I am convinced that Dugan's insight bears witness to the fact that bringing students to concentrate on the linguistic layers of Djebar's writing provides them with invaluable tools for teasing out the multiple meanings of language, even—or perhaps especially—in translation.

NOTES

[1]Students are often impressed by the replacement of the word *silence* with *death* in the English translation of the passage from *L'amour*. This observation usually provokes productive discussion about whether or not there is a connection between silence and death, and what the relation between the two might be for a woman writer from Algeria.

[2]Although this double meaning exists in both French and English, *langue* is a nearly inescapable homonym in French, whereas in English *tongue* is usually considered an intentional synonym. It is not uncommon to use the word *tongue* to refer to language in English, but this usage is most often limited to certain fixed expressions (such as "mother tongue"), and people generally choose *language* on a regular basis.

[3]I share with students other reflections by Djebar that address the difficulty of rendering the words of Algerian women in the French-language text, such as this quotation from *L'amour*: "Ta voix s'est prise au piège; mon parler français la déguise sans l'habiller. À peine si je frôle l'ombre de ton pas!" (202; "I have captured your voice; disguised it with my French without clothing it. I barely brush the shadow of your footsteps!" [142]). I put students in touch with the original French and explore with them other possible English versions. Students typically emphasize the notion of *piège* ("trap") in the original and seek a formulation that fully renders it in English. For them, *capture* has positive overtones that they do not believe Djebar was attempting to convey.

How to Teach Assia Djebar: An Afterword

Gayatri Chakravorty Spivak

The second time we met, on a long walk through the streets of Paris, Djebar called me her twin sister. I have tried to rise to that responsibility here, to encounter myself in her texts.

For me, it is difficult to restrict Djebar to any one approach or any one context. Commenting on some archive footage of the 1960s anticolonial struggles in Mozambique and Angola, I wrote, a couple of days ago:

> Although liberation struggles force women into an apparent equality—starting with the nineteenth century or even earlier—when the dust settles, the so-called postcolonial nation goes back to the invisible long-term structures of gendering. The most moving shot of this film is the black Venus, reminding us of the Venus of Milo with her arm gone, who is also a black Madonna, suckling a child with bare breasts. This icon must remind us all that the endorsement of rape continues not only in war but also, irrespective of whether a nation is developing or developed, in women fighting in legitimized armies. Colonizer and colonized are united in the violence of gendering, which often celebrates motherhood with genuine pathos.

I realized later that this entire insight came to me from Djebar in "Forbidden Gaze, Severed Sound." This is the nature of my debt to Djebar. In many different contexts lessons learned from her writings crop up to help me to think. Who can forget such tremendous insights as the locked steel car with the modern Algerian woman driving as still a veil? Beyond the veil, the insight travels into the gated community as prison.

These essays come from *Women of Algiers in Their Apartment*, a jeweled, personal book, presenting Algeria as a space of desire. Yet, just as W. E. B. Du Bois should not be defined on the basis of his jewel-like *Souls*, so should Assia Djebar not be defined on the basis of this iconic text alone.

Djebar is consistently taught as part of francophone literature. Indeed, she was professor of francophone literature in her last academic position. But her most important stance is against identitarianism. If you cannot say yes to the enemy, you cannot practice freedom—this is imaginative activism.

Thus in the beginning of *Fantasia*, she tries to gaze at her hometown as the conqueror did. You cannot enter the conqueror's mind-set—capture his gaze—without sympathy. This is the opening of her book, and it makes a tremendous impact on the careful reader—invites the reader to a sort of imaginative activism, which is a complicity, a folded-togetherness between metropolitan French and the francophone world, if you like. Her embrace of Camus, full of nuanced detail, is a mark of this complicity. The double bind of *francophonie* for an Arab woman of her generation, denied entry into written Arabic, is of course part of Djebar's theme. French is manifest because Arabic as writing medium can only be desired. That desire describes a huge *paraphe* all across her work, broken by an early decision that legitimized a mere polarization: I will not write in French but make a film. The result is the exquisite *Nouba of Women from Mount Chenoua*, which won the Fipresci (International Federation of Film Critics) Prize at Venice, and *Zerda and the Songs of Forgetting*, winning a prize in Berlin in 1983.

Of course she could not remain within that unproblematic ritualization of the split between the verbal and the visual. In 1982 she starts her magisterial Algeria quartet. At the close of *Fantasia*, the first novel, she gives us the best metaphor for the double bind of *francophonie*: her father's traditional decision to marry her off, as a child bride, to the French language. Wow! This so resonates with my more feebly expressed conviction that the bride in traditional exogamy is the originary diasporic, redefining exile, that I rejoice.

Typically, Djebar genders exile, breaks it between دين (din; "faith") and دنيا (dunya; "world"). "Il n'y a pas d'exil" ("There Is No Exile"), says the man of faith, as the devout woman reports. The worldly woman, the same one, defines true exile. The sequence is split by a wordless woman's voice, outside the frame (*Women* 72–73). This already enriches Said's sense of the exilic, and, if there is no out-text (Derrida, *Of Grammatology* 158), there are texts of many weaves in Djebar. In the rest of *Fantasia*, a plethora of metaphors stages the inability to grip this double bind in a single articulation. The autobiographical subject's personal reaction to women's orality is just as doubly bound. But collectively it is seen as memory chains—not history but the *longue durée* in fiction, its appropriate habitat—imaginatively recreating the ancestress of ancestresses whom no soldier was to describe. Literature is not evidence but an instrument for imaginative training. A defense of fiction, if you like, over against the coarser contemporary trend to privatize historiography by so-called cultural memory.

This fiction has a broad field. "My first stirrings of religious feeling go back much further," to the "Ballad of Abraham" in the village, which gives to Sarah "her say" (*Women* 170–71). Read this with Jacques Derrida and Gianni Vattimo locating the ethical moment of the Abrahamic there in the negotiation between God and Abraham regarding Ishmael. (Incidentally, she was not influenced by Lacan and Derrida, except insofar as they were in the Parisian air; on a humbler scale comparable to my relation to the work of Edward Said.) Toni Morrison had maternalized the story and made the murder happen. So does Djebar's text in other ways. The women's chants make Sarah speak. *Francophonie* is the textual blank in her story—so that we are obliged to look at the interstices where Arabic makes its entrance, as with Lla Zohra's intervention (186–88), rewriting Friedrich Nietzsche's Baubo (8)—postreproductive women—into figureheads at the prow of memory; riffing Islamic feminism in reporting the aunt's triumphal repetition of a verse in the Qur'an that would prove to her that "woman was historically the first to adhere to the Islamic faith" (172); and the mother's publicly passing on the Qur'anic injunction to read to a girl child; trumping Salman Rushdie in acknowledging pre-Islamic goddesses available through her second mother tongue: Lybico-Berber. I have laid out other connections with Derrida in "Ghostwriting." Her excavating reimagining through musical form is most specifically true, of course, of *Far from Madina*, but as a theme it is present and beckoning in all her writing, as the essays in this collection note in many ways. Djebar's main intent is thus not, specifically, to be true to her Arabic sources in *Madina*, but rather respectfully to transgress and imagine and flesh out the moments where women make their appearance. Her opera *Daughters of Ishmael in Wind and Storm*, shown in Rome and New York, gives us a sense of this intent.

From her *Children of the New World*, which should be read with Frantz Fanon's *Wretched of the Earth* to gender the scene, to *The Tongue's Blood Does Not Run Dry*, written in 1997, belonging to the trajectory where fiction and historiography merge and the inevitable failure of decolonization is spelled out, her work calls for an "absolute reader," as Djebar remarks in the afterword to *The Tongue's Blood*, echoing Francis Ponge, a male French writer. The self-inflicted death of the absolute reader—an extreme image of reading—will assuage nothing (214, 215). History will continue to hurt. Such an exhortation should be remembered by every reader of a how-to-read book, for every "correct" reading will by that very claim undo itself: fiction's greatest lesson—who wins loses. So much said, let us also offer a description in the most abject formula, today trivialized in the United States: This book shows what "the personal is political" can really mean. Mature sexuality, women as teachers, daughters, mothers, wives, sisters of brothers, French gone Arab gone Berber gone French, and so on indefinitely. The history that can heal but will not be allowed to because men under colonization have had no practice of freedom and will kill. The double bind of the commitment to the named country—which is yet emptied of its name, becoming what a Lacanian might call a *parole vide* ("an empty word"), pushing into a Paris of exile—runs through many permutations.

The emptying of the name of Algeria is consummated at the end of *So Vast the Prison*. Djebar takes enormous risks here, laying out the themes of her fiction in a cinematic style, keeping the responsible reader working at transitions: a detailed account of sexuality, a plunge into the *longue durée* of history, filmmaking as turning the حيك (haik; a traditional Algerian women's covering) inside out in the camera's little eye, Carthage and the Berber script, and finally the bloody Algeria of retaliatory violence. If women's suffering is vast and generalized, death by torture, knife, bullet, throttling, and rape is narrow. We are brought here by way of many effacements (as in the section titles) to the imagined death—but also a historical fact—of the Berber hero Jugurtha in a Roman dungeon more than two thousand years ago, uttered in the tongue of the Berbers. Now narrow equals vast equals narrow in an abyssal structure of internal and external violence. In Jugurtha, as in Eugène Delacroix's painting, she touches continental Africa. In the painting, it is the walking stance of the black woman that will lead us out of the freeze. And Jugurtha is the first African Lumumba, betrayed by his own kind in collusion with the imperialists. "The blood of History and . . . the oppression of women," she writes in parenthesis at the end of this anguished book that took her seven years to write (*So Vast* 347). In the end, she makes the narrator—Isma, "the name" (341), and that naming is staged in the staggering last movement—act out absolute readership, wounding her body's voice machinery deeper and deeper with a knife. Her exile is now described bitterly as "fugitive and knowing it" (359).

(Djebar is not an essentialist in her depiction of women's desire. This is not expository prose, nor straightforward autobiography, if there is such a thing. The sentiments belong to Isma, a narrative character. And what is the pun between *arable* and *Arabe*, with the "l" (*elle*; "she") in between? Only by way of the structural labor of the author as sign must we connect it to Assia Djebar, moving on to Fatima Zohra Imalhayene (Djebar's name at birth), remembering that the intertextuality of life and fiction is elusive and must be worked at, elaborated. This is where most criticism of Djebar goes astray, taking the staging of autobiography as autobiography as such.)

If in *So Vast the Prison* absolute readership is staged, it prepares us for *Algerian White*, where Djebar, as mourner graduating from solitude to collectivity, is herself the absolute reader of that "blurred and broken white [from which she] reconstructs the margin" (229; trans. modified), as she writes, quoting André du Bouchet. It is hard to advise a way to read this book: as if, as readers, we are eavesdropping? The beginning is an intimate act of mourning, addressing three friends recently assassinated by Islamists in Algeria. But then, from the personal she turns to the political of the *longue durée*, the recounting of the facts of death, even as Fatna lets her assassinated husband be given over to the immensely extended family for burial, not the nuclearity of only wife and children. From this recounting she goes to the minutiae of the failure of decolonization already lurking in the tremendous treacheries of the nationalist struggle. The form is a procession of the dead. In the manner of Ernesto Cardenal's "Prayer for Marilyn Monroe," she mingles the assassinated with the "naturally" dead, those who died of disease, accident, suicide. As in all her work, she transforms the wisdom song, reminding us of African writers such as Ama Ata Aidoo. She comes out of the somewhat single-issue woman focus that she has sometimes had: "It is no longer just the night of women separated, isolated, exploited as mere child-bearers . . ." (*So Vast* 217). Here more than ever, Djebar, an abiding pacifist obliged to inhabit violence, brings colonial and postcolonial violence together, exclaiming, with Josie Fanon, Frantz's widow, in October, 1988: "*Once more, O Frantz, the 'wretched of the earth!'*" (92).

The question of language, as the essays in this collection have noted in many different ways, is all over the consideration of colonialism passing into the failure of decolonization. Languages of power: Latin, Arabic, Turkish, and now the confected Arabic that is the "national language" of Algeria. She closes with a mysterious question: "The white of writing in a non-translated Algeria?" (229). We cannot catalog Djebar only under *francophonie*. Her French shares more with Édouard Glissant's *créolisation* ("creolization"). And it is significant that she records it not only via the written Andalusian dialect دارجة (darija) of her mother's ancestry but also via Dante:

> Already six and a half centuries ago, someone called Dante, permanently exiled from his city, Florence, was to call this language "the illustrious common speech." "We call it illustrious because, illuminating and illuminated, it shines forth," he added. . . . So it is, my friends, when they speak to me, and if I could catch at least a little of their language "linked with poetry"; Dante compares this language of the absent dear to us, who in order to approach us defy the refrigerating frontier of our lives behind which we take on weight, Dante compares this language—which is like yours, when, impalpably, you come back to me—to the "perfumed panther," the mythical animal of medieval bestiaries. (52; trans. modified)

(I received a letter yesterday from Davide Messina, an Italian now teaching at the University of Edinburgh, saying, "I remember that you asked me what I thought of Dante's idea of 'creolization'" in *De vulgari eloquentia*—I had not read *Algerian White* yet—"and, to be honest, I had never considered this. Only after a while I realized how important this open critical view was for my approach to Italian studies." Resonance.)

Nulle part dans la maison de mon père ("No Place in My Father's House") is dedicated to me. At the beginning of our friendship, in the late eighties, I had been drawn to Djebar because she had acknowledged Bengali as an Islamic language in her *Women of Algiers*, drawn not so much on my behalf as on behalf of my friend Farhad Mazhar, whose brilliant poem of taking Bengali away from Allah, turning the general nonrecognition of Bengali around quite as the eye of the camera turns the *haik* around for Djebar, I had translated. In *Nulle part*, thinking that I could share in her predicament, she considers the double-edged gift of the veil of the French language and culture from her father, without access to either the women's or the men's world fully, and she generalizes her intensely private story. The theme of self-effacement is center stage. To respond to this responsibility, I point to my development of the idea of being married to colonialism in the very same essay ("Situating") in which I present the thought of the bride as diasporic.

How to teach Assia Djebar? This collection provides many important approaches and deeply contextual information. Much of what I have written is repetition. I have not written for scholarly annotation but rather to insist that teaching reading is imaginative training for epistemological performance. Most of the essays in this collection are aware of this need, but it bears repetition. Arab students, Arab American students, Algerian students, Algerian American students, male students, female students, religious students, secular students, religious-secular students, ideologically "American" students, ideologically "radical" students, Left students, hexagonal students, French American students, French Empire students, French Empire–American students, feminist students, just-managing-an-easy-elective students, comparative literature students, francophone studies students, Research 1 University students, liberal arts college students—all will react differently to her texts, of course. These are the exhilarating risks and challenges of acknowledging the global diversities of new histories, new geographies. I have therefore used my privilege as afterworder to try to speak to the contingency of her writing rather than to its categorizability—a supplement to the essays in this collection. The essays themselves will be altogether more useful in the classroom (and useful to me when I teach not only Djebar but other texts in translation).

Assia Djebar was a cosmopolitan, a star, a francophone writer, a feminist. In this afterword, I have also tried to suggest that each of these descriptions is problematized in her work, as indeed the writers of these essays have suggested. To be a star is to be nowhere in her father's house. To be a feminist is to generalize women's oppression. *Francophonie* is a labyrinth of double binds, an enabling violation, a distancing from the oral, the originary. And cosmopolitanism—where her rescuers are Ibn Khaldun, Augustine, and Pauline Rolland—is the choice of an elsewhere, as Djebar makes clear in *Algerian White*. Keep these problems alive as you necessarily solve them in order to teach her; she is herself your best guide. I say this because in my global peregrinations I see unconditional ethics transformed into knowledge management with toolkits. In Djebar's defense of fiction (and mine too, يا [ya] Assia), we hold out for the imagination.

NOTE

A shorter version of this piece appeared in *Frontier*, vol. 48, nos. 14–17, 11 Oct.–7 Nov. 2015, and in the fall 2016 issue of *Romanic Review*.

NOTES ON CONTRIBUTORS

Diya Abdo is associate professor of English at Guilford College. Her recent research and publications focus on Arab women writers' narrative strategies, Islamic feminism, and life writing. She is the founder of Every Campus a Refuge.

Maria Bobroff is associate professor of French at Guilford College. Her research focuses on eighteenth-century French theater and language pedagogy.

Carine Bourget is professor of French and francophone studies at the University of Arizona. She is the author of *Coran et tradition islamique dans la littérature maghrébine* and *The Star, the Cross, and the Crescent: Religions and Conflicts in Francophone Literature from the Arab World*.

Maya Boutaghou is assistant professor of French at the University of Virginia. She is the author of *Occidentalismes*: *Romans historiques post-coloniaux et identités nationales*.

Valérie J. Budig-Markin is professor emerita of French and francophone studies and chair of the Department of World Languages and Cultures at Humboldt State University. She is the coauthor, with James Gaasch, of *Diversité: La nouvelle francophone à travers le monde*.

Thérèse De Raedt is associate professor of French at the University of Utah. Her research has focused on the representation of Africans in eighteenth- and nineteenth-century French literature and visual arts, holiday resorts conceived as postcolonial utopian spaces, and French and francophone cross-cultural relations.

Anne Donadey is professor of French and francophone studies and of women's studies at San Diego State University. She is the author of *Recasting Postcolonialism: Women Writing between Worlds*, coeditor of *Postcolonial Theory and Francophone Literary Studies*, and coeditor of the second edition of *Women in Culture: An Intersectional Anthology for Gender and Women's Studies*.

Hanan Elsayed is assistant professor of French and Arabic at Occidental College. She is the author of *L'histoire sacrée de l'Islam dans la fiction maghrébine* (2016). She is the coeditor, with Warren Montag, of a collection on the work of Etienne Balibar titled *Balibar and the Citizen Subject* (2017).

Dominique D. Fisher is professor of French and francophone studies at the University of North Carolina, Chapel Hill. She is the author of *Écrire l'urgence* and articles on the literatures and films of the Maghreb, Lebanon, and Québec. She is presently working on a book on franco-arabophone films.

Martine Guyot-Bender is professor of French literature and cultures at Hamilton College. She is the author of *Mémoire en derive: Poétique et politique de l'ambiguïté chez Patrick Modiano* and coauthor of *Paradigms of Memory: The Occupation and Other Hi/Stories in Patrick Modiano's Fiction*. She specializes in modern novels and documentary films that focus on the memory of war, social conflict, and trauma.

Christa Jones is associate professor of French and associate department head of Languages, Philosophy, and Communication Studies at Utah State University. She is the author of *Cave Culture in Maghrebi Literature: Imagining Self and Nation* (2012), the coeditor of *Women from the Maghreb* (2014), and the coeditor of *New Approaches to Teaching Folk- and Fairy Tales* (2016).

Kathryn Lachman is associate professor of French and comparative literature at the University of Massachusetts, Amherst. She is the author of *Borrowed Forms: The Music and Ethics of Transnational Fiction* (2014) and the coeditor of *Feasting on Words: Maryse Condé, Cannibalism, and the Caribbean Text*.

Mildred Mortimer is professor emerita in the Department of French and Italian at the University of Colorado, Boulder, and research associate in the Department of European Languages at the University of Pretoria, South Africa. Her most recent books are *Writing from the Hearth: Public, Domestic and Imaginative Space in Francophone Women's Fiction of Africa and the Caribbean* and the edited volume *Maghrebian Mosaic: A Literature in Transition*.

Najat Rahman is professor of comparative literature at the University of Montreal. She is the author of *In the Wake of the Poetic: Palestinian Artists after Darwish* and *Literary Disinheritance: The Writing of Home in the Work of Mahmoud Darwish and Assia Djebar*.

Alison Rice is associate professor of French and francophone studies at the University of Notre Dame. She is the author of *Time Signatures: Contextualizing Contemporary Autobiographical Writing from the Maghreb* and *Polygraphies: Francophone Women Writing Algeria*.

Annica Schjött Vonèche holds a PhD in French and francophone studies and an MA in learning sciences from Northwestern University. She has taught language and literature classes at Northwestern and at the University of Paris 1 Panthéon-Sorbonne and is currently working at Boston University.

Gayatri Chakravorty Spivak is University Professor at Columbia University. Her latest books are *Other Asias*, *An Aesthetic Education in the Era of Globalization*, and *Readings*.

Dana Strand is Andrew W. Mellon Professor of French and the Humanities emerita at Carleton College. Her research interests include film, North African literature, and postcolonial studies.

Vlatka Velčić is professor of comparative literature at California State University, Long Beach. She is the author of essays on the Croatian writer Dubravka Ugrešić and the Serbian filmmaker Emir Kusturica.

SURVEY PARTICIPANTS

Wendy W. Allen, Saint Olaf College
Susan Andrade, University of Pittsburgh
Yifen Beus, Brigham Young University, Hawai'i
Maria Bobroff, Guilford College
Maya Boutaghou, Florida International University
Katharine (Kate) Conley, Dartmouth College
Hanan Elsayed, Occidental College
Dominique D. Fisher, University of North Carolina, Chapel Hill
Martine Guyot-Bender, Hamilton College
Irene Ivantcheva-Merjanska, University of Cincinnati
Timothy B. Johns, Murray State University
Christa Jones, Utah State University
Mildred Mortimer, University of Colorado, Boulder
Jessica Nyamugusha, Glenelg Country High School, MD
Valérie K. Orlando, University of Maryland, College Park
Dayna Oscherwitz, Southern Methodist University
Thérèse De Raedt, University of Utah
Najat Rahman, Université de Montréal
Felisa V. Reynolds, University of Saint Thomas
Alison Rice, University of Notre Dame
Dana Strand, Carleton College
Vlatka Velčić, California State University, Long Beach

WORKS CITED

"À Alger, Hollande reconnaît les souffrances de la colonisation." *Le point*. Le Point, 20 Dec. 2012. Web. 26 Nov. 2015. <http://www.lepoint.fr/politique/le-discours-de-francois-hollande-a-alger-accueilli-positivement-20–12-2012–1604413_20>.

Abu-Lughod, Lila. *Veiled Sentiments. Honor and Poetry in a Bedouin Society*. Berkeley: U of California P, 2000. Print.

Accad, Evelyne. "Assia Djebar's Contribution to Arab Women's Literature: Rebellion, Maturity, Vision." *World Literature Today* 70.4 (1996): 801–12. Print.

Achebe, Chinua. "The African Writer and the English Language." Williams and Chrisman 428–34.

———. *Things Fall Apart*. New York: Anchor, 1994. Print.

ACTFL Proficiency Guidelines 2012. ACTFL, n.d. Web. 26 Nov. 2015.

Ahmed, Leila. "Feminism and Cross-Cultural Inquiry: The Terms of the Discourse in Islam." *Coming to Terms: Feminism, Theory, Politics*. Ed. Elizabeth Weed. New York: Routledge, 1989. 143–51. Print.

———. Interview. *Women and Islam*. Films for the Humanities and Sciences, 1994. Videocassette.

———. *A Quiet Revolution: The Veil's Resurgence, from the Middle East to America*. New Haven: Yale UP, 2011. Print.

———. "Western Ethnocentrism and Perceptions of the Harem." *Feminist Studies* 8.3 (1982): 521–34. Print.

———. *Women and Gender in Islam: Historical Roots of a Modern Debate*. New Haven: Yale UP, 1992. Print.

Aïcha. Dir. Yamina Benguigui. Perf. Biyouna, Rabia Mokkedem, and Farida Khelfa. Paris: France Télévision Distribution, 2009. DVD.

Algeria: The Life and Death of Algerian Journalists. Dir. Merzak Allouache and John Matshikiza. Cape Town: Common Ground Productions, 1997. VHS.

Algeria: Women at War. Dir. Parminder Vir. Women Make Movies, 1992. Film.

Algérie, 1998–2000: Autopsie d'une tragédie. Dir. Séverine Labat and Malik Aït-Aoudia. Paris: Compagnie des Phares et Balises, 2003–05. DVD.

Algérie(s). Dir. Thierry Leclère, Malek Bensmaïl, and Patrice Barrat. Paris: Montparnasse, 2004. DVD.

Algiers, 1957: The Lady Carriers of Fire. Dir. Faouzia Fekiri. BFC productions; France 3, 2007. Film.

Allende, Isabel. *The House of the Spirits*. New York: Bantam, 1993. Print.

Alloula, Malek. *The Colonial Harem*. Trans. Myrna Godzich and Wlad Godzich. Minneapolis: U of Minnesota P, 1986. Print.

———. *Le harem colonial: Images d'un sous-érotisme*. Geneva: Slatkine, 1981. Print.

Al-Nakib, Mai. "Assia Djebar's Musical Ekphrasis." *Comparative Literature Studies* 42.4 (2005): 253–76. Print.

Altes, Liesbeth Korthals. "Identité, mémoire, fantasme dans *L'amour, la fantasia* de Assia Djebar." *Colonizer and Colonized*. Ed. Theo d'Haen and Patricia Krüs. Amsterdam: Rodopi, 1999. 433–49. Print.

Amireh, Amal. "Writing the Difference: Feminists' Invention of the 'Arab Woman.'" *Interventions: Feminist Dialogues on the Third World Women's Literature and Film*. Ed. Brinda Bose and Bishnupriya Ghosh. New York: Garland, 1997. 185–211. Print.

Amrane-Minne, Danièle Djamila. *Les femmes algériennes dans la guerre*. Paris: Plon, 1991. Print.

———. "Women and Politics in Algeria from the War of Independence to Our Day." *Research in African Literatures* 30.3 (1999): 62–77. Print.

———. "Women at War: The Representation of Women in *The Battle of Algiers*." Trans. Alistair Clarke. *Interventions* 9.3 (2007): 340–49. Print.

Amrouche, Jean. *Chants Berbères de Kabylie*. 1942. Paris: L'Harmattan, 1986. Print.

Apter, Emily. "On Translation in a Global Market." *Public Culture* 13.1 (2001): 1–12. Print.

———. "Out of Character: Camus's French Algerian Subjects." *Modern Language Notes* 112.4 (1997): 499–516. Print.

———. *The Translation Zone: A New Comparative Literature*. Princeton: Princeton UP, 2006. Print.

Ashcroft, Bill, Gareth Griffiths, and Helen Tiffin. *The Empire Writes Back: Theory and Practice in Postcolonial Literatures*. Abingdon: Routledge, 1989. Print.

Asholt, Wolfgang, Mireille Calle-Gruber, and Dominique Combe, eds. *Assia Djebar, littérature et transmission*. Paris: Sorbonne Nouvelle, 2010. Print.

Assia Djebar: Entre ombre et soleil. Dir. Kamal Dehane. CBA; ENPA; Zeaux, 1992. Videocassette.

Assia Djebar: 1996 Neustadt International Prize for Literature. Spec. issue of *World Literature Today* 70.4 (1996): 777–1040. Print.

Austin, John L. *How to Do Things with Words*. Ed. J. O. Urmson. Oxford: Clarendon, 1962. Print.

Bab El Oued City. Dir. Merzak Allouache. Perf. Nadia Kaci, Mohamed Ourdache, Hassan Abdou, Messaoud Hattou, Michel Such, and Nadia Samir. Blaq Out, 1994. DVD.

Bab el Web. Dir. Mezak Allouache. Perf. Samy Naceri, Faudel, Julie Gayet, Valmont, and D. J. Abdel. France 3, 2005. DVD.

Badawi, M. M. "Islam in Modern Egyptian Literature." *Journal of Arabic Literature* 2 (1971): 154–76. Print.

Badran, Margot. "Feminisms and Islamisms." *Journal of Women's History* 10.4 (1999): 196–204. Print.

———. *Islamic Feminism Revisited*. Countercurrents.org, 10 Feb. 2006. Web. 19 Feb. 2013.

———. "Islamic Feminism: What's in a Name?" *Al-Ahram Weekly* 56 (2002): 17–23. Print.

Badran, Margot, and Miriam Cooke, eds. *Opening the Gates: A Century of Arab Feminist Writing*. Bloomington: Indiana UP, 1990. Print.

Balzac, Honoré de. *La fille aux yeux d'or*. Paris: Slatkine, 1996. Print.

Barakat! Dir. Djamila Sahraoui. Perf. Rachida Brakni, Fettouma Bouamari, and Zahir Bouzrar. First Run Features, 2006. DVD.

Barthes, Roland. *Mythologies*. 1957. Paris: Seuil, 1970. Print.

———. *S/Z*. Trans. Richard Miller. Malden: Blackwell, 1990. Print.

The Battle of Algiers. Dir. Gillo Pontecorvo. 1966. Film.

Bazin, André. "Every Film Is a Social Documentary." Trans. Paul Fileri. *Film Comment* 44.6 (2008): 40–41. Print.

Beaumont, Peter. "Albert Camus, the Outsider, Is Still Dividing Opinion in Algeria Fifty Years after His Death." *Guardian*. Guardian News and Media, 27 Feb. 2010. Web. 26 Nov. 2015.

Bedjaoui, Youcef, et al., eds. *An Inquiry into the Algerian Massacres*. Plan-les-Ouates: Hoggar, 1999. Print.

Benjamin, Walter. "The Task of the Translator." Trans. Harry Zohn. Venuti 15–23.

Ben Jelloun, Tahar. *L'enfant de sable*. Paris: Seuil, 1985. Print.

———. *La fiancée de l'eau suivi de Entretien avec Monsieur Saïd Hammadi, ouvrier algérien*. Paradou: Actes Sud, 1984. Print.

———. *The Sand Child*. Trans. Alan Sheridan. London: Quartet, 1988. Print.

Benlyazid, Farida, dir. *Ruses de femmes (Keid Ensa / Women's Wiles)*. Brussels Avenue, 1999. Film.

Bennoune, Karima. *Your Fatwa Does Not Apply Here: Untold Stories from the Fight against Muslim Fundamentalism*. London: Norton, 2013. Print.

Bensmaia, Reda. "*La nouba des femmes du Mont Chenoua*: Introduction to the Cinematic Fragment." Trans. Jennifer Curtiss Gage. *World Literature Today* 70.4 (1996): 877–84. Print.

Berger, Anne-Emmanuelle, ed. *Algeria in Others' Languages*. Ithaca: Cornell UP, 2002. Print.

Bernard, Philippe, and Nathaniel Herzberg, eds. *Lettres d'Algérie*. Paris: Gallimard, 1998. Print.

Bigelow, Gordon. "Revolution and Modernity: Assia Djebar's *Les enfants du nouveau monde*." *Research in African Literatures* 34.2 (2003): 13–27. Print.

Bint al-Shati'. تراجم سيدات بيت النبوة [Tarajim sayyidat bayt al-nubuwwa; "Biographies of the Women of the Prophet's Household"]. 5 vols. Cairo: Dar al-Hilal and Shirkat al-ʿArabiyya; Beirut: Dar al-Kitab al-ʿArabi, 1956–84. Print.

Bourdieu, Pierre. *The Algerians*. Trans. Alan C. M. Ross. Boston: Beacon, 1962. Print.

———. *Sociologie de l'Algérie*. Paris: PUF, 1963. Print.

Bourget, Carine. *Coran et tradition islamique dans la littérature maghrébine*. Paris: Karthala, 2002. Print.

———. "*Kaidakunna ʿadhimoun* Revisited: Farida Benlyazid's *Ruses de femmes* and Assia Djebar's *La beauté de Joseph*." *French Review* 86.1 (2012): 147–59. Print.

———. "La réédition de *Femmes d'Alger dans leur appartement*." *L'Esprit Créateur* 48.4 (2008): 92–103. Print.

Boutaghou, Maya. "Le style en arabesque d'Assia Djebar." *French Studies* 67.2 (2013): 216–31. Print.

Caillé, Patricia. "The Illegitimate Legitimacy of the Battle of Algiers in French Culture." *Interventions* 9.3 (2007): 371–88. Print.

Calle-Gruber, Mireille. *Assia Djebar*. Paris: Association pour la Diffusion de la Pensée Française, 2006. Print.

———, ed. *Assia Djebar, nomade entre les murs: Pour une poétique transfrontalière*. Paris: Maisonneuve, 2005. Print.

———. *Assia Djebar ou la résistance de l'écriture: Regards d'un écrivain d'Algérie*. Paris: Maisonneuve, 2001. Print.

Camus, Albert. *L'étranger*. Paris: Gallimard, 1942. Print.

———. *The First Man*. Trans. David Hapgood. New York: Knopf, 1995. Print.

———. *La peste*. Paris: Gallimard, 1947. Print.

———. *Le premier homme*. Paris: Gallimard, 1994. Print.

Cardenal, Ernesto. "Prayer for Marilyn Monroe." Trans. Jonathan Cohen. *Ricardo Blanco's Blog*. Richard Gwyn, n.d. Web. 7 Feb. 2016.

Caruth, Cathy. *Unclaimed Experience: Trauma, Narrative, and History*. Baltimore: Johns Hopkins UP, 1996. Print.

Çelik, Zeynep. *Urban Forms and Colonial Confrontations: Algiers under French Rule*. Berkeley: U of California P, 1997. Print.

Ceylac, Catherine, and Assia Djebar. "Thé ou café." France 2 (Saturday, 15 Dec. 2007, 7–8 p.m.). Television interview.

Charrad, Mounira M. "Family Law Reforms in the Arab World: Tunisia and Morocco." Report for the United Nations Department of Economic and Social Affairs (UNDESA) Division for Social Policy and Development Expert Group Meeting Good Practices in Family Policy Making: Development, Monitoring and Implementation: Lessons Learnt. United Nations, New York, 15 May 2012. Address.

Chatelard, Marie-Claire. "L'Algérie entre la violence et la parole: Réflexions sur *Oran, langue morte* d'Assia Djebar." *Francophonie et identités culturelles*. Ed. Christine Albert. Paris: Karthala, 1999. 227–40. Print.

Chikhi, Beïda. *Les romans d'Assia Djebar*. Alger: Office des PU, 1990. Print.

Chomsky, Noam. Foreword. Bedjaoui et al. xiii–xv.

Cixous, Hélène. "Bare Feet." *An Algerian Childhood: Collection of Autobiographical Narratives*. Ed. Leïla Sebbar. Trans. Marjolijn de Jager. St. Paul: Ruminator, 2001. 49–60. Print.

———. "My Algeriance, in Other Words: To Depart Not to Arrive from Algeria." Trans. Eric Prenowitz. *Stigmata: Escaping Texts*. New York: Routledge, 1998. 153–72. Print.

———. "Pieds nus." *Enfances algériennes*. Ed. Leïla Sebbar. Paris: Gallimard, 1997. 53–63. Print.

———. *Rêveries de la femme sauvage: Scènes primitives*. Paris: Galilée, 2000. Print.

———. *Reveries of the Wild Woman: Primal Scenes*. Trans. Beverley Bie Brahic. Evanston: Northwestern UP, 2006. Print.

Cooke, Miriam. "Multiple Critique: Islamic Feminist Rhetorical Strategies." *Nepantla: Views from South* 1.1 (2000): 91–110. Print.

Cuddon, J. A. *The Penguin Dictionary of Literary Terms and Literary Theory*. London: Penguin, 1998. Print.

Daeninckx, Didier. *Meurtres pour mémoire*. Paris: Gallimard, 1998. Print.

———. *Murder in Memoriam*. Trans. Liz Heron. Brooklyn: Melville, 2012. Print.

Damrosch, David. "What Is World Literature?" *World Literature: A Reader*. Ed. Theo D'haen, César Domínguez, and Mads Rosendahl Thomsen. London: Routledge, 2013. 198–206. Print.

Daoud, Kamel. *Meursault contre-enquête*. Arles: Actes Sud, 2014. Print.

Darraj, Susan Muaddi. "Understanding the Other Sister: The Case of Arab Feminism." *Monthly Review* 53.10 (2002): 15–25. Print.

Déjeux, Jean. *Assia Djebar: Romancière algérienne, cinéaste arabe*. Sherbrooke: Naaman, 1984. Print.

Delacroix, Eugène. *Death of Sardanapalus*. 1827. Musée du Louvre. Media Commons, n.d. Web. 25 Mar. 2016. < https://commons.wikimedia.org/wiki/File:Eug%C3%A8ne_Delacroix_-_The_Death_of_Sardanapalus_-_WGA6173.jpg>.

———. *Liberty Leading the People*. 1830. Musée du Louvre. Media Commons, n.d. Web. 14 Mar. 2016. <https://commons.wikimedia.org/wiki/File:Eug%C3%A8ne_Delacroix_-_Liberty_Leading_the_People_%2828th_July_1830%29_-_WGA6177.jpg>.

———. *The Massacre at Chios*. 1824. Musée du Louvre. Media Commons, n.d. Web. 14 Mar. 2016. <https://commons.wikimedia.org/wiki/File:Eug%C3%A8ne_Delacroix_-_The_Massacre_at_Chios_-_WGA6163.jpg>.

———. *Odalisque Reclining on a Divan*. 1827 or 1828. Fitzwilliam Museum. Media Commons, n.d. Web. 23 June 2016. < https://commons.wikimedia.org/wiki/File:Eug%C3%A8ne_Delacroix_-_Odalisque_Reclining_on_a_Divan_-_WGA06172.jpg>.

———. *Women of Algiers in Their Apartment*. 1834. Musée du Louvre. Media Commons, n.d. Web. 25 Nov. 2015. <http://commons.wikimedia.org/wiki/File:Eug%C3%A8ne_Delacroix_-_Les_Femmes_d%27Alger.jpg>.

———. *Women of Algiers in Their Apartment*. 1849. Musée Fabre, n.d. Web. 25 Nov. 2015. <http://floramusee.montpellier-agglo.com/flora/servlet/LoginServlet>.

Delbo, Charlotte. *Days and Memory*. Trans. Rosette Lamont. Marlboro: Marlboro, 1990. Print.

———. *La mémoire et les jours*. Paris: Berg Intl., 1985. Print.

Derrida, Jacques. *Limited Inc*. Trans. Samuel Weber and Jeffrey Mehlman. Evanston: Northwestern UP, 1988. Print.

———. *Le monolinguisme de l'autre, ou, La prothèse d'origine*. Paris: Galilée, 1996. Print.

———. *The Monolingualism of the Other*. Trans. Patrick Mensah. Palo Alto: Stanford UP, 1998. Print.

———. *Of Grammatology*. Trans. Gayatri Chakravorty Spivak. Baltimore: Johns Hopkins UP, 1997. Print.

Derrida, Jacques, and Gianni Vattimo, eds. *Religion : Cultural Memory in the Present*. Stanford: Stanford UP, 1996. Print.

Des hommes et des dieux / Of Gods and Men. Dir. Xavier Beauvois. Perf. Jacques Herlin, Lambert Wilson, Michael Lonsdale, Olivier Rabourdin, and Philippe Laudenbach. Artificial Eye, 2011. DVD.

Djaout, Tahar. *Le dernier été de la raison*. Paris: Seuil, 1999. Print.

———. *The Last Summer of Reason*. Trans. Marjolijn de Jager. Lincoln: U of Nebraska P, 2007. Print.

Djebar, Assia. *Algerian White: A Narrative*. Trans. David Kelley and Marjolijn de Jager. New York: Seven Stories, 2000. Print.

———. *Les alouettes naïves*. Paris: Julliard, 1967. Print.

———. *L'amour, la fantasia*. 1985. Paris: Michel; Librairie Générale Française, 1995. Print.

———. "Anamnesis in the Language of Writing." Trans. Anne Donadey with Christi Merrill. *Studies in Twentieth-Century Literature* 23.1 (1999): 179–89. Print.

———. "The Arab Woman as Historian." Humboldt State U. 20 Feb. 1995. Address.

———. "Assia Djebar: Écrire dans la langue *adverse*." Interview by Marguerite Le Clézio. *Contemporary French Civilization* 9.2 (1985): 230–43. Print.

———. *La beauté de Joseph*. Arles: Actes Sud, 1998. Print.

———. *Le blanc de l'Algérie*. Paris: Michel, 1995. Print.

———. *Ces voix qui m'assiègent: En marge de ma francophonie*. Paris: Michel, 1999. Print.

———. *Children of the New World: A Novel of the Algerian War*. Trans. Marjolijn de Jager. New York: Feminist, 2005. Print.

———. "Discours d'entrée à l'Académie Française." Asholt, Calle-Gruber, and Combe 403–18.

———. "Le discours de Francfort." *Études* 395.3 (2001): 235–46. Print.

———. "Le discours de Francfort." *Études* 395.3 (2001): n. pag. Cairn.info, n.d. Web. 13 June 2016. <http://www.cairn.info/revue-etudes-2001–9-page-235.htm>.

———. *Discours de réception, et réponse de Pierre-Jean Rémy*. Académie Française, 22 June 2006. Web. 23 Dec. 2013. < http://academie-francaise.fr /discours-de-reception-et-reponse-de-pierre-jean-remy>.

———. *La disparition de la langue française*. 2003. Paris: Michel; Librairie Générale Française, 2006. Print.

———. *Les enfants du nouveau monde*. 1962. Paris: Seuil, 2012. Print. Collection Points.

———. "Entretien avec Assia Djebar, écrivain algérien." Interview by Mildred Mortimer. *Research in African Literatures* 19.2 (1988): 197–205. Print.

———. "Entretien avec Assia Djebar le 30 mai 1975." By Wadi Bouzar. *Lectures maghrébines*. Algiers: Office des PU; Publisud, 1984. 155–61. Print.

———. *Fantasia: An Algerian Cavalcade*. Trans. and introd. Dorothy S. Blair. London: Quartet, 1989. Print.

———. *Far from Madina: Daughters of Ishmael*. Trans. Dorothy S. Blair. London: Quartet, 1994. Print.

———. *La femme sans sépulture*. Paris: Michel; Librairie Générale Française, 2002. Print.

———. *Femmes d'Alger dans leur appartement*. 1980. Paris: Michel; Librairie Générale Française, 2002. Print.

———. *Filles d'Ismaël dans le vent et la tempête / Figlie di Ismaele, nel vento e nella tempesta*. Firenze: Giunti, 2000. Print.

———. "Forbidden Gaze, Severed Sound." Djebar, *Women* 133–53.

———. *Les impatients*. Paris: Julliard, 1958. Print.

———. *Loin de Médine: Filles d'Ismaël*. Paris: Michel; Librairie Générale Française, 1991. Print.

———. *The Mischief*. Trans. Frances Frenaye. New York: Simon, 1958. Print.

———, dir. *La nouba des femmes du Mont Chenoua*. 1978. Women Make Movies, 2007. DVD.

———. "Les nuits de Ramadan." Preface. *Ramadan: Voyage au cœur d'un rite*. By Angela Grünert and Christel Becker-Rau. Paris: La Martinière, 2001. 10–13. Print.

———. *Les nuits de Strasbourg*. Arles: Actes Sud, 1997. Print.

———. *Nulle part dans la maison de mon père*. Paris: Fayard, 2007. Print.

———. *Ombre sultane*. 1987. Paris: Michel; Librairie Générale Française, 2006. Print.

———. *Oran, langue morte*. Arles: Actes Sud, 1997. Print.

———. *Poèmes pour l'Algérie heureuse*. Algiers: SNED, 1969. Print.

———. "'Silence on Silk'; or, Writing in Flight." Trans. Farida Abu-Haidar. *L'Esprit Créateur* 48.4 (2008): 129–32. Print.

———. *A Sister to Scheherazade*. Trans. Dorothy S. Blair. London: Quartet, 1987. Print.

———. *So Vast the Prison*. Trans. Betsy Wing. New York: Seven Stories, 1999. Print.

———. *La soif*. Paris: Julliard, 1957. Print.

———. "Territoire des langues: Assia Djebar." Interview by Lise Gauvin. *L'écrivain francophone à la croisée des langues: Entretiens*. Paris: Karthala, 1997. 17–34. Print.

———. *The Tongue's Blood Does Not Run Dry: Algerian Stories*. Trans. Tegan Raleigh. New York: Seven Stories, 2006. Print.

———. *Vaste est la prison*. Paris: Michel, 1995. Print.

———. *Women of Algiers in Their Apartment*. Trans. Marjolijn de Jager. Charlottesville: Caraf; UP of Virginia, 1992. Print.

———. *La zerda et les chants de l'oubli*. 1982. YouTube, 9 Nov. 2012. Web. 25 Nov. 2015. <http://www.youtube.com/watch?v=rTid3V6D3gI>.

Djebar, Assia, and Walid Garn. *Rouge l'aube*. Algiers: SNED, 1969. Print.

Dobie, Madeleine. "Francophone Studies and the Linguistic Diversity of the Maghreb." *Comparative Studies of South Asia, Africa and the Middle East* 23.1–2 (2003): 32–40. Print.

Donadey, Anne. "African American and Francophone Postcolonial Memory: Octavia Butler's *Kindred* and Assia Djebar's *La femme sans sépulture*." *Research in African Literatures* 39.3 (2008): 65–81. Print.

———, ed. *Assia Djebar*: L'amour, la fantasia—*avant et après*. Spec. ed. of *L'Esprit Créateur* 48.4 (2008): 1–134. Print.

———. "L'expression littéraire de la transmission du traumatisme dans *La femme sans sépulture* d'Assia Djebar." Asholt, Calle-Gruber, and Combe 67–80.

———. "Introjection and Incorporation in Assia Djebar's *La femme sans sépulture*." *L'Esprit créateur* 48.4 (2008): 81–91. Print.

———. "The Multilingual Strategies of Postcolonial Literature: Assia Djebar's Algerian Palimpsest." *World Literature Today* 74.1 (2000): 27–36. Print.

———. "Overlapping and Interlocking Frames for Humanities Literary Studies: Assia Djebar, Tsitsi Dangarembga, Gloria Anzaldúa." *College Literature* 34.4 (2007): 22–42. Print.

———. *Recasting Postcolonialism: Women Writing between Worlds*. Portsmouth: Heinemann, 2001. Print.

Donner, Fred M. Translator's foreword. *The Conquest of Arabia: The Riddah Wars*. Ed. Donner. Albany: State U of New York P, 1985. xi–xxiii. Print. Vol. 10 of *The History of al-Ṭabarī*.

Dorbani Bouabdellah, Malika. *Femmes d'Alger dans leur appartement*. Paris: Musée du Louvre, 2008. Print.

Ducrot, Oswald, and Jean-Marie Schaeffer. *Nouveau dictionnaire encyclopédique des sciences du langage*. Paris: Seuil, 1995. Print.

Dugan, Thomas. "Cultural Conundrum: The Identity Dilemma in Franco-Algerian Literature." U of Notre Dame. 18 Dec. 2007. TS.

Duras, Marguerite. *Hiroshima, Mon Amour*. Trans. Richard Seaver. New York: Grove, 1994. Print.

El Saadawi, Nawal. "Arab Women and Western Feminism: An Interview with Nawal Al-Saadawi." *Race and Class* 22 (1980): 175–82. Print.

Elsayed, Hanan. "'Silence' and Historical Tradition in Assia Djebar's *Loin de Médine*." *Research in African Literatures* 44.1 (2013): 91–105. Print.

Erickson, John. *Islam and Postcolonial Narrative*. New York: Cambridge UP, 1998. Print.

———. "Translating the Untranslated: Djebar's *Le blanc de l'Algérie*." *Research in African Literatures* 30.3 (1999): 95–107. Print.

Ette, Ottmar. "Expériences sur le savoir-vivre ensemble: Assia Djebar et *Les nuits de Strasbourg*." Trans. Sylvie Mutet. Asholt, Calle-Gruber, and Combe 331–47.

Exils. Dir. Tony Gatlif. Perf. Romain Duris, Lubna Azabal, and Zouhir Gacem. TF1 Vidéos, 2004. DVD.

Fanon, Frantz. "Algeria Unveiled." *A Dying Colonialism*. Trans. Haakon Chevalier. New York: Grove, 1965. 35–67. Print.

———. "L'Algérie se dévoile." *Sociologie d'une révolution: L'an V de la révolution algérienne*. Paris: Maspéro, 1968. 16–50. Print.

———. *The Wretched of the Earth*. Trans. Richard Philcox. New York: Grove, 1963. Print.

Faulkner, Rita. "Psychoanalysis and Anamnesis in the National Allegory of Nawal El Saadawi and Assia Djebar." *L'Esprit Créateur* 48.4 (2008): 69–80. Print.

Fernandes, Martine Manuela. *Les écrivaines francophones en liberté: Farida Belghoul, Maryse Condé, Assia Djebar, Calixthe Beyala: Écritures de l'hybridité postcoloniale et métaphores cognitives*. Paris: L'Harmattan, 2007. Print.

Fisher, Dominique D. *Écrire l'urgence: Assia Djebar et Tahar Djaout*. Paris: L'Harmattan, 2007. Print.

Fromentin, Eugène. *Sahara et Sahel: Un été dans le Sahara [and] Une année dans le Sahel*. Paris: Méditerranée, 2004. Print.

Gaasch, James, and Valérie Budig-Markin. *Diversité: La nouvelle francophone à travers le monde*. Boston: Houghton, 2000. Print.

Gabara, Rachel. *From Split Selves to Screened Selves: French and Francophone Autobiography in the Third Person*. Stanford: Stanford UP, 2006. Print.

Gafaiti, Hafid. "Écriture autobiographique dans l'œuvre d'Assia Djebar: *L'amour, la fantasia*." *Itinéraires et contacts de cultures* 13 (1991): 95–101. Print.

———. *Les femmes dans le roman algérien: Histoire, discours et texte*. Paris: L'Harmattan, 1996. Print.

Gauvin, Lise. "Assia au pays du langage." Calle-Gruber, *Assia Djebar, nomade* 219–29.

Geesey, Patricia. "Collective Autobiography: Algerian Women and History in Assia Djebar's *L'amour, la fantasia*." *Dalhousie French Studies* 35 (1996): 153–67. Print.

Genette, Gérard. *Fiction and Diction*. Ithaca: Cornell UP, 1993. Print.

———. *Paratexts: Thresholds of Interpretation*. Cambridge: Cambridge UP, 1997. Print.

Glissant, Édouard. *Créolisation*. Edouardglissant.fr, n.d. Web. 7 Feb. 2016.

Graebner, Seth. *History's Place: Nostalgia and the City in French Algerian Literature*. Lanham: Lexington, 2007. Print.

Green, Mary Jean. "Assia Djebar in the Twenty-First Century: Rewriting Identities." *Contemporary French and Francophone Studies* 17.1 (2013): 49–57. Print.

Guerre d'Algérie, histoire de l'OAS. *YouTube*. YouTube, 2 Apr. 2010. Web. 26 Nov. 2015. <http://www.youtube.com/watch?v=jw4f4uIqh9k>.

Hammadou, Ghania. "L'auteur répond aux questions d'Algérie." *Littérature / Action* 12–13 (1997): 127–31. Print.

Hanort, Juliet. *La madone de Bentalha: Histoire d'une photographie*. Paris: Colin, 2012. Print.

Harbi, Mohamed. "Violence, nationalisme, islamisme." *Les temps modernes* 580 (1995): 24–33. Print.

Harrison, Nicholas. *Postcolonial Criticism: History, Theory, and the Work of Fiction*. Cambridge: Polity, 2003. Print.

Hassen, Rim. "Translating Women in Assia Djebar's *Far from Madina*." *Palimpsestes* 22 (2009): 61–82. Print.

Hayes, Jarrod. *Queer Nations: Marginal Sexualities in the Maghreb*. Chicago: U of Chicago P, 2000. Print.

Hiddleston, Jane. *Assia Djebar: Out of Algeria*. Liverpool: Liverpool UP, 2006. Print.

———. "The Mother as Other: Intimacy and Separation in the Maternal Memories of Assia Djebar's *Nulle part dans la maison de mon père*." *Journal of Romance Studies* 11.2 (2011): 21–33. Print.

Hodgson, Marshall G. S. *The Venture of Islam*. Vol. 1. Chicago: U of Chicago P, 1974. Print.

Hollywood Harems. Dir. Tania Kamal-Eldin. Women Make Movies, 1999. Film.

Horne, Alistair. *A Savage War of Peace: Algeria, 1954–1962*. London: Macmillan, 1977. Print.

Hornung, Alfred, and Ernstpeter Ruhe, eds. *Postcolonialisme et autobiographie: Albert Memmi, Assia Djebar, Daniel Maximin*. Amsterdam: Rodopi, 1998. Print.

Humphries, Jeff. "A Brief Conversation with Assia Djebar." Trans. Daniel Simon. *World Literature Today* 80.4 (2006): 15. Print.

Hutcheon, Linda. *A Poetics of Postmodernism: History, Theory, Fiction*. New York: Routledge, 1988. Print.

Ibn Hisham, ʿAbd al-malik, ed. السيرة النبوية [Al-sira al-nabawiyyah; "The Biography of the Prophet"]. 4 vols. Ed. Mustapha al-Saqqa. Beirut: Daral-Maʿrifa, 2007. Print.

Ibn Saʿd, Muhammad. كتاب الطبقات [Kitab al-Tabaqat; "The Book of Generations"]. 2 vols. Ed. Ihsan ʿAbbas. Beirut: Dar Sader, 1998. Print.

Inch' Allah Dimanche. Dir. Yamina Benguigui. Perf. Fejria Deliba, Zinedine Soualem, and Marie-France Pisier. Film Movement, 2001. DVD.

"Interlanguage." Def. 2. *American Heritage Dictionary of the English Language*. Boston: Houghton, 2009. Print.

———. *The Free Dictionary*. Farlex, n.d. Web. 3 Feb. 2016. < http://www.thefreedictionary.com/interlanguage>.

Jameson, Fredric. *The Prison-House of Language*. Princeton: Princeton UP, 1975. Print.

Joubert, Jean-Louis, ed. *Littérature francophone: Anthologie*. Paris: Nathan, 1992. Print.

Kashani-Sabet, Firoozeh. "The Swinging Pendulum: Linguistic Controversy in Post-colonial Algeria." *Middle Eastern Studies* 32.4 (1996): 264–80. Print.

Kassam, Tazim R. "Teaching Religion in the Twenty-First Century." *Teaching Islam*. Ed. Brannon Wheeler. New York: Oxford UP, 2003. 191–215. Print.

Kateb Yacine. *Nedjma*. Paris: Seuil, 1956. Print.

Kelly, Debra. *Autobiography and Independence: Selfhood and Creativity in North African Postcolonial Writing in French*. Liverpool: Liverpool UP, 2005. Print.

———. "'An Unfinished Death': The Legacy of Albert Camus and the Work of Textual Memory in Contemporary European and Algerian Literatures." *International Journal of Francophone Studies* 10.1–2 (2007): 217–35. Print.

Kemp, Anna. *Voices and Veils: Feminism and Islam in French Women's Writing and Activism*. London: Legenda; Maney, 2010. Print.

Képis bleus: La guerre d'Algérie. By Patrick Buisson. Paris: Michel, 2009. DVD.

Khalidi, Tarif. *Arabic Historical Thought in the Classical Period*. Cambridge: Cambridge UP, 1994. Print.

Khanna, Ranjana. *Algeria Cuts: Women and Representation, 1830 to the Present*. Stanford: Stanford UP, 2008. Print.

Khatibi, Abdelkebir. *Amour bilingue*. Montpellier: Fata Morgana, 1983. Print.

———. *Maghreb pluriel*. Paris: Denoël, 1983. Print.

Kian, Soheila. *Écritures et transgressions d'Assia Djebar et de Leïla Sebbar: Les traversées des frontières*. Paris: L'Harmattan, 2009. Print.

Knight, Diana. "Barthes and Orientalism." *New Literary History* 24.3 (1993): 617–33. Print.

Kouchkar Ferchouli, Fatma-Zohra. "Émergence du parler féminin arabe dans la langue française dans le roman d'Assia Djebar: *L'amour, la fantasia*." Ed. Meriem Bedjaoui. *Actes du Colloque Langues: Cultures et Traduction*. Alger: El-hikma, 2001. 101–16. Print.

Kristeva, Julia. *Étrangers à nous-mêmes*. Paris: Fayard, 1988. Print.

Lachman, Kathryn. *Borrowed Forms*. Liverpool: Liverpool UP, 2014. Print.

———. "Echo's Legacy: Autobiography and Intertextuality in Assia Djebar's *Nulle part dans la maison de mon père*." *Conventions and Conversions: Generic Innovations in African Literatures / Innovations génériques dans les littératures africaines*. Ed. Susanne Gehrmann and Flora Veit-Wild. Trier, Germany: Wissenschaftlicher, 2012. 87–103. Print.

Laghouati, Sofiane. "Assia Djebar: Quand l'écriture est une route à ouvrir, un territoire entre les langues . . . : Prolégomènes pour une 'diglossie littéraire.'" Asholt, Calle-Gruber, and Combe 97–118.

Lançon, Daniel. "L'invention de l'auteur: Assia Djebar entre 1957 et 1969 ou l'Orient second en français." Asholt, Calle-Gruber, and Combe 119–39.

Lazarus, Joyce. "Writing as Resistance: Assia Djebar's *Vaste est la prison*." *Journal of International Women's Studies* 11.4 (2010): 83–90. Print.

Lazreg, Marnia. "Feminism and Difference: The Perils of Writing as a Woman on Women in Algeria." *Feminist Studies* 14.1 (1988): 81–107. Print.

Le Bris, Michel, and Jean Rouaud, eds. *Pour une littérature-monde*. Paris: Gallimard, 2007. Print.

Lewis, Reina, and Sara Mills, eds. *Feminist Postcolonial Theory: A Reader*. New York: Routledge, 2003. Print.

Linton, Anne. "Allegory and Exoticism: Balzac's Allusion to La Liberté guidant le peuple in *La fille aux yeux d'or*." *Nineteenth-Century French Studies* 39.1–2 (2010–11): 46–61. Print.

Lionnet, Françoise. *Autobiographical Voices: Race, Gender, Self-Portraiture*. Ithaca: Cornell UP, 1989. Print.

———. "Ces voix au fil de soi(e): Le détour du poétique." *L'Esprit Créateur* 48.4 (2008): 104–16. Print.

———. *Postcolonial Representations: Women, Literature, Identity*. Ithaca: Cornell UP, 1995. Print.

Lioult, Jean-Luc. *À l'enseigne du réél: Penser le documentaire*. Aix en Provence: PU de Provence, 2004. Print.

Mabanckou, Alain. "Le chant de l'oiseau migrateur." Le Bris and Rouaud 55–66.

Mack, Mehammed. "Kamel Daoud: Sexual Demonization and the Secularist Select." *Jadaliyya*. Arab Studies Inst., 9 Mar. 2016. Web. 6 June 2016. <http://maghreb.jadaliyya.com/pages/index/24029/kamel-daoud_sexual-demonization-and-the-secularist>.

Majid, Anouar. "The Politics of Feminism in Islam." Saliba, Allen, and Howard 53–93.

Martin, Florence. "The Poetics of Memory in Assia Djebar's *La femme sans sépulture*: A Study in Paradoxes." *Memory, Empire and Postcolonialism: Legacies of French Colonialism*. Ed. Alec G. Hargreaves. Lanham: Lexington, 2005. 160–73. Print.

Mernissi, Fatima. *Beyond the Veil: Male-Female Dynamics in Modern Muslim Society*. Bloomington: Indiana UP, 1987. Print.

———. *Le harem politique: Le Prophète et les femmes*. Paris: Michel, 1987. Print.

———. *Sexe, idéologie, islam*. Paris: Tierce, 1983. Print.

———. *The Veil and the Male Elite: A Feminist Interpretation of Women's Rights in Islam*. Trans. Mary Jo Lakeland. Reading: Addison, 1991. Print.

Metz, Christian. *Imaginary Signifier: Psychoanalysis and the Cinema*. Trans. Ben Brewster. Bloomington: Indiana UP, 1986. Print.

Milkovitch-Rioux, Catherine. "Les fables du deuil dans l'œuvre d'Assia Djebar." *Écrire le deuil dans les littératures des XXe-XXIe siècles*. Ed. Bernadette Hidalgo-Bachs and Milkovitch-Rioux. Clermont-Ferrand: PU Blaise Pascal, 2014. 557–73. Print.

Moghadam, Valentine. "Islamic Feminism and Its Discontents: Towards a Resolution of the Debate." Saliba, Allen, and Howard 15–51.

Mohammedi-Tabti, Bouba. "Assia Djebar: *Les enfants du nouveau monde* ou la clôture du lieu." *Assia Djebar*. Redouane and Bénayoun-Szmidt 115–28.

Mohanty, Chandra Talpade. "Under Western Eyes: Feminist Scholarship and Colonial Discourses." *Third World Women and the Politics of Feminism*. Ed. Mohanty, Ann Russo, and Lourdes Torres. Bloomington: Indiana UP, 1991. 51–80. Print.

———. "'Under Western Eyes' Revisited: Feminist Solidarity through Anticapitalist Struggles." *Feminism without Borders: Decolonizing Theory, Practicing Solidarity*. Durham: Duke UP, 2003. 221–73. Print.

La moitié du ciel d'Allah. Dir. Djamila Sahraoui. CNC; Images de la culture, 1995. DVD.

Mortimer, Mildred. *Assia Djebar*. Philadelphia: CELFAN, 1988. Print.

———. "Edward Said and Assia Djebar: A Contrapuntal Reading." *Research in African Literatures* 36.3 (2005): 53–67. Print.

———. "Tortured Bodies, Resilient Souls: Algeria's Women Combatants Depicted by Danièle Djamila Amrane-Minne, Louisette Ighilahriz, and Assia Djebar." *Research in African Literatures* 43.1 (2012): 101–17. Print.

———. "Writing the Personal: The Evolution of Assia Djebar's Autobiographical Project from *L'amour, la fantasia* to *Nulle part dans la maison de mon père*." *Journal of Women's History* 25.2 (2013): 111–29. Print.

Murdoch, H. Adlai. "Rewriting Writing: Identity, Exile and Renewal in Assia Djebar's *L'amour, la fantasia*." *Yale French Studies* 83 (1993): 71–92. Print.

Murdoch, H. Adlai, and Anne Donadey, eds. *Postcolonial Theory and Francophone Literary Studies*. Gainesville: UP of Florida, 2005. Print.

Murray, Alison. "Women, Nostalgia, Memory: *Chocolat*, *Outremer*, and *Indochine*." *Research in African Literatures* 33.2 (2002): 235–44. Print.

Murray, Jenny. "'La mort inachevée': Writing, Remembering, and Forgetting in Assia Djebar's *Le blanc de l'Algérie* and *Nulle part dans la maison de mon père*." *Anamnesia: Private and Public Memory in Modern French Culture*. Ed. Peter Collier, Anna Magdalena Elsner, and Olga Smith. Bern: Lang, 2009. 71–83. Print.

———. *Remembering the (Post)Colonial Self: Memory and Identity in the Novels of Assia Djebar*. Oxford: Lang, 2008. Print.

Musulmans de France de 1904 à nos jours. Dir. Karim Miské, Emmanuel Blanchard, and Mohamed Joseph Paris: France Télévisions Distribution, 2010. DVD.

Nader, Laura. "Orientalism, Occidentalism, and the Control of Women." *Cultural Dynamics* 11.3 (1989): 323–35. Print.

Ngũgĩ wa Thiong'o. "The Language of African Literature." Williams and Chrisman 435–55.

Nietzsche, Friedrich. *The Gay Science*. Ed. Bernard Williams. Trans. Josefine Nauckhoff. Cambridge: Cambridge UP, 2001. Print.

Niney, François. *Le documentaire et ses faux-semblants*. Paris: Klincksieck, 2009. Print.

Ortiz, Fernando. *Cuban Counterpoint: Tobacco and Sugar*. Trans. Harriet de Onis. Durham: Duke UP, 1995. Print.

Page, Andrea. "Rape or Obscene Copulation? Ambivalence and Complicity in Djebar's *L'amour, la fantasia*." *Women in French Studies* 2 (1994): 42–54. Print.

Pappas, Sara. "Opening the Door: Reinterpreting Interior Space and Transpositions of Art in *La fille aux yeux d'or* via Assia Djebar." *Symposium* 64.3 (2010): 169–86. Print.

Pépé le Moko. Dir. Julien Duvivier. 1936. Home Vision Entertainment, 2003. DVD. Criterion Collection.

Pervillé, Guy. *Pour une histoire de la guerre d'Algérie, 1954–1962*. Paris: Picard, 2002. Print.

Picasso, Pablo. *Women of Algiers*. Version G. 18 Jan. 1955. Pablo-ruiz-picasso.net, n.d. Web. 26 Nov. 2015.

———. *Women of Algiers*. Version O. 14 Feb. 1955. Pablo-ruiz-picasso.net, n.d. Web. 26 Nov. 2015.

Prabhu, Anjali. "Sisterhood and Rivalry in-between the Shadow and the Sultana: A Problematic of Representation in *Ombre sultane*." *Research in African Literatures* 33.3 (2002): 69–96. Print.

Preamble. *République algérienne démocratique et populaire: Constitution de 1963*. Conseil Constitutionnel, n.d. Web. 13 July 2015. <http://www.conseil-constitutionnel.dz/Constituion1963.htm#Preambule>.

Rachida. Dir. Yamina Bachir-Chouikh. First Run Features, 2002. DVD.

Rahman, Najat. *Literary Disinheritance: The Writing of Home in the Work of Mahmoud Darwish and Assia Djebar*. Lanham: Lexington, 2007. Print.

Reber, Michel. *L'Islam*. 1996. Toulouse, France: Milan, 2005. Print.

Redouane, Najib, and Yvette Bénayoun-Szmidt, eds. *Assia Djebar*. Paris: L'Harmattan, 2008. Print.

Le repenti. Dir. Merzak Allouache. Perf. Adila Bendimerad, Nabil Asli, and Khaled Benaissa. Sophie Dulac Distribution. 2013. DVD.

Rice, Alison. "Algerrance: Envois et envols." Calle-Gruber, *Assia Djebar, nomade* 247–52.

———. *Polygraphies: Francophone Women Writing Algeria*. Charlottesville: U of Virginia P, 2012. Print.

Rights and Wrongs: The Story of Women in Islam. Dir. Corine Huq et al. Women Make Movies, 2011. DVD.

Rocca, Anna. *Assia Djebar, le corps invisible: Voir sans être vue*. Paris: L'Harmattan, 2004. Print.

Rolot, Christian, and Francis Ramirez. "La casbah des insoumis: Alger dans *Pépé le Moko* de Julien Duvivier." *Alger, une ville et ses discours*. Ed. Naget Khadda and Paul Siblot. Montpellier: Praxilig; U Paul Valéry–Montpellier III, 1996. 379–90. Print.

Rosello, Mireille. *France and the Maghreb: Performative Encounters*. Gainesville: UP of Florida, 2005. Print.

Rosenthal, Franz. *A History of Muslim Historiography*. Leiden: Brill, 1968. Print.

Roy, Arundhati. *The God of Small Things*. New York: Harper, 1998. Print.

Ruhe, Ernstpeter. *Assia Djebar*. Würzburg: Könighausen, 2001. Print.

Ruses de femmes [*Keid Ensa*; *Women's Wiles*]. Dir. Farida Benlyazid. Brussels Avenue, 1999. Videocassette.

Rushdie, Salman. *The Satanic Verses*. New York: Viking, 1989. Print.

Sabbagh, Suha. *Arab Women: Between Defiance and Restraint*. New York: Olive Branch, 1996. Print.

Said, Edward W. *Beginnings: Intention and Method*. New York: Columbia UP, 1985. Print.

———. *Culture and Imperialism*. New York: Vintage, 1993. Print.

———. *On Late Style: Music and Literature against the Grain*. New York: Vintage, 2006. Print.

———. *Orientalism*. New York: Vintage, 1979. Print.

———. *Orientalism*. London: Penguin, 2003. Print.

Said, Edward, Sut Jhally, and Sanjay Talreja. *Edward Said on Orientalism*. Media Educ. Foundation, 1998. DVD.

Saliba, Therese. "Arab Feminism at the Millenium" *Signs* 25.4 (2000): 1087–92. Print.

Saliba, Therese, Carolyn Allen, and Judith Howard, eds. *Gender, Politics, and Islam*. Chicago: U of Chicago P, 2002. Print.

Salut Cousin! Dir. Merzak Allouache. Perf. Gad Elmaleh, Messaoud Hattou, and Magaly Berty. Gaumont, 1996. DVD.

Sansal, Boualem. *The German Mujahid*. Trans. Frank Wynne. New York: Europa, 2009. Print.

———. *Le village de l'Allemand, ou le journal des frères Schiller*. Paris: Gallimard, 2008. Print.

Schneider, Günther, and Peter Lenz. *A Bank of Descriptors for Self-Assessment in European Language Portfolios, 2004*. Council of Europe, n.d. Web. 26 Nov. 2015. <www.coe.int/t/dg4/education/elp/elp-reg/cefr_scale_EN.asp>.

School of Babel. Dir. Julie Bertuccelli. Icarus Films, 2015. DVD.

Schuchardt, Béatrice. "Manifestion d'une esthétique interstitielle dans *La disparition de la langue française* d'Assia Djebar." Asholt, Calle-Gruber, and Combe 365–82.

Searle, John R. "Reiterating the Differences: A Reply to Derrida." *NINE* (1977): 198–208. Print.

———. *Speech Acts: An Essay in the Philosophy of Language*. Cambridge: Cambridge UP, 1969. Print.

Sebbar, Leïla. *La Seine était rouge: Paris, Octobre 1961*. Paris: Magnier, 1999. Print.

———. *The Seine Was Red: Paris, October 1961*. Trans. Mildred Mortimer. Bloomington: Indiana UP, 2008. Print.

Siegel, Robert. "Novelist Kamel Daoud, Finding Dignity in the Absurd." *NPR Books*. NPR, 21 Aug. 2015. Web. 6 June 2016. <http://www.npr.org/2015/08/21/432618805/novelist-kamel-daoud-finding-dignity-in-the-absurd>. Muslim Artists, Now.

Silences of the Palace. Dir. Moufida Tlatli. Tunisia-France, 1994. Film.

Siskind, Mariano. "The Globalization of the Novel and the Novelization of the Global: A Critique of World Literature." *Comparative Literature* 62.4 (2010): 336–60. Print.

Spivak, Gayatri Chakravorty. "Acting Bits / Identity Talk." *Critical Inquiry* 18.4 (1992): 770–803. Print.

———. *An Aesthetic Education in the Era of Globalization*. Cambridge: Harvard UP, 2012. Print.

———. "Can the Subaltern Speak?" Williams and Chrisman 66–111.

———. "Echo." *New Literary History* 24.1 (1993): 17–43. Print.

———. "Examples to Fit the Title." *American Imago* 51.2 (1994): 161–96. Print.

———. "Ghostwriting." *Diacritics* 25.2 (1995): 64–84. Print.

———. "The Politics of Translation." Venuti 397–416.

———. "Situating Feminisms." MS.

Stewart, Susan. *On Longing: Narratives of the Miniature, the Gigantic, the Souvenir, the Collection*. Baltimore: Johns Hopkins UP, 1984. Print.

Stora, Benjamin. *La gangrène et l'oubli: La mémoire de la guerre d'Algérie*. Paris: La Découverte, 1991. Print.

———. *La guerre invisible: Algérie, années 90*. Paris: Sciences Po, 2001. Print.

Stora, Benjamin, and Gabriel Le Bomin. *Guerre d'Algérie: La déchirure*. Nilaya; Ina, 2012. DVD.

Stora, Benjamin, and Tramor Quemeneur. *Algérie, 1954–1962: Lettres, carnets et récits des Français et des Algériens dans la guerre*. Paris: Arènes, 2010. Print.

Strand, Dana. "Assia Djebar's *La femme sans sépulture* as Postcolonial Primer." *Contemporary French and Francophone Studies* 13.3 (2009): 339–47. Print.

Suleiman, Susan Rubin. Introduction. *Exile and Creativity: Signposts, Travelers, Outsiders, Backward Glances*. Ed. Suleiman. Durham: Duke UP, 1998. 1–6. Print.

Tabari, Abu Jaʿfar. *The History of al-Ṭabarī*. 39 vols. Gen. ed. Ehsan Yar-Shater. Albany: State U of New York P, 1985–99. Print.

Tageldin, Shaden M. "Which *Qalam* for Algeria? Colonialism, Liberation, and Language in Djebar's *L'amour, la fantasia* and Mustaghanimi's *Dhakirat al-Jasad*." *Comparative Literature Studies* 46.3 (2009): 467–97. Print.

Taha, Rachid. *Tékitoi*. Wrasse Records, 2004. CD and DVD.

Taraud, Christelle. *La prostitution coloniale: Algérie, Tunisie, Maroc, 1830–1962*. Paris: Payot, 2003. Print.

Thatcher, Nicole. "La mémoire de la deuxième guerre mondiale en France et la voix contestataire de Charlotte Delbo." *French Forum* 26.2 (2001): 91–110. Print.

Thiel, Veronika. *Assia Djebar: La polyphonie comme principe générateur de ses textes*. Vienna: Praesens, 2005. Print.

———. "La querelle des discours: Techniques formelles de la réécriture de l'histoire dans *L'amour, la fantasia*." *L'Esprit Créateur* 48.4 (2008): 34–46. Print.

Tlatli, Soraya. "L'ambivalence linguistique dans la littérature maghrébine d'expression française." *French Review* 72.2 (1998): 297–307. Print.

Venuti, Lawrence, ed. *The Translation Studies Reader*. London: Routledge, 2000. Print.

Vernet, Horace. *Capture of the Smalah of Abd-el-Kader by the Duc d'Aumale, May 16, 1843*. Media Commons, n.d. 14 Mar. 2016. <https://commons.wikimedia.org/wiki/File:Prise_de_la_smalah_d_Abd-El-Kader_a_Taguin_16_mai_1843_Horace_Vernet.jpg>.

Vincendeau, Ginette. *Pépé le Moko*. London: BFI, 1998. Print.

Vogl, Mary B. "Using the Arts to Teach Assia Djebar's 'Femmes d'Alger dans leur appartement.'" *French Review* 76.4 (2003): 692–720. Print.

Wadud, Amina. *Qurʾan and Woman: Rereading the Sacred Text from a Woman's Perspective*. 2nd ed. New York: Oxford UP, 1999. Print.

Watt, W. Montgomery. "ʿĀʾisha Bint Abī Bakr." *Encyclopaedia of Islam Online*. 2nd ed. Brill, n.d. Web. 13 Mar. 2013.

Weber-Fève, Stacey. *Rehybridizing Transnational Domesticity and Femininity: Women's Contemporary Filmmaking and Lifewriting in France, Algeria, and Tunisia*. Lanham: Lexington, 2010. Print.

Williams, Patrick, and Laura Chrisman, eds. *Colonial Discourse and Post-colonial Theory: A Reader*. New York: Routledge, 1994. Print.

Woodhull, Winifred. *Transfigurations of the Maghreb: Feminism, Decolonization, and Literatures*. Minneapolis: U of Minnesota P, 1993. Print.

Young, Robert. *White Mythologies: Writing History and the West*. London: Routledge, 2004. Print.

Zimra, Clarisse. Afterword. Djebar, *Children* 201–33.

———. Afterword. Djebar, *Women* 159–211.

———. "Disorienting the Subject in Djebar's *L'amour, la fantasia*." *Yale French Studies* 87 (1995): 149–70. Print.

———. "Hearing Voices; or, Who You Calling Postcolonial? The Evolution of Djebar's Poetics." *Research in African Literatures* 35.4 (2004) 149–59. Print.

———. "In Her Own Write: The Circular Structures of Linguistic Alienation in Assia Djebar's Early Novels." *Research in African Literatures* 11.2 (1980): 206–23. Print.

———. "Sounding off the Absent Body: Intertextual Resonances in 'La femme qui pleure' and 'La femme en morceaux.'" *Research in African Literatures* 30.3 (1999): 108–24. Print.

———. "Still Besieged by Voices: Djebar's Poetics of the Threshold." *Postcolonial Poetics: Genre and Form*. Ed. Patrick Crowley and Jane Hiddleston. Liverpool: Liverpool UP, 2011. 109–28. Print.

———. "Writing Woman: The Novels of Assia Djebar." *SubStance* 21.3 (1992): 68–84. Print.

Žižek, Slavoj. *Violence: Six Sideways Reflections*. New York: Picador, 2008. Print.

INDEX